MW01087948

THE SUPREME ADVENTURE

OTHER WORKS BY DR. ROBERT CROOKALL:

Coal Measure Plants. Edward Arnold & Co. Ltd., 1929.

The Kidston Collection of Fossil Plants. H.M. Stationery Office, 1938.

Fossil Plants of the Carboniferous Rocks of Great Britain. H.M. Stationery Office, Part I, 1955; Part II, 1959; Part III, 1964; Part IV, 1966; Part V, 1968; Part VI, 1969.

The Study and Practice of Astral Projection. Aquarian Press, 1960. American Edition, University Books, Inc., New Hyde Park, New York, U.S.A., 1966.

More Astral Projections. Aquarian Press, 1964.

The Techniques of Astral Projection. Aquarian Press, 1964.

The Supreme Adventure. James Clarke & Co. Ltd., 1961.

Intimations of Immortality. James Clarke & Co. Ltd., 1965.

During Sleep. The Possibility of "Co-operation". Theosophical Publishing House (London), 1964.

The Next World—and the Next. Ghostly Garments. Theosophical Publishing House (London), 1966.

Events on the Threshold of the After-life. Darshana International, Moradabad, India, 1967.

The Mechanism of Astral Projection. Ibid., 1968.

The Interpretation of Cosmic and Mystical Experiences. James Clarke, 1969.

The Jung-Jaffe View of Out-of-the-body Experiences. World Fellowship Press, 1970.

Out-of-the-body Experiences. A Fourth Analysis. University Books, Inc., N.Y., U.S.A., 1970.

A Case Book of Astral Projection. Ibid., 1972.

Ecstasy, Darshana International, India, 1973.

"Dreams" of High Significance, ibid., 1973.

Scientific papers in:

> *The Geological Magazine*
> *The Annals of Botany*
> *Memoirs of the Geological Survey of Great Britain*
> *The Naturalist*
> *Memoirs and Proceedings of the Manchester Literary and Philosophic Society*
> *Proceedings of the Geologists' Association*
> *Proceedings of the Royal Society of Edinburgh*
> *Proceedings of the Royal Physical Society*
> *Proceedings of the Cotteswold Naturalist and Field Club*
> *Proceedings of the Institute of Mining Engineers*
> *Proceedings of the South Wales Institute of Engineers*
> *Fuel*
> *Colliery Guardian*
> *Darshana International*
> *Psychics International*
> *World Science Review*
> *The British Association for the Advancement of Science,* etc.

With Dr. F. B. A. Welch:

BRITISH REGIONAL GEOLOGY—*Bristol and Gloucester District.* H.M. Stationery Office, 1935.

With Canon J. D. Pearce-Higgins and Rev. G. Stanley Whitby: *Life, Death & Psychical Research,* Rider, 1973.

THE
SUPREME ADVENTURE

Analyses of Psychic Communications

by

ROBERT CROOKALL, B.Sc. (Psychology), D.Sc., Ph.D.

Late Principal Geologist, H.M. Geological Survey, London (Department of Scientific and Industrial Research).
Formerly Lecturer in Botany, University of Aberdeen.
Member of the Society for Psychical Research.
Hon. Member of the Indian Society for Psychical and Yogic Research.
Member of the Churches' Fellowship for Psychical and Spiritual Studies.
Hon. Member of the American Society for Psychical Research.

Published for the Churches' Fellowship
for Psychical Study by
JAMES CLARKE & CO. LIMITED
7 All Saints Passage,
Cambridge.

First published 1961
© Robert Crookall

Second edition 1974

ISBN 0227 67606 8

GENERAL EDITOR FOR SERIES:
Rev. John D. Pearce-Higgins, M.A.

Printed and bound in Great Britain by
REDWOOD BURN LIMITED
Trowbridge & Esher

"He that answereth a matter before he heareth it, it is a shame and a folly unto him."—*Solomon*.

"Read not to contradict and confute, nor to believe and take for granted, but to weigh and consider."—*Bacon*

"Is it not a fact that, until Western Society utilises the findings of parapsychology, it has little with which to attack the materialistic state-philosophy of the U.S.S.R.? Freedom, morality, democracy, etc., are tied to our conception of man's relation to matter."—*Professor J. B. Rhine*.

"The pharisaical scepticism which denies without investigation is quite as perilous and much more contemptible than the blind credulity which accepts all that it is taught without inquiry: it is, indeed, but another form of ignorance assuming to be knowledge."—*Catherine Crowe*.

"The proper meaning of orthodoxy is simply 'true', or 'right opinion'. In practical affairs everyone recognises the value of having true opinions. . . . Life itself is a practical affair and we are unlikely to make much of it if we have false opinions concerning the world, our nature and our relations with God. . . . The mistake which 'orthodox' people make is to suppose that they have all the truth and that nothing more can be known."—*Dr. W. R. Matthews*.

"To believe that any past generation held the monopoly of truth, or was able to give it final expression, is not only inconsistent with the teaching of history, but is a flat denial of the Holy Spirit, which was promised to guide us progressively into all truth."—*Dr. Cyril Alington*.

INTRODUCTION

By Rev. John D. Pearce-Higgins, M.A.,
*Hon. C. F. Vicar of Putney, and Vice-Chairman of the Churches'
Fellowship for Psychical Study*

I am very glad to have reached the point of writing the introduction to what I hope is the first book in a long and notable
series of studies whose publication is planned under the auspices
of the Churches' Fellowship for Psychical Study. The publication of such a series is an ambition which the Council of the
C.F.P.S. has cherished for some years, but whose fulfilment
has not been possible until we could find a publisher who was
sufficiently interested in our work to be prepared to make a
venture of faith. The venture has now been made and it is up
to the members of the Fellowship to play their part in support-
ing it by the purchase of the books, as well as by making them
as widely known as possible.

The Churches' Fellowship has come into being for a variety
of excellent reasons and performs a diversity of functions. It is
meeting a personal need felt by many people for further study
in a difficult field of which they know a little and would like to
know more. It is enabling those who already have had personal
experiences of a psychic or spiritual nature to share these
experiences with others, and to submit them to the test of strict
but sympathetic criticism inside the fellowship, and with
reference to the teachings of the Christian Church. It also has
its genesis, as Sir Cyril Atkinson has hinted in his Foreword, in
the tensions between the ancient churches and certain newer
movements of the spirit, such as Spiritualism, which claims to
shed new light on the problem of survival, and Christian
Science which has opened up again the whole question of
spiritual healing. But viewed from a wider angle, the C.F.P.S.
aims at making a scientific and philosophical contribution
towards the now century-old battle between Science and Religion. In the latter aspect it may have an unusual role to play,
acting rather as Socrates did in ancient Athens, as a 'gadfly'
and reminding men both of Science and Religion that here is a
valid field of study, and one which, in spite of the heavy pressure

of tradition and orthodoxy in both field, and also of the innate *vis inertiae* of the mind, they cannot afford to neglect.

'Study' is the operative word which lies at the back of the Fellowship's work, and which is emphasised in the presentation to the public of *The Supreme Adventure*, and the books which are to follow it. We plan in this series to provide material for study not only for our own members, whether as individuals or members of the Study Groups, but also for others investigating this field, and we have already accumulated sufficient remarkable material to enable us to continue this series for some years. This will include both much hitherto unpublished evidence (and this, of course, is being added to daily) and also from time to time works which endeavour, as does this brilliant book of Dr. Crookall, to reassess existing evidence in the light of increasing knowledge and new techniques.

The books, although published under the auspices of the Fellowship, will not in any sense bear the *imprimatur* of the Fellowship or express any 'official' point of view. The C.F.P.S. has no official point of view. In this it resembles the older societies for investigation whose members carry out their researches on individual lines, and express personal opinions of all shades. Because, however, of the religious affiliations and beliefs of our writers, this series is likely to favour a positive rather than a negative interpretation of the evidence, where it is scientifically admissible, while avoiding, I hope, both the almost pathological and in fact not truly scientific prejudices in favour of scepticism shown in some quarters, and also the credulity displayed in others.

If this universe is merely a collection of material particles—a fact which physicists are now beginning to doubt—and if consciousness is merely an ephemeral by-product of the swirling contents of the space-time continuum, then not only psychical, but all other human studies are valueless, and existence is, as Ecclesiastes suggested, 'vanity'. But if the universe is primarily a manifestation of Mind, and is peopled by spiritual beings, under the aegis of a Spiritual Power—GOD—then clearly we are right in seeking evidence for the purpose of our existence and for the continued development of these spirits beyond the "bourne of time and space". Our enquiry will not only lead us to study such evidence, but also to enquire into the nature of such continued existence after that great watershed which we call 'death'. And we have reason to believe that we shall make more progress in our studies if we display a sympathetic approach, rather than turn the familiar Nelsonian 'blind eye' to the evidence as do so many scientists and theologians.

Dr. Crookall's massive array of facts may not prove convincing to some people, though I feel that they will be hard put to it to ascribe such a widespread and consistent body of human experience to purely subjective causes. His work forms a remarkable synthesis of a great mass of evidence which has never so far been correlated, let alone interpreted. His work is scientific in the best sense of the word—it is internally coherent, and provides a hypothesis which is consonant with the sciences, with philosophy and theology. Those who like myself find this book impressive and convincing will find here a well-stocked armoury of facts and interpretations which make the *materialist interpretation* of the universe unthinkable. Indeed it is only by turning a blind eye to the facts of psychic science that a materialist interpretation is at all possible. I hope that Dr Crookall's book will draw such forceful attention to them that neither scientists nor clergy nor teachers will be able to neglect them any longer.

Churches Fellowship for Psychical Study,
   November 7th, 1960

CONTENTS

Stages not of dicing
Three on dicing

ILLUSTRATIONS

ACKNOWLEDGMENTS

For permission to make brief extracts from copyright material the writer tenders grateful thanks to the following publishers and authors:

Alfred A. Knopf: Wilfred Brandon, *Open the Door*, 1935, p. 27.
—— Edward C. Randall, *Frontiers of the After-life*, 1932, pp. 31, 34, 43.
Andrew Dakers Ltd.: Alice Gilbert, *Philip in Two Worlds*, 1948, pp. 89, 102, 103, 120, 137, 139, 162, 201.
Aquarian Press Ltd.: Alice Gilbert, *Philip in the Spheres*, 1952, p. xxii, xxiv, 35.
—— Geraldine Cummins, *Mind in Life and Death*, 1956, p. 32.
Arrowsmith & Co. Ltd.: Mrs. C. A. Dawson-Scott, *From Four Who are Dead*, 1926, pp. 13, 47, 95, 153.
Arthurs Press Ltd.: Dr. Nandor Fodor, *Encyclopedia of Psychic Science*, 1933, p. 394.
Basil Blackwood: Miss L. M. Bazett, *Beyond the Five Senses*, 1946.
Besant & Co. Ltd.: Lieut.-Colonel A. E. Powell, *The After-death Life*, 1929.
Cassell & Co. Ltd.: Harold Bailey, *The Undiscovered Country*, 1918, p. 68.
—— J. Arthur Hill, *Man is a Spirit*, 1918, p. 156.
Charles Taylor: F. Heslop, *Life Worth Living*, pp. 26, 28, 29.
Chatto and Windus: Aldous Huxley, *The Doors of Perception*, 1954; *Heaven and Hell*, 1956.
Church Assembly: 'Report Towards the Conversion of England', 1945, p. 35.
Collins & Co. Ltd.: J. I. Macnair, *Livingstone the Liberator*, p. 83.
—— The Rev. C. Drayton Thomas, *Life Beyond Death with Evidence*, 1928, pp. 60, 112, 268.
—— Dr. Charles Richet, *Thirty Years of Psychical Research*, 1923.
Colby and Rich Ltd.: Dr. J. Peebles, *Immortality*, 1887.
Constable & Co. Ltd.: Doris and Hilary Severn, *In the Next Room*, 1911, p. 29.

Curtiss, San Francisco: A. C. and F. H. Curtiss, *Realms of the Living Dead*, pp. 67, 68, 169.

Creative Press Inc.: Mrs. Eileen J. Garrett, *Awareness*, 1943, p. 213.

The C. W. Daniel Co. Ltd.: A. B., *One Step Higher*, 1937, pp. 52, 53, 54, 100, 143.

—— Constance Wiley, *A Star of Hope*, 1938, pp. 7, 22, 48, 169.

David Stott: Anon, *I Awoke*, 1895, p. 153.

Dent & Co. Ltd.: Dr. Harry Roberts, *Everyman in Health and Sickness*, 1935.

Duckworth & Co. Ltd.: Canon Knight, *Spiritualism, Reincarnation and Immortality*, 1950.

—— Dr. Grey Walter, *The Living Brain*, 1953.

Dunstan: *Letters from Lancelot*, 1931, pp. 35, 53, 61, 75, 86.

English Universities Press Ltd.: Dr. C. Raynor Johnson, *Psychical Research*, 1955, p. 29.

—— D. H. C. Read, *The Christian Faith*, 1956, p. 163.

F. V. White: Florence Marryat, *The Spirit World*, 1894.

Faber and Faber Ltd.: Phoebe Payne and L. J. Bendit, *The Psychic Sense*, 1943, p. 120.

—— Sir Ernest Bennett, *Apparitions and Haunted Houses*, 1939.

—— Warner Allen, *The Timeless Moment*, 1946, pp. 31-3.

Feature Books Ltd.: Anthony Borgia, *A.B.C. of Life*, pp. 35, 38, 40.

Fernie: A. L. Fernie, *Not Silent if Dead*, 1890, p. 25.

Frederick Muller Ltd.: L. M. Geldert, *Thy Son Liveth*, 1946, pp. 12, 19, 33, 39.

F. W. Allen: Anon., *The Life Beyond the Grave*, 1876, pp. 6, 45, 104, 108.

G. Bell & Sons Ltd.: Eric Cudden, *Hypnosis and Its Meaning and Practice*, 1955.

George Allen and Unwin Ltd.: Edward C. Randall, *The Dead Have Never Died*, 1918, pp. 54, 160.

—— G. N. M. Tyrrell, *The Nature of Human Personality*, 1954.

—— W. O. Stevens, *The Mystery of Dreams*, 1950.

—— Dr. L. P. Jacks, *Near the Brink*, 1952.

—— Edward Carpenter, *The Drama of Love and Death*, 1925.

George Redway: Dr. Carl du Prel, *The Philosophy of Mysticism*, 1889.

—— Mme. d. Esperance, *Shadow Land*, 1897.

—— Adolphe d'Assier, *Posthumous Humanity*, 1887.

George Harrap: Lieut.-Colonel Reginald M. Lester, *Towards the Hereafter*, 1956, p. 183.

Grant Richards Ltd.: The Rev. C. L. Tweedale, *Man's Survival after Death*, 2nd ed., 1920, p. 39.

Greater World Assoc.: Joy Snell, *The Ministry of Angels*, 1950, p. 27.

Greber, N.Y.: Johannes Greber, *Communications with the Spirit World*, 1932, pp. 40, 53, 84, 96.

Harcourt, Brace & Co. Ltd.: Professor C. D. Broad, *Religion, Philosophy and Psychical Research*, 1954.

Helix Press: Eileen J. Garrett, *Does Man Survive Death?* 1957, p. 16.

Hillside Press Ltd.: Montgomery Smith, *Life and Work in the Spiritual Body*, p. 57.

Hodder and Stoughton Ltd.: Sir Arthur Conan Doyle, *The New Revelation*, 1918, p. 88.

Holywell Press, Oxford: E.L.B.S., *Realities of the Future Life*, 1908.

Hutchinson and Co. Ltd.: Anon. (King's Counsel), *Bear Witness*.

—— F. W. Fitzsimons, *Opening the Psychic Door*, 1933, pp. 35, 57, 73, 89, 172, 302.

—— 'W. T. Stead' (via Hester Dowden), *The Blue Island*, 1922, p. 94.

Independent Press Ltd.: Stephen Hobhouse, *A Discourse on the Life to Come*, 1954.

International Record of Medicine and General Practice Clinics, Vol. 169, 1956, p. 529.

Ivor Nicholson and Watson Ltd.: Geraldine Cummins, *The Road to Immortality*, 1932, pp. 25, 32, 59, 85, 89, 151; *Beyond Human Personality*, 1935, pp. 24, 29, 44, 71, 124, 130, 193.

Kegan Paul, Trench, Trubner and Co. Ltd.: Anon. (King's Counsel), *I Heard a Voice*, 1928, p. 2.

—— A. Campbell Holms, *The Facts of Psychic Science and Philosophy*, 1925, pp. 27, 381.

—— Dr. Hereward Garrington, *Your Psychic Powers and how to Develop Them*, 1920, p. 252.

—— P. E. Cornillier, *The Survival of the Soul*, 1921, pp. 122, 185, 202, 236, 241, 262, 269, 275, 378, 380, 423, 456.

Kegan Paul, Trench, Trubner and Co. Ltd.: E. Gurney, F. W. H. Myers and F. Fodmore, *Phantasms of the Living*, 1886, p. 428.

—— Professor G. Henslow, *The Proofs of the Truths of Spiritualism*, 1919, p. 237.

—— Dr. W. J. Kilner, *The Human Atmosphere*, 1920.

Journ. S.P.R., xxxix, 1957, pp. 32, 92.

Journ. American S.P.R., 1908, 1945.

Lancet, 1884, p. 1,058; 1910, p. 148.

Lectures Universal Ltd.: The Rev. C. Drayton Thomas, *In the Dawn Beyond Death*, pp. 20, 34, 64, 66, 67, 133.

Light, vol. xxxiv, 1914, p. 262.

L. N. Fowler and Co. Ltd.: Yoga Ramacharka, *The Life Beyond Death*.

L.S.A. Publications Ltd.: Helen Alex Dallas, *Human Survival and Its Implications*, 1930, p. 32.

—— Olive C. Pixley, *Listening In*, 1928.

—— Helen Macgregor and Margaret Underhill, *The Psychic Faculties and Their Development*, 1934, pp. 63, 90.

L. S. Publications: G. Vivian, *Love Conquers Death*, pp. 9, 19, 91, 117.

Longmans, Green and Co. Ltd.: F. W. H. Myers, *Human Personality and Its Survival of Bodily Death*, 1916, pp. 232, 238, 245, 252.

—— Lady Barrett, *Personality Survives Death*, 1937, p. 114.

Lucis Publishing Co. Ltd.: Anon., *The Science of Initiates*, 1934, p. 164.

Macmillan and Co. Ltd.: Sadhu Sundar Singh, *Visions of the Spiritual World*, 1926, p. 6.

Methuen and Co. Ltd.: Sir Wm. Barrett, *Death-bed Visions*, 1926, p. 49.

—— Sir Oliver J. Lodge, *The Survival of Man*, 1909, pp. 288, 292, 298, 302; *Raymond*, 1916, pp. 127, 159, 183, 195, 196.

—— Th. Besterman, *An Enquiry Into the Unknown*, 1954.

—— Whately Carington, *Telepathy*, 1945.

The Month, 1935, pp. 49, 126.

Nay Nesbit and Co. Ltd.: David Duguid, *Hafed, Prince of Persia*, 1893.

Omega Press Ltd.: George Sandwith, *Magical Mission*, 1955.

—— A. W. Osborn, *The Expansion of Awareness*, 1955.

Pelican Books Ltd.: Dr. Cyril Garbett, *The Age of Revolt*, 1956, pp. 105, 263.

Philip Allen and Co. Ltd.: Kate Wingfield, *More Guidance from Beyond*, 1928, p. 41.

Prediction, December, 1952; March, 1955.

Proc. S.P.R.: iii, 301; v, 408, 888-9; vi, 429; xii, 405; xiii, 28, 484; xiv, 12; xxi, 233; xxiv, 351; xxv, 560, 1,181; xxviii, 200; xxxi, 188; xliii, 232; xlvii, 281.

Psychic Book Club: Carl A. Wickland, *The Gateway of Understanding*, pp. 16, 65.

—— Mrs. Kelway Bamber, *Claude's Book*, 1918, p. 2.

—— Dr. Margaret Vivian, *The Doorway*, 1941, p. 15.

Psychic News: January 22, 1955; April 28, 1956; July 17, 1956; January 19, 1957.

Psychic Press Ltd.: A. T. Baird, *A Case Book for Survival*, p. 140.

—— Geraldine Cummins, *Travellers in Eternity*, 1948, pp. 20, 122.

—— J. Arthur Findlay, *Where Two Worlds Meet*, 1951, p. 599.

—— W. S. Montgomery-Smith and E. M. Taylor, *Light in Our Darkness*, 1936, p. 99.

—— The Rev. C. Drayton Thomas, *Beyond Life's Sunset*, p. 48.

Psychical Research, March, 1931.

Rider and Co. Ltd.: Cesar de Vesme, *Primitive Man*, vol. 1, 1931, p. 238.

—— Mrs. Eileen J. Garrett, *My Life as a Search for the Meaning of Mediumship*, 1939, p. 15.

—— Elsa Barker, *Letters from a Living Dead Man*, 1914, pp. 39, 45, 63, 184, 194, 266.

—— Frank Lind, *My Occult Case Book*, 1953.

—— G. N. M. Tyrrell, *Grades of Significances*, 1930, p. 196.

—— Geoffrey Hodson, *The Science of Seership*, p. 132.

—— Geraldine Cummins, *They Survive*, pp. 42, 49, 105; *Unseen Adventures*, 1951, pp. 45, 75, 156.

—— Dr. Hereward Carrington, *The Story of Psychic Science*, 1930, p. 93.

—— Isabelle Major Evans, *The History of Benjamin Kennicott*, 1932, p. 55.

—— 'J.V.H.', *Death's Door Ajar*, 1934, pp. 100, 105.

—— Jane Sherwood, *The Country Beyond*, pp. 24, 26, 34, 73, 125; *The Psychic Bridge*, pp. 26, 27, 38, 40, 47, 61.

Rider and Co. Ltd., J. Arthur Findlay, *On the Edge of the Etheric*, 1931, pp. 71, 148.

—— Leon Dennis, *Here and Hereafter*, 1910, p. 218.

—— J. S. M. Ward, *Gone West*, 1917, pp. 28, 31.

—— Lord Dowding, *Lychgate*, pp. 35, 37.

—— Oliver Fox, *Astral Projection*, p. 106.

—— Mrs. Rhys Davids, *What Is Your Will?*, pp. 168, 169.

—— The Rev. C. Drayton Thomas, *From Life to Life*, p. 65.

—— Roy Dixon-Smith, *New Light on Survival*, 1952.

—— Sylvan J. Muldoon and Dr. Hereward Carrington, *The Projection of the Astral Body*, 1929, pp. 38, 69; *The Phenomena of Astral Projection*, 1951.

—— Ralph Shirley, *The Mystery of the Human Double*, p. 33.

—— Dr. Wm. Wilson, *After Life*, p. 82.

Rosicrucian Fellowship Calif.: Max Heindel, *The Rosicrucian Cosmo-conception*, 1911, p. 66.

Routledge and Co. Ltd.: Catherine Crocre, *The Night Side of Nature*, 1904, p. 133.

Sands and Co. Ltd.: Anon., *The Dangers of Spiritualism*, 1901, p. 92.

Samiska, ix, 1955, p. 3.

Spencer, Coimbatore: M. K. Spencer, *The Other World*.

Stead's Publishing House: W. T. Stead, *Afrer Death*, 1897, p. 87.

Secker and Warburg Ltd.: Frederick Grisewood, *The World Goes By*, 1952.

Simpkin Marshall: Starr Daily, *Release*.

Swan Sonnenschein: Wm. Tebb and Dr. E. P. Vollum, *Premature Burial*, 1896.

The Society for Communion: Rev. J. W. Potter, *From Beyond the Clouds*, 1927, p. 430.

Swedenborgian Society, Inc.: E. Swedenborg, *Heaven and Hell*, 1937.

T. Fisher Unwin Ltd.: Cesare Lombroso, *After Death—What?*, 1909.

—— C. Flammarion, *Death and Its Mystery*, vol. *iii*, 1923, p. 113.

—— Professor James Hyslop, *Psychical Research and the Resurrection*, 1908, pp. 163, 175, 195, 305.

—— J. D. Parsons, *The Nature and Purpose of the Universe*, 1906, p. 107.

The Progressive Thinker Publishing House: Franchezzo (transl. Farnese), *A Wanderer in Spirit Land*, 1910, p. 76.

The Spiritualist, 1875, p. 292.

Theosophical Publishing House: Geoffrey Hodson, *Clairvoyant Research and the Life After Death*, 1935.

—— Phoebe and Dr. L. J. Bendit, *Man Incarnate*, 1957, pp. 5, 14, 114.

Two Worlds, August, 1952.

Two Worlds Publishing Co. Ltd.: Dr. Hereward Carrington, *Psychic Science and Survival*, 1930, p. 37.

T. Werner Laurie: H. Dennis Bradley, *Towards the Stars*, 1924.

—— Dr. Hereward Carrington, *Psychical Phenomena and the War*, 1918, pp. 231, 249, 251, 254.

Victor Gollancz: R. H. Ward, *A Drug-taker's Notes*, 1957, pp. 15, 37.

Watkins and Co. Ltd.: Anon., *Christ in You*, 1910, pp. 79, 82, 89, 134; *Letters from the Other Side*, 1919, pp. 2, 33.

—— Mary Bruce Wallace, *The Coming Light*, 1924, pp. 69, 70, 166.

—— Mrs. May Wright Sewall, *Neither Dead nor Sleeping*, 1921, pp. 29, 306.

—— W. T. Pole, *Private Dowding*, 1917, pp. 13, 16, 22, 33, 88, 157.

Watts and Co. Ltd.: Usborne Moore, *Glimpses of the Next State*, 1911.

Women's Printing Society Ltd.: 'A.L.E.H.,' *Fragments from My Messages*, 1929, pp. 14, 26, 34, 52, 60, 198.

Wright and Brown: 'W. T. Stead' via Hester Travers Smith (Dowden), *Life Eternal*, 1933, p. 170.

—— Ivan Cooke, *Thy Kingdom Come*, 1932, pp. 74, 82, 109, 149, 156.

William Isbester Ltd.: Dr. E. H. Plumtree, *The Spirits in Prison*, 1887.

PREFACE

THE writer considers that, by means of analyses of psychic communications (examples of which are cited in this book), it is possible to pierce the veil that obscures death and the immediate hereafter. Such analyses not only indicate *survival:* they also provide a means by which we can envisage *the general conditions under which we survive* and enable us to adduce *reasons why certain experiences are undergone at certain stages in the process of disembodiment.*

While mediumistic communications in general doubtless reflect a "climate of thought", we venture to suggest that certain of them, and particularly those descriptive of *experiences*, are significant. The admissibility of the evidence is considered in Appendix I.

The data examined in this book, then, are primarily the accounts of supposed *experiences*. The explanations proffered of those experiences are of important secondary value. The concordances that occur in numerous independent accounts seem to be explicable only if those accounts did, in fact, emanate from the 'dead' and if they do bear a close relationship to the truth. (Statements are abbreviated wherever possible. Those portions that are printed in italics are so emphasised by the present writer. Where an explanatory note has been inserted, the fact is indicated by its inclusion in square brackets.)

The books from which these communications were taken were not selected in any way. This claim can easily be tested: let the same, or similar, communications be analysed (as regards the *experiences* described) and, without doubt, the results will accord with those here obtained.

The 'official' attitude of psychical researchers to the numerous books containing automatic writings, etc., is noteworthy. Many such books include statements that their writers received evidence of identity which was of too private a nature to be disclosed. The psychical researchers, having no means of assessing the value of such evidence, conclude that the vast majority of these books—even those which include information of a supernormal type—are purely 'sub-conscious productions' of their writers. Our analyses indicate that they often include valuable material.

In the main, then, the communications here analysed are from 'popular' books which are rejected by most psychical researchers as having no value. Some of them were not produced in connection with acknowledged psychics. But it is to be noted that the *experiences* described by communicators through first-class mediums (e.g. Mrs. Piper, Mrs. Leonard, Mrs. Willett, Geraldine Cummins, etc.) are identical with those in the 'popular' books.

It is desirable to distinguish between theory and practice in these matters. The writer is convinced that the survival of bodily death (and of the communication of survivors with mortals) is as well established as the theory of evolution. The direct evidence is reviewed in many books and does not here concern us.

So much for the doctrine. The practice of attempting communication with those who have 'passed on' may be undertaken by so many different kinds of people, with so many different motives and under so many different conditions that no simple statement concerning its desirability is possible (see Appendices III, IV and V). We naturally disagree with the holding of indiscriminate séances, the forcible development of the psychic faculties, too frequent and too prolonged periods of receptivity, and the development of mediumship by people who are unhealthy in mind or body. These, however, are only special cases of the need for common sense and balance in all things. Again, the true motives of psychics, and of those who consult them, are important. They are important in all things. The frequent recourse to psychics for purely personal messages is undesirable.

There are dangers everywhere, and psychic investigations are not exempt. Those who are unqualified should not undertake psychical research or any other technical investigation. This, of course, refers to practice and not to theory. All things must be judged by their 'fruits'.

Sensitiveness to psychical impressions is said to apply to us all in varying degrees. Awareness of the receipt of the impressions comes *naturally* (under certain conditions) to some people. These may find it advantageous to seek the education of the psychical faculties. If they do so, experienced and qualified persons should be consulted.

There is, however, no necessary connection between the truth (or falsity) of statements and the methods by which they were obtained. Vivisection is an obnoxious method of investigation, but it has revealed truths that are valuable not only to man, but also to animals. Similarly, certain forms (or instances) of mediumship may be more or less obnoxious, but they may yield facts of great value.

In the following pages, therefore, the writer is primarily concerned with the *experiences* described by the 'dead', chiefly, though not invariably, through mediums. He does not presume to sit in judgment upon the latter or on those who consulted them.

R. CROOKALL.

GLOSSARY

Astral Body.—This term is used with different meanings by different authors and should be discarded. In some cases it refers to the vehicle of vitality, in others to the Soul Body and in still others to a combination of the two.

Astral Plane.—This also has various meanings in various books: it is sometimes applied to 'Hades' conditions, sometimes to 'Paradise' conditions and sometimes to both.

'Butterfly' State.—Begins with life in the Soul Body, in 'Paradise' conditions.

Christ-spirit.—The 'Father'-in-manifestation, "by whom all things were made" (John i. 3), the 'True Vine' (John xv. 1) of which the 'Father' is the 'Life' (John i. 4, v, 26, vi. 33, 47, 48, 54, x 10, xi. 25, xiv. 6), and of which the Greater Selves of men are the 'branches' or partial manifestations (John xv. 5).

'Chrysalis' State.—Corresponds to 'Hades' (not 'hell'=torment) conditions, with the vehicle of vitality enshrouding the Soul Body, immediately after physical death.

Double.—The Physical Body is sometimes said to have a 'double', but the latter is primary and the Physical Body is a 'condensation' of it, i.e. it is the Soul Body which has a 'double'—namely, the Physical Body. The vehicle of vitality properly belongs to the Physical Body, but since at death it leaves the latter along with the Soul Body, for a time (an average of from three to four days) the total after-death 'double' consists of (*a*) the vehicle of vitality *plus* (*b*) the Soul Body. The former is shed (at the 'second death') and the 'double' then consists of the Soul Body only.

'Earthbound'.—Those who, having died, remain an unduly long time with the vehicle of vitality enshrouding the Soul Body, i.e. in 'Hades' conditions, are said to be 'earthbound'. Some are sensual or wicked, others merely weak or ignorant.

Eschatology.—Teachings concerning death, the Judgment, Heaven, Hell, etc.

Etheric Body.—The same remarks apply as to the Astral body.

'Etheric double' (*of Theosophy*).—This is the vehicle of vitality.

God the 'Father'.—The 'Father' is beyond time, space, form, matter and human understanding: He is Transcendent, Infinite, Absolute, Unmanifest, purely 'subjective'. He manifests as the *Logos* or Christ-spirit.

Greater Self.—The 'Spirit', Divine Self in man: the Over-soul, the Christ-in-you of St. Paul (Col. i. 27). See p. 57.

'Hades' state.—The condition immediately after death, when the Soul Body is enveiled by the vehicle of vitality: the "Plane of Illusion".

Hallucination.—A sensory perception in the absence of a corresponding physical stimulus.

Hypnagogic.—Dream-images which may be seen in the early sleep-state (which is related to 'Hades' state).

Lesser self.—That (small) portion of the Greater Self which filters through the physical body and brain: the personality.

Man.—Confusion arises when this word is used in different senses. The perfectly true statement, by the zoologist, that 'man' evolved from ape-like animals applies to his *earthly body and its mental correlates* (instinct, incipient reason, etc.). The equally true statement, by theologians, that 'man' was made "in the image of God" and originally dwelt in 'Heaven' apply to the *Greater Self, Over-Soul or 'Spirit', a Cosmic Being.* The latter (in the Spiritual Body) undergoes a process of *involution*, a 'fall' or 'descent' into 'matter' that is denser than that of the Spiritual Body. First, 'He' assumes the Soul Body (with the formation of a psychic self, or 'soul'), corresponding to 'the Garden of Eden', or 'Paradise'), then an earthly body (with the formation of a lesser self, or personality). The important point is that man's physical body had been evolved by the animals (in whom *both* body and consciousness are in process of *evolution*. The temporary assumption, by the Greater Self, of an animal body facilitates individualisation. Thereafter 'man' can co-operate with the basic plan (including the evolution of plants and animals).

Medium.—A sensitive, psychic, automatist or interpreter.

'Paradise' State.—The normal 'next' world of the average and above-average 'dead'. The Soul Body corresponds to this environment. It is 'semi-physical' and is not the 'super-physical' true 'Heavens' of the Bible (which is entered

after the 'Third Death', i.e. the shedding of the Soul Body).

Psychical Body.—This is the Soul Body (the 'psychical' body of St. Paul was unfortunately translated 'natural').

Psycho-kinesis.—*See* tele-kinesis.

'Second death'.—The shedding of the vehicle of vitality from the Soul Body.

Soul Body.—Corresponds to 'Paradise' conditions and produces 'mental' psychical phenomena (i.e. telepathy, clairvoyance, foreknowledge, etc.).

Spirit Body.—Remarks as for Astral Body.

Spiritual Body.—Ditto. The 'Spiritual', 'Divine' or 'Celestial' Body of St. Paul (II Cor. v. 1), the 'highest', most subtle and responsive of man's bodies, the 'body' of the Greater Self, is scarcely organised in average men: When consciousness does operate through it, mystical or cosmic experiences are produced. It corresponds with the True 'Heavens' of the Bible.

Tele-kinesis.—The movement of physical objects without physical contact.

'Third-death.'—Shedding the Soul Body at end of 'Paradise' state (when true 'Heavens' are entered). Thereafter, direct communication with mortals is impossible.

'Thought-forms'.—Mental images (which, in the 'Hades' state, may be mistaken for actual objects).

Vehicle of Vitality.—This, 'the nerve spirit' of German communicators, the 'vital body' of the Rosicrucians, the 'etheric double' of the Theosophists, and the 'Bardo Body' of Tibetans, is part (the 'magnetic' or ultra-gaseous part) of the total Physical Body. If 'loose', it can give off 'ectoplasm' and produce such 'physical' phenomena as 'raps', levitation, direct voice, tele-kinesis and 'materialisations'.

'Veil.'—Since at death the vehicle of vitality leaves the Physical Body along with the Soul Body, it 'enveils' the latter until shed (at 'the second death'). It causes temporary 'sub-normal' consciousness.

FIRST PART

THE SUCCESSION OF EXPERIENCES

"We cannot but speak the things we have seen and heard."—*SS. Peter and John* (Acts iv. 20).

"Whatever the humblest men affirm from their own experience is always worth listening to, but what even the cleverest of men, in their ignorance, deny, is never worth a moment's attention."—*Sir William Barrett.*

"Human experience, which is constantly contradicting theory, is the great test of truth."—*Dr. Samuel Johnson.*

"All our most real convictions are born and brought up in . . . personal experiences. Communication is always, of necessity, personal, so it is always incredible until personally experienced. Once realised, it is unforgettable and indestructible."—*Robertson Ballard.*

"Evolution is the product of knowledge acquired by personal experience. One only knows what one has experienced. Beyond this there is only belief. So long as you have not gone to Versailles you do not *know* that Versailles exists; you may *believe* it from reports, but you will not know it from experience."—*P. E. Cornillier.*

INTRODUCTORY

A FEW decades ago Sir Oliver Lodge, Sir William Barrett, F. W. H. Myers, Dr. Richard Hodgson, Mrs. Sidgwick and many other psychical researchers concluded that survival was a proven fact. Today, a canvass of those best able to judge would give a probability not of 100 per cent, but one of about 90 per cent: survival is not now considered by many psychical researchers to be absolutely proven on evidential grounds. Why is this?

Let us take a typical (imaginary) case. Suppose Mr. Jones 'loses' his brother and wants to know if he has survived death. He goes to a medium, sensitive or psychic who transmits from the 'brother' all sorts of 'messages' that include memories of his earth-life: these memories are verified by Jones. "Yes," he says, "I believe we are indeed in touch with my brother." Then he puts a test: "Ask my brother what I said to him when we were alone together on the boat on Lake Windermere on August 1, 1940." (Now, this was a very strange and unusual expression, one which could not possibly be guessed.) The sensitive transmits the phrase correctly. Jones, highly satisfied, goes to a sceptical friend, gives him an account of the proceedings, and concludes, "My brother is still alive: no one knew about that strange expression but we two." "Ah," replies his friend, "but *you* knew, and the sensitive might have obtained it from *your* mind by telepathy. I grant you that the probabilities are nine to one that it was your brother, but there remains the odd chance that it was telepathy. His survival is very probable, but not certain."

Jones returns to the sensitive for further evidence. "Your brother," says the sensitive, "wants to convince you. He wants to transmit something that you did not know, that nobody in the world but himself knew. When you were boys there was a wood behind your house and in that wood was an old fountain around which you used to play. Your brother says that he once began a game which he never finished, in fact, circumstances arose in which he could not finish it. He had forgotten it until now, when searching for something really evidential. He put a penny beneath the big stone behind the fountain. Go back to your old home and you will find the coin: it was dated 1890."

Jones goes back to his childhood home, enters the wood, finds the fountain, raises the stone and there is the old penny, dated 1890. He returns to his friend and tells of this new evidence. "No," replies his friend; "again I will grant you a high degree of probability, say nine to one, but sensitives in trance may be almost omniscient, they may be able to read some kind of Memory of Nature or some kind of Collective Unconscious. Your brother's survival is highly likely but not absolutely certain."

Jones's friend is quite right. In fact some psychical researchers now maintain that the problem of survival must be shelved until more is known about the supernormal capabilities of mediums, psychics or sensitives. They consider that there is a deadlock on this important question. Dr. Gardner Murphy[1] said, "The case for survival rests upon dead centre, waiting for evidence so good, or objections so sound, as to warrant the formation of a judgment." Dr. D. J. West[2] took much the same view. Professor J. B. Rhine spoke of "a stalemate".

Half a century ago, Professor Henri Bergson suggested a different method of approach to this problem: he suggested that, instead of seeking for verifiable earth-memories of people who have 'passed on', we should examine other, though non-verifiable, statements that purport to come from the 'dead'. These, he thought, might provide evidence in support of the theory of survival. Sir Oliver Lodge agreed. But no systematic work has been done on these lines. Why is this?

We suggest three main reasons. First, the 'communications' contain many *contradictions* and this naturally arouses doubt. But we would point out that, in material of this kind, we ought to expect to find contradictions which, however, on closer examination, prove to be apparent and not real.

Let us suppose there are Martians and that their bodies are egg-shaped. They say, "Can there be any intelligent creatures on earth?" They send one of their number to earth. He lands in Alaska and returns to describe intelligent creatures who are

[1] *Journ. American S.P.R.*, 1945.   [2] *Psychical Research Today*, Duckworth, 1954.

white, who live dressed in furs among snow and ice, and who eat chiefly fish. Another Martian makes the journey to earth. He lands in Africa and goes back to describe the intelligent creatures who are black, who wear no clothes and who eat fruit. A third lands in China, where he sees yellow men who wear flowing robes and live on rice. A fourth lands in the Red Indian Reserve of U.S.A. and sees red men who spend their time in the chase and live on the animals they catch. A fifth reaches London and reports white men with clothes, activities, food, etc., that are different from any of those hitherto described. When these reports are compared back on Mars, although *we* know that each and every one was accurate, *they* would find a preponderance of contradictions. In fact, there might be only one feature common to all the narratives —all the intelligent creatures described as seen on earth possessed two arms and two legs! This would be significant, since (we are supposing) Martians are not so constructed—it is highly unlikely that this common feature would be either imagined or invented by a number of independent observers. The contradictions reported, though numerous, were apparent and not real: the similarities, though few, were highly significant.

The second reason why unverifiable 'communications' have been neglected is that the *similarities* which they contain are dismissed as due to the 'fact' that the 'sub-conscious minds' of mediums, psychics or sensitives tend to think in the same way —they are attributed to 'a mediumistic climate of thought'. This procedure has been fatal to progress.

'Communications' of the unverifiable type deal with in-numerable subjects—the supposed conditions of the after-life, the 'spheres', 'planes' or environments in which the 'dead' live, their occupations and activities, their relationships to each other and to us mortals, the methods by which they communicate with us, their 'lecture halls', 'libraries', 'hospitals', etc. Many who have made a study of the numerous independent accounts of such matters have pointed out that they exhibit remarkable similarities and that, although they cannot be taken as literally true and exact descriptions, they must, presumably, refer to reality of some sort. A study of such matters will not, however, contribute towards a demonstration of survival. But there is, we suggest, one element in communications that is in a different category and that may—in fact, does—help in this problem.

All people, however learned, however untutored, know what happens to themselves—when they fall down, when they get up, when they go to sleep, when they wake up, when they remember something, etc. The present writer, therefore, in the first instance, selects from the great mass of unverifiable 'messages' what the 'dead' say they *experienced* at (and soon after) death. Collections of such experiences would be expected to contain apparent contradictions. The contradictions that occurred in the reports of our Martians had no bearing on the question of the existence of men or earth; they merely reflected the different conditions in which men live. In the same way, contradictions in the reports from 'the other side' may not indicate that they do not emanate from the living dead, but merely reflect the fact that 'the other side' includes 'many mansions', i.e. abiding-places (John xiv. 2).

In these circumstances our second task is to make some kind of a sieve which will let through the (? apparent) contradictions for subsequent inspection but retain the significant similarities as of immediate significance and value.

Two sets of factors affect all who die and may cause them to have different (i.e. apparently contradictory) experiences. We may expect that, while a great saint will have experiences that differ markedly from those of a great sinner (as, indeed, we are informed in the Scriptures—Luke xvi. 19, etc.), one person of average moral and spiritual development will have experiences that are, in general, similar to those of another person of average type. Our method, so far as status is concerned, is therefore to concentrate on the experiences described by *average* men.

The second set of factors that may cause (? apparent) contradictions in narratives from 'beyond' is represented by the nature of the transition that is undergone: this varies greatly, with all gradations between two extremes (*a*) natural death (typically in old age) and (*b*) enforced death in the prime of life—a soldier killed in battle. (In deaths of the average type the person concerned is neither suddenly and forcibly ejected from the body in his prime nor does he reach the full 'three score years and ten' of the Psalmist (Ps. xc. 10): on the contrary, he shortens his life, perhaps by a few months or years only, by unwise living, such as by over- or under-eating, over- or under-working, etc.). So far as this group of factors is concerned, our method is to avoid the confusing average and concentrate on the experiences described under *the two extreme conditions of 'passing'* (Fig. 1)

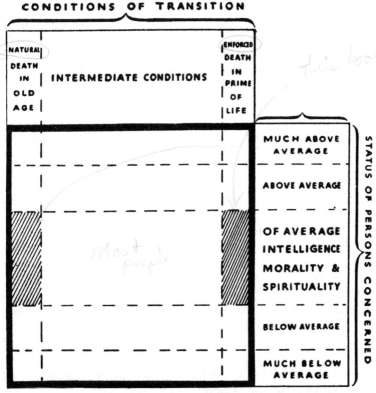

FIG. 1. Showing (*a*) average people who died naturally (in old age) and (*b*) average people whose death was enforced in the prime of life.

We therefore compare what is described by men of average type (*a*) who died naturally in old age and (*b*) whose death was enforced in the prime of life. In doing this, we follow the procedure which was adopted by medical scientists in the study of physical birth: they did not investigate the innumerable possible variations *en masse*; on the contrary, they studied the chief factors separately—different physical and mental types of women, different types of delivery, etc. If they had not adopted this method the process of physical birth would have remained obscure, since one factor (e.g. good or bad heredity) might modify, even nullify, another factor (e.g. good or bad diet) and must cause apparent contradictions.

It seems strange that psychologists and psychical researchers have not applied some method of this type to the 'communications' that purport to describe the birth which we call death, instead of dismissing them *in toto*. Had they done so they would not only have obtained supplementary evidence for survival, but, in addition, information concerning the conditions of the early after-life. Our method is seen to be particularly helpful concerning the after-death 'sleep' (see p. 136).

A third factor which has tended to prevent any serious study of unverifiable mediumistic communications is that their intellectual content is often (though by no means always) of poor quality. But the average person (who provides the bulk of the 'messages' studied) is not highly intellectual. Nevertheless, he is just as well aware of what happens to him, of what he *experiences*, as the intellectuals. When, instead of demanding that supposed communicators prove their reality by "telling us something we don't know", "something about God", "new scientific facts", etc.—we make an unbiased study of what they do say that they *experienced* (at, and soon after, death), their narratives are seen to be highly significant, since they exhibit "internal consistency" to a quite remarkable degree. Moreover, while they have no "antecedent improbability", they clearly have considerable "inherent probability", agreeing, as they do, with many of the facts and theories of psychological and psychical science. There is an Arab proverb which runs: "Do not ask of the book-learned man who has not been there—ask the ordinary fellow who has!"

In this book, then, we provisionally assume that there is "an ordinary fellow" on 'the other side' who has told us, among other things, how he fared in the birth which we call death and we clarify our study by concentrating on the statement of those who claim to have 'passed' under the two extreme conditions (Fig. 1). Our procedure yields many 'pointers' to survival.

The meaning of the term 'pointer', as here used, may be illustrated by reference to another sphere of exploration, the geographical field. In early times, when the Mediterranean Sea was the centre of civilisation, explorers occasionally sailed through the Straits of Gibraltar and along the coast of northern Africa. Many of the descriptions they brought back were, no doubt, exaggerations; some were doubtless inventions. However, one venturesome captain, on returning from such a voyage, not only described landscapes, peoples, animals, etc., but also made the statement that eventually the sun had shone from the north! Just as creatures with two arms, two legs were unknown to our Martians, this phenomenon was unknown to Mediterranean peoples. The captain was laughed to scorn. But today we cannot doubt that he had been where he claimed to have been—that he had, in fact, sailed south of the equator. His statement was a 'pointer'; though we lack direct evidence on the matter, this indirect evidence shows that this traveller's tale was true.

The 'pointers' in our analyses of 'communications' bypass the 'deadlock' or 'stalemate' in the direct evidence for survival; they are independent of ecclesiastical or scientific authority, of the good faith of any mediums and of the nature of any 'controls' concerned. These 'travellers' tales' also are clearly true (see Appendix II).

THE FIRST EXPERIENCE: THE 'CALL'

NATURAL DEATH

A PERSON who is in course of natural transition is said, in communications from 'beyond', to send out a kind of 'call' to friends and relatives who have 'gone before'. This 'Call' sometimes consists of deliberate and conscious thoughts; sometimes it is more or less instinctive and subconscious.

(1) The communicator of Wilfred Brandon (*Open the Door*), Alfred A. Knopf, 1935, p. 27) stated: "Usually friends or relatives take the newly-dead man in charge. This is sure to be so if, before death, he has sent out thoughts of them." This statement occurs in a book of a 'popular' type, but similar ones occur in *Proc. S.P.R.* For example, 'Bennie' told his parents, "When you are called to this beautiful world, I shall be the first to greet and help you"[1] (presumably in response to the 'Call').

(2) 'W. T. Stead', communicating, said, "In this land we are much more sensitive than whilst on earth and when thoughts are directed to us by mortals we have a direct call . . . and we are practically always able to come in close contact with the person who is thinking of us.[2]

(3) Winifred Graham, in the Foreword to her book of communications, stated, "It is the bond of love which bridges the gulf". She added, "I firmly believe that all who are bound by love may communicate (even if they cannot write) by mind-impressions"[3] [=telepathy and communion rather than by verbal communications].

It is also significant that the converse statement is independently communicated. Thus: "Being self-centred, he was unable to send out the urgent 'Call' that is always picked up and answered."[4]

---

[1] *Proc. S.P.R.*, xxiv, 351.
[2] *The Blue Island*, Hutchinson & Co. Ltd., 1922, p. 94.
[3] *My Letters from Heaven*, Rider & Co. Ltd.
[4] Geraldine Cummins, *Travellers in Eternity*, Psychic Press Ltd., 1948, p. 122.

ENFORCED DEATH

Whereas references to the 'Call' commonly occur in connection with natural transitions, we have seen no case whatever in connection with soldiers who were killed in battle, etc.

THE SECOND EXPERIENCE:
A REVIEW OF THE PAST LIFE

NATURAL AND ENFORCED DEATH

COMMUNICATORS often declare that, in the early stages of transition, they experienced a panoramic review of their past earth-lives. This applies to both natural and enforced types of transition. It was impersonal and non-emotional in nature.

In addition to the following examples, the 'review' is mentioned incidentally when other experiences are being described—there are four references to it under Experience No. 3 and three under Experience No. 6.

(1) Findlay was told: "The scenes of the past life are . . . often revealed to those who are just passing, at the last moment."[1]

(2) "I was unconscious for just a moment [=the momentary coma due to shedding the Physical Body, i.e. Experience No. 3B]. Then my entire life unreeled itself. . . ."[2]

(3) "The first thing they find when they come here is the record of their past life."[3]

(4) "One of the first things noticed is that, without mental effort, everything we have done . . . comes before us as a present memory."[4]

(5) "I saw clearer and clearer the events of my past life pass, in a long procession, before me. . . ."[5]

(6) "I saw my life unfold before me in a procession of images."[6]

Similar statements were made by 'Myers' through Geraldine Cummins. "In the life after death he enters an intermediate stage, and . . . his soul perceives, at intervals, the episodes of

[1] J. Arthur Findlay, *Where Two Worlds Meet*, Psychic Press Ltd., 1951, p. 599.

[2] Philip Paul, *Psychic News*, January 22, 1955.

[3] F. Heslop, *Speaking Across the Border Line*, Chas. Taylor, 1912.

[4] A. Campbell Holms, *The Facts of Psychic Science and Philosophy*, Kegan Paul, Trench, Trubner and Co. Ltd., 1925, p. 27.

[5] Franchezzo, *op. cit.*, 1910, p. 76.

[6] 'A.L.E.H.', *Fragments from my Messages*, Women's Printing Society, 1929, p. 198.

the past existence."[1] Again, "I seemed to be . . . seeing pictures of my life. . . ."[2]

(7) 'W. T. Stead', communicating, said: "My memory of earth functioned at this time . . . I felt for the moment all the joys and griefs of a lifetime."[3]

(8) 'Scott' told Jane Sherwood that his thoughts "raced over the record of a whole long lifetime". He continued: "I reviewed it as though I had no responsibility for it."[4]

(9) Another communicator told Jane Sherwood that the 'review' was like "a film shown backwards."[5]

(10) 'Major P.', communicating to W. T. Pole while he was in process of transition, said: "I have been laid up a long time. I seem to be standing in an open doorway. All the events of my life are portrayed before me in symbolic form. I can see myself as a child, as a boy, as a man."[6]

(11) Our last reference to the 'review' takes us back twenty-five centuries. According to Edouard Schure (*Pythagoras*, Paris, 1926), the great Greek philosopher Pythagoras (who was "entitled to be called 'the Father of Science' "), taught that, at death, the soul "sees, over and over again, its earthly existence, the scenes succeeding one another with startling clearness."

[1] Geraldine Cummins, *Beyond Human Personality*, Ivor Nicholson and Watson, 1935, p. 29.
[2] Geraldine Cummins, *They Survive*, Rider and Co. Ltd., p. 42.
[3] *Life Eternal*, Wright and Brown, 1933, p. 73.
[4] *The Psychic Bridge*, Rider & Co. Ltd., p. 48.
[5] *The Country Beyond*, Rider & Co. Ltd., p. 24.
[6] *Private Dowding*, Watkins, 1943, p. 107.

THE THIRD GROUP OF EXPERIENCES:
SHEDDING THE BODY

NATURAL DEATH

ACCORDING to communications from supposed discarnates whose 'passing' was of the natural type, the act of shedding the physical body caused the various experiences indicated below (a-e). Some examples of these are also given incidentally under other experiences, notably under Experience No. 2 (one example) and Experience No. 5 (four examples).

(a) A sensation of rising and falling

(1) "*I had a sinking feeling*. The daylight seemed to go. I swayed about in the dark and felt slightly giddy. Then the atmosphere became light and I heard the voices of my dear boys [who had 'passed on']. After a time of unconsciousness I suddenly became clearer . . . and saw my boys, my brothers and many others round me."[1]

(2) "At the moment of death the soul finds itself entirely unconscious beyond *a feeling of sinking away*."[2]

(3) "I saw about me those that had been dead for a long time. . . . *Then I seemed to rise up out of my body and come down quietly on the floor*. . . . There seemed to be two of me, one on the bed and one beside the bed. . . . My pain was gone. Some of those whom I recognised as persons who had died asked me to go. . . . My next thought was that it was a dream. . . . I was gently told what had happened."[3]

(4) "I was dimly conscious of figures moving round the bed. Then I saw that *I was not lying in the bed, but floating in the air, a little above it*. I saw the body, stretched out straight. My first idea was that I might re-enter it, but all desire to do this soon left me—the tie [=the 'silver cord'] was broken. I stood on the floor. . . . Close to me was my father's father; he had been with

---

[1] The Rev. C. Drayton Thomas, *In the Dawn Beyond Death*, Lectures Universal Ltd., p. 20.

[2] H. Dennis Bradley, *Towards the Stars*, T. Werner Laurie, 1924.

[3] Edward C. Randall, *Frontiers of the After Life*, Alfred A. Knopf, 1932, p. 34.

me all through. I also saw my relatives still in earth-life [='dual consciousness']. I spoke to them. They took no notice."[1]

(5) "*I seemed to be lifted above the usual surroundings.* I was not only with those who had passed over recently, but with my father and mother, whom I had not seen for a long time. I was not conscious of any change or of anything abrupt. . . . Then I passed into a peaceful sleep. *I hear now that I slept for three or four days* [=Experience No. 4]. I knew I was not on earth because of the long-lost people now around me again and the brilliancy of the atmosphere."[2]

(6) "*I felt myself floating.* . . . I found myself in a pearly mist."[3]

(7) Although 'J. V. Wilson', communicating to A. J. Davis (*The Physician*, 1850) did not say that he felt the sensation of rising above his body, he said that he found himself "over the head of the body".

(b) A momentary coma, passing through a 'doorway', a 'tunnel', etc.

Many communications experienced leaving the body as a coma, 'blackout', etc., and when this was more than momentary, described it as like passing through a 'tunnel', 'door', 'passage', etc.

(1) A boy who was dying, "was full of excitement about *a door* he could see at the corner of his room". . . and said, "When it is open wide, I shall go through it."[4]

(2) A communicator from 'beyond' said he felt as though he had gone through "*a door*".[5]

(3) "I remember a curious opening, as if one had passed through subterranean passages and found oneself near the mouth of *a cave*. . . . The light was much stronger outside."[6]

(4) A communicator stated that he and his discarnate friends helped people who were in course of transition (i.e.,

[1] Helen Alex Dallas, *Human Survival and Its Implications*, L.S.A. Publications Ltd., 1930, p. 32.

[2] The Rev. C. Drayton Thomas, *In the Dawn Beyond Death*, p. 66.

[3] *Light*, vol. xlvii, 1927, p. 314.

[4] Sir Wm. Barrett, *Death-bed Visions*, Methuen, 1926, p. 49.

[5] Jane Sherwood, *The Country Beyond*, Rider & Co. Ltd., p. 125.

[6] The Rev. C. Drayton Thomas, *In the Dawn Beyond Death*, Lectures Universal Ltd., p. 133.

that they operated as 'deliverers'): he said they tried "to make this passage through *the tunnel* as happy as possible.[1]

(c) An expansion of consciousness

The shedding of the Physical Body was often found to bring an 'expansion' of consciousness.

(1) "A great darkness swooped down on me like a bird [=shedding the Physical Body, i.e. Experience No. 3, B]. *Then there was relief, expansion,* a sense of being freed from an intolerable weight. I came out into a strange clearness and could not believe that I had died."[2]

(2) 'Conan Doyle' stated: "The narrowed conscious daily life of man is immeasurably *broadened and expanded* beyond death. . . ."[3]

(3) 'J. V. Wilson', communication to A. J. Davis (*The Physician*) said that, as death approached, "Thought became too intense and elevated for the body". He went to bed and "felt the evidences of transformation . . .". He stated, "The transition was interesting and *delightful. I expanded* in every direction. I was boundless, was infinite. . . ."

(4) Another of Davis's communicators mentioned "*expanding thoughts*" and said: "A *super-consciousness* pervaded me and my Spirit was endowed with immortal sensibilities." He continued: "Lo! instead of seeing the external forms of my friends [mourners], I beheld their interior life and read their inmost thoughts. . . . Directing my perceptions to where I saw them gaze, I beheld (in their thoughts) the body which I myself had worn! I strove to tell them that the deserted tenement was nothing, and that *I possessed a body* and stood among them: but there could be no communication between us."

(5) 'A.B''s communicator (*One Step Higher*, The C. W. Daniel Co. Ltd., 1937, pp. 22, 76, 115) said that when he died his soul "*expanded*", his consciousness "*widened*": "time stood still and space meant nothing".

(6) "I have been laid up a long time. . . . *I seem to be standing in an open doorway.* . . . All the events of my life are portrayed before me . . . [=the first review, i.e. Experience No. 2]. Now I see myself [=the double] lying there asleep among the

---

[1] Anon., *Talks with Spirit Friends Bench and Bar*, Watkins, 1931, p. 79.

[2] Geraldine Cummins, *They Survive*, Rider & Co. Ltd., p. 49.

[3] Ivan Cooke, *Thy Kingdom Come*, Wright and Brown, p. 109.

THE THIRD GROUP OF EXPERIENCES: SHEDDING THE BODY

trees in that fair land. . . . And still I [=the Physical Body] am
in bed [='dual consciousness']. They have injected something
and I am being forcibly held down. If they only knew and
would let me go! [=reluctance to return]. Their voices sound
faint and the room recedes. I am in bed, yes, yet I am also in
that *doorway*—on the threshold, nearly ready, nearly. . . . It
is as if I were extracting the real 'me' [the double] from the
unreal 'me' [=the body]. . . . Where am I? Is this my real
self, lying so quietly here with flowers and green around
me. . . .? I have slept again [=shedding the 'vehicle of
'vitality' =the 'second death']. *I am where I am, yet I am everywhere! I am a self that is far greater and vaster than what I thought
and felt myself to be.*"[1]

(7) "How does it feel to be 'dead'? One can't explain,
because there's nothing in it. I simply felt free and light. My
being seemed to have *expanded*."[2]

(8) "After you die *the soul suddenly seems to expand*."[3]

The after-death 'expansion' is discussed in the Third Part
under Statements 22-4 and 34.

(d) Glimpses of discarnate friends

A constant feature of the experiences described in natural
death is the fact that the person concerned was 'met', aided and
welcomed by friends and relatives who had 'gone before'.
Many insisted that the act of dying involved no pain, and said
that they saw the Physical Body lying on the bed, reminding
them of a discarded garment. Everything was so natural
that the fact of transition was often unrealised at first. They
found that they could not be seen or heard by (non-psychic)
friends still in the flesh. Meanwhile any undue grief on the
part of the latter enveloped the newly-dead in gloom and
despondency.

The Indian Christian mystic, Sadhu Sundar Singh (like the
well-known Methodist journalist, John Oxenham) maintained
that the visions that he saw and the voices that he heard differed
essentially from those described by others—that they were
characteristically of a Christian type. The Sadhu said that the
messages and signs received by others are "fragmentary and
unintelligible", while those which he received were "vivid

---

[1] W. T. Pole, *Private Dowding*, Watkins, 1917, p. 107.   [2] *Ibid.*, p. 16.
[3] 'W. T. Stead' in *Life Eternal*, Wright and Brown, 1933, p. 170.

and clear in every detail" and represented "rational elucida-
tions" of his problems. All accounts, however, are identical.
In particular the Sadhu was told, "Death is like sleep. There is
no pain in the passing over, except in the case of a few bodily
diseases and mental conditions. . . . Many only with great
difficulty realise that they have left the material world. . . .
They imagine that they are visiting some country of the
physical world. It is only when they have been more fully
instructed that they realise their 'passing'. Loved ones who
have died before are permitted to attend the death-beds of
believers. On entering the world of spirits they at once feel
at home—their friends are about them and they had long
been preparing themselves for that home while on earth".[1]

(e) The 'silver cord'

Many communicators say that they observed a feature that
clearly corresponds to the 'silver cord' mentioned by Ecclesiastes (xii, 6), a non-physical tie, link or extension that unites
the Physical Body to the double whenever they are separated
during earth-life (and the severance of which is the irrevocable
feature of death).

(1) "I began to feel a heavy weight. Gradually I realised
that this weight was slipping away from me—or, rather, I was
sliding out from it, as if someone were drawing his hand out
from a wet glove. Then I began to feel free at one end, so to
speak, and then I began to see again. I saw once more the
room and the people in it. Then I was free! I saw myself
lying stretched out on the bed, and *from my mouth came, as it
were, a cord of light. It vibrated for a moment, then snapped.* At that
moment someone said, "I think he has gone". . . . Then the
room seemed to fade away. I was in the most exquisite scenery
imaginable. . . ."[2]

(2) "I lapsed into a state of semi-consciousness . . . the nurse
gradually receded; other forms came nearer, and I discerned
Mother and Father and many others. *Even then I still held on
to my body.* . . . This was the process of my leaving the body.
There were a few moments of total unconsciousness [=the
coma while shedding the Physical Body, i.e. Experience
No. 3B]; then it seemed that a strong hand was stretched out

[1] Sadhu Sundar Singh, *Visions of the Spiritual World*, Macmillan, 1926.
[2] S. M. Ward, *Gone West*, Rider and Co. Ltd., 1917, p. 28.

and I was lifted [by 'deliverers']. I came to consciousness with *my new body resting parallel over my old one and about a yard away, immediately above it.* . . . *A cord from the solar plexus linked me to my old body.* I remained floating and swaying, realising that I was still bound. . . . Then something seemed to snap, and I began to take an upright position. *Then I saw that the cord had snapped.* I was free, a new man in a new body. I was surrounded by all the dear ones . . . born again!"[1]

(3) "Without dreaming, without delirium, I actually saw 'J.' and she spoke to me. It was a dreamy consciousness, for I was affected by the exhaustion of my Physical Body. *I felt a connection* with it [=the 'silver cord'], severed as I was. The mourners around my bed wept. I seemed to feel the force of their grief and I longed to assuage it. Unconsciousness then came [=Experience No. 3B]. I awoke on a wonderful plain."[2]

(4) 'Felicia Scatcherd', communicating, said: "I felt myself *floating* [=Experience No. 3A] . . . in a kind of buoyant mist. Those who came to me ['deliverers'] said they must slowly help me out of my body—*breaking those threads.* I kept very quiet and . . . all the threads broke easily and naturally. I got quite away from my body and was not half-caught, as some are."

(5) 'A.L.E.H.' was promised, "I shall be able to free your spirit from *the many tiny threads* that bind it to the body. . . . Then you will be able to leave this cast-off garment and will not hang about it as so many do. . . . Last of all *the silver cord of life* is severed."

(6) 'Abraham Ackley, M.D.' of Ohio, was quoted by Mrs. de Morgan thus: "In most cases there is little or no . . . suffering; even when there is a struggle, it is only an effort, painless in character, by the spirit to burst *the bonds* that have bound it to the physical body. This was my own experience. . . . I learned, after my spirit was free from its *connection* with the external body, that these were produced by it in its attempts to sever this *connection* which in all cases is more or less difficult. The vital points of contact being suddenly broken by disease, the union of the other portions of the system is necessarily

[1] F. T. Robertson, *Celestial Voices*, H. M. Greaves Ltd., p. 265.
[2] Anon. ('King's Counsel'), *Bear Witness*, Hutchinson & Co.
[3] *Light*, XLVII, 1927, p. 314.   [4] 'A.L.E.H.', *op. cit.*, 1929, p. 14.

severed by violence, but, so far as I have learned, without . . .
pain. Like many others, I was unable to leave the form at
once. I could feel myself gradually raised from my body
[=Experience No. 3A] and in a dreamy . . . state. It seems as
though . . . I was separated into two parts, and yet . . . there
seemed to be an indissoluble *connecting-link*. My spirit was
freed a short time after the organs of my physical body had
ceased to function. My spiritual form was then united into one
and *I was raised a short distance above the body*. . . . Two spirits
['deliverers'] . . . conducted me from the room. . . . As
consciousness returned, the scenes of my whole life moved
before me like a panorama. So rapidly did it pass that I had
little time for reflection [=the first review, i.e. Experience
No. 2]. . . ."[1]

There are innumerable general statements in the literature
that agree with the individual statements cited above. The
following are typical.

(1) 'Myers', communicating through Geraldine Cummins,
stated: "During sleep, the soul exists within the double while
the body is recharged with nervous energy. . . . The double is
an exact counterpart of the physical shape. *The two are bound
together by many little threads, by two silver cords.* One of these
makes contact with the solar plexus, the other with the brain.
. . . Death occurs when these two principal communicating
lines are severed. . . . Life occasionally lingers in certain cells
of the body after the soul has fled. There is a simple explanation
for it. *The double still adheres to the physical shell by means of certain
threads which have not yet been broken. The newly-dead man has,
thereby, a greater awareness of the immediate surroundings of his
physical body . . . power to perceive his friends wherever his physical
body lies* [i.e. until the 'silver cord' and all subsidiary threads
are severed, a newly-dead man may have 'dual consciousness',
with some awareness of his physical body (and its environment)
and some of his double (and its environment)]. *As a rule,
however, he obtains complete freedom . . . [i.e. all cords and threads
break*] within an hour, or a few hours, of death."[2]

(2) Mrs. Rhys Davids said: "*For an hour, roughly speaking, before
the heart stops, the 'man' will have left his dying body and be standing
near, 'encased' in the emerged other-body*" [Soul Body]. Any

[1] *From Matter to Spirit*, Longmans, Green & Co. Ltd., 1863, p. 142.
[2] Geraldine Cummins, *The Road to Immortality*, Ivor Nicholson and Watson, 1932.

commotions of a purely physical nature in the dying body are purely 'reflex'. Of these, the man feels nothing."[1]

(3) 'Heslop' affirmed: "*The act of dying is absolutely painless. The contortions frequently witnessed are purely muscular: the dying man does not feel them as pain. . . . The process . . . begins at the feet and . . . emerges from the head.* Occasionally, the spiritual counterpart [=double], when released, assumes a perpendicular position, but more *generally it floats horizontally above the dying form.* It may remain some time in this position, for *it is attached to the body by a fine filmy cord* [the 'silver cord']. *Death does not take place until this cord has been severed.* In most cases . . . beloved arisen friends of the one who dies [i.e. 'deliverers'] come about him at the last to break this cord and bear him away. . . ."[2]

(4) Another communicator said: "Much of the apparent suffering of a deathbed is not felt. . . . *His real life is already half-retired from the body.*"[3]

(5) Another stated: "Death, which seems so painful to those who watch it, is not painful to us; no more painful than the convulsions of the medium are to her when trance is coming on. *The soul, in both cases, is cast out of the body:* the action of the body is merely a reflex action." He added: "The soul can actually look at the body as it dies."[4]

(A) ENFORCED DEATH OTHER THAN BY EXPLOSION

Descriptions of the experience of enforced death mainly come from those who passed out in war and we are here chiefly concerned with death from a blow (bullet, etc.) from a fall, or from drowning. But many communicators independently say that death from explosion involves a distinctive feature and we deal with such statements separately (p. 30).

Some of the statements made by those whose death was enforced are similar to those made by men who died naturally (e.g. (1) they felt little, if any, physical pain; (2) the shedding of the body caused no more than a momentary coma, 'blackout', etc.; (3) the fact that they had permanently vacated the body ('died') was often unrealised for some time; (4)

[1] Mrs. Rhys Davids, *What is Your Will?*, Rider & Co. Ltd., p. 168.
[2] F. Heslop, *Life Worth Living*, Charles Taylor, p. 26.
[3] Jane Sherwood, *The Country Beyond*, Rider & Co. Ltd., p. 26.
[4] 'A.B.', *One Step Higher*, The C. W. Daniel Co. Ltd., 1937, p. 33.

many saw their own bodies; (5) they suffered from any undue grief on the part of still-embodied friends; (6) they could not make (non-psychic) mortals see or hear them and (7) some at first wondered if they might be dreaming.

But people who died in the prime of life typically made other statements that are markedly different from those of those who died naturally. They are as follows: (1) the natural death of average men is typically followed by a 'sleep' but in enforced death the person concerned tended to be awake and alert at once or almost at once; (2) in natural death consciousness was characterised by such words as 'peace', 'security', 'happiness', 'freedom', etc.; in enforced death it was at first 'confused', 'bewildered', etc.; (3) whereas in natural transition the environment was described as 'beautiful', 'clear', 'light', and 'brilliant', in enforced death it was often (at first) 'misty', 'foggy' even 'watery'; (4) whereas many who died naturally were conscious of having seen (or felt the presence of) the 'silver cord', that feature is very seldom mentioned by those whose death was enforced; (5) whereas men who died naturally were often aware that they were met by discarnate friends (and death-bed visions are common in natural transitions), there was some delay on the part of men whose death was enforced in seeing those who met them (and none described pre-death visions of discarnate friends).

The Rev. J. W. Potter's communicator indicated two differences between natural and enforced death: in the former, "there is a cord between spirit and body for a short time"; in the latter, the cord "is instantly snapped" and sleep "is long in coming".[1]

The following are typical statements by those whose death was enforced. (1) "I awoke from a deep sleep [=shedding the Physical Body, i.e. Experience No. 3B]. *Bewildered, I got to my feet, and, looking down, saw my body among many others on the ground.* I remembered the battle, but did not realise I had been shot. *I was apart from, yet I still seemed held in some way [by the 'silver cord'] to the body. My condition was one of terrible unrest; how was it that I was alive and had a body [=the double] and was not yet apart from the covering I had thought constituted my body?* I looked about. Others of the seeming dead moved. Then many of them stood up and, like me, seemed to emerge from their Physical

---

[1] *From Beyond the Clouds*, The Society of Communion, 1927, p. 430.

Bodies, for their old forms still lay upon the field. Soon I found myself among thousands in a similar mental state: none knew just what had happened. I did not know then, as I know now, that I always possessed a Spirit Body and that the Physical Body was only the garment it wore in earth-life. *While the passing-out from this old body is without pain, it is a terrible thing to drive a strong spirit from a healthy body, to tear it from its covering.* It is un-natural, and the sensation following re-adjustment is awful. In a short time I became easier, but *I was still bewildered.* It was neither night nor day; about us all was gloom. Something like an atmosphere, dark and red, enveloped us all. *We seemed to hear one another think.* Soon there was a ray of light that grew brighter each moment and then a great concourse of men with kindly faces came and, with comforting words, told us not to fear—that we had made the great change, that the war for us was over. . . . I will not tell you of the sorrow that came with such realisation, sorrow for the wife. *Her great grief, when she learned what had happened, bound me to her condition. We sorrowed together.* I could not progress [*via* the 'second death', out of the dream-like 'Hades' into 'Paradise' conditions], or find happiness, until time had healed her sorrow."[1]

(2) "*We are extra-sensitive to the thoughts of those on earth,* especially in the early days when our minds hover between the earth and the new land. . . . In that between condition [= 'Hades' state, corresponding to the 'vehicle of vitality'] we need . . . constructive, helpful, loving thoughts."[2]

(3) "There is no horror in death. I was one minute in the thick of things and the next minute Lieutenant Wells said, 'Our command has crossed: let us go!' I thought he meant the river and followed him up a hillside that I had not noticed before—a clean spot, not blackened by guns. Lots of our fellows were there, and strange troops. But they looked queer. [He was noting incongruities between his recent (physical) environment and his present ('Hades') environment.] . . . I overtook Wells. 'What is the matter with me, with us all?' I asked. *He said, 'Bob, we're dead!' I didn't believe it at first. I felt all right. . . . The soul leaves the body as a boy jumps out of a school-door, that is, suddenly and with joy. But there is a period of confusion*

[1] Edward C. Randall, *Frontiers of the After Life*, Alfred A. Knopf, 1922.
[2] Lady Barrett, *Personality Survives Death*, Longmans, Green & Co., 1937.

when a fellow needs a friend. . . . The easiest thing in life is death.''[1]

(4) *"There was a crash and a blackness* [=*shedding body,* i.e. Experience No. 3B]. *It was not really pain as most people think of pain—a rending crash and then gone.* . . . I lay quiet and pictures came before me of myself as a little boy . . . [=the first review, i.e. Experience No. 2]. I opened my eyes again. I was surprised that I had no bruises: I felt myself all over. [He was noting incongruities between the (physical) environment he had just left and his present ('Hades') environment]. Then I saw a car coming. I saw it brake and push something along the road. *I looked, and it was my body. I looked at myself and saw my own body* [*double*] *seeming quite real and solid.* . . . *Suddenly I saw Grandpapa, standing smiling all lit up, and knew I was killed. I* said at once, 'Then mother was right—I have got an etheric body!' *I felt terribly muddled and confused.* Then came the thought of you . . . so I began to walk along the road. . . . You opened the window and called, but did not see me. *Yet I could see what you were thinking—how frightened you were! Suddenly I remembered what you said—that spirits can go through matter. I said, 'Here goes! and ran at the door—and passed right through it. I tried it two or three times.* . . . *I shall be at the funeral tomorrow.* . . . *I am still mixed up with the earth* [=the 'vehicle of vitality' still enshrouded the Soul Body]."[2]

(5) "The shock of an unnatural death sets one in a *mad turmoil.* . . . *One finds oneself in a fantastic dream-world with no . . . proper framework of space and time.*"[3]

(6) "When as the result of a fall, Joyce aged 18, 'passed over', she *didn't feel much pain;* transition seemed *'very natural'.* She told her incarnate mother, 'I had regrets which seemed all centred in you—I found *I could visit you but couldn't understand why you didn't talk to me. I saw a lot of people when I was passing, but they weren't clear. I was not able to think at first: I merely felt things were happening.* It never occurred to me that I was dead. . . . I had no sensation of travelling when I passed over. I rested for a bit [=the 'sleep' phase, i.e. Experience No. 4] yet it was not sleep in the ordinary sense, for I was seeing people all the time."[4]

[1] L. M. Geldert, *Thy Son Liveth*, Frederick Muller, Ltd., 1944, p. 12.
[2] Alice Gilbert, *Philip in Two Worlds*, Andrew Dakers Ltd., 1948, p. 89.
[3] Jane Sherwood, *The Country Beyond*, Rider & Co. Ltd., p. 24.
[4] G. Vivian, *Love Conquers Death*, L. S. Publications, pp. 19, 91.

(7) "*I felt a terrible blow on my head, a sensation of dizziness and of falling, then nothing more* [=momentary coma, i.e. Experience No. 3]. . . . Consciousness returned. . . . My body [=double] seemed to have become light. I wondered if I were in hospital. . . . A kindly doctor came to my bedside and said, 'I want to have a talk with you. . . . You have passed out of the physical body and are in the state you used to know as having died.' I could not believe him. . . . Then a gentleman came to speak to me who, I was told, was my grandfather. But I had never seen him before and was not convinced. *I felt as if I were living in a dream.* . . . The doctor promised that I should be sent to you [his incarnate mother], that the truth might be proved to me. . . . Two friends guided me through the astral plane [here ='Hades'] to the earth. *As we came nearer the earth the atmosphere became thicker and misty and the houses and everything seemed indistinct.* The view disappeared. I found myself standing in your room. . . . I called, '*Mummy, I'm here! Can't you see or hear me?*' *You made no reply.* . . . You have only to concentrate your thoughts on me and they will reach me [=the 'Call', i.e. Experience No. 1 in reverse].[1]

(8) "Something struck hard. . . . I fell and found myself outside myself! What a small incident this dying is! One moment I was alive, in the earthly sense, looking over the trench parapet, unalarmed, normal. Five seconds later I was standing outside my body. You see what a small thing death is, even the violent death of war! As in my case, *thousands of soldiers pass over without knowing it.* If there be a shock, it is not the shock of physical death. Shock comes later when comprehension dawns: 'Where is my body? Surely I am not dead?'. . . . I was so little dead that I imagined I was still [physically] alive. I had been struck by a shell-splinter. *There was no pain.* It was as if I had been running hard until, hot and breathless, I had thrown my overcoat away. The coat was my body. I felt free and light. I am still evidently in a body of some sort [=the double]. After I had recovered from the shock of realising I was dead, *I was above the battlefield. It seemed as if I were floating in a mist that muffled sound and blurred the vision. Everything was distant, misty, unreal.* [Since he had not, as yet, shed the 'vehicle of vitality', his consciousness remained

[1] Mrs. L. Kelway Bamber, *Claude's Book*, Psychic Book Club, 1918, p. 2.

enshrouded and therefore 'sub-normal', while his environment
was the illusory 'Hades' conditions]. I think I fell asleep for
the second time [=a second momentary coma, the 'second
death', due to shedding the 'vehicle of vitality']. At last
I awoke [in the un-enshrouded Soul Body]. I am alive. . . .
'Life' [in 'Paradise' conditions] is strangely similar to earth-
life."[1]

(9) "*Gradually I found that my real self was being separated from
my body, until I was floating in the air above it* [=Experience
No. 3A]. *I tried to free myself from the cord* [=*the silver 'cord'*]
*that still held me to my useless body, and it became gradually thinner
until at last it snapped.* . . . I succeeded in assuming an erect
position, floating in the air just above the ground. *I spoke to
a man but he did not hear me. Then I saw friends who had been dead
some time* [=‘dual consciousness’]. I lost consciousness and woke
to find myself in hospital. *I was puzzled, having no idea I had been
killed.*"[2]

(10) "I was suddenly shot out of the body. *I felt no pain.
I had a good look at my body.* I could not wrench myself away
from it immediately. I accompanied it when it was carried
off by stretcher-bearers."[3]

(11) "*I felt nothing, only a nasty knock, and turned to look for
the fellow who had struck me. I knew no more. I fell asleep* [=shed-
ding the body, i.e. Experience No. 3B]. Then I saw lots of
my friends, all smiling at me. A brother officer stretched out
his hand, saying, 'Come along, old chap!' I took his hand
and knew that I had passed to where war is no more. . . .
Things seemed familiar. Many places I had often visited in my
dreams [=‘astral projections’, not mere fantasies]. . . ."[4]

(12) "We went 'over the top'. . . . It was twenty minutes
before I realised that I had 'passed over'. During that time,
although my Physical Body was lying on the field, I went on
with the attacking party, thinking I was still alive [=in
physical embodiment]. *I then found that those around me could
not see me and went back and saw my body, lying dead.*"[5]

(13) "*I went out suddenly, in full strength, consequently it did not*

[1] W. T. Pole, *Private Dowding*, Watkins, 1917, p. 13.

[2] Margaret Vivian, *The Doorway*, Psychic Book Club, 1941, p. 15.

[3] Dr. Hereward Carrington, *Psychical Phenomena and the War*, T. Werner Laurie,
Ltd., 1918, p. 249.

[4] Lilian Walbrook, *The Case of Lester Coltman*, Hutchinson & Co., 1924, p. xiv.

[5] *Ibid.*, p. 25.

take long for me to awaken. . . . The shock was terrible. . . . I was at home in my father's house as much as ever I was. I heard every word uttered, saw the sadness, and, as it were, lived it. *I could not make myself known.*"[1]

(14) "*There came first a mere sense of identity* . . . [a 'partial awakening'] and next *a tumult of emotions* [=confusion] and the *unrolling of memories* [=the review of the past life, i.e. Experience No. 2]. Then . . . a dream-like awareness of people on earth. . . . Then . . . 'Hades', a dim and formless world. . . . Finally . . . a growing awareness of . . . people moving about in a *glorious world* [='Paradise' conditions]."[2]

(15) "*They must not think I really suffered.* . . . I couldn't feel the controls, but I was still in flight. Awfully queer it seemed— no pain and all this blackness. Suddenly it lifted and then I saw I *was floating* through what seemed space without a parachute. I soon met people who told me I had survived in another life."[3]

(16) "My mind became blank. . . . *I was falling down and through something, as one does in sleep.*"[4]

(17) 'Nigel', killed in a 'plane, had "no recollection of agonising pain." He saw "a blaze of light" and then "thought he was travelling down a *dark tunnel*".[5]

(18) "The 'plane crashed into the sea, but he was out of his body *before* it touched the water."[6]

General accounts of enforced death are similar to the individual accounts exemplified above. A few are given below:

(1) "The matter of the etheric double [here =the vehicle of vitality] adulterates the astral body [here =the Soul Body] for *three days* or so after death. We wander in the mists of un-reality in a dreamy, half-way state, with vague glimpses of the earth and the astral world [here ='Hades' conditions], superimposed on each other like a double-exposed photograph. This is the land of dreams into which we enter in our sleep,

[1] Dr. Hereward Carrington, *Psychical Phenomena and the War*, T. Werner Laurie, Ltd., 1918, p. 23.

[2] Jane Sherwood, *The Country Beyond*, Rider & Co. Ltd., p. 24.

[3] Geraldine Cummins, *Mind in Life and Death*, Aquarian Press Ltd., 1956.

[4] *Journ. S.P.R.*, vol. 39, 1958, p. 32.

[5] Geraldine Cummins, *Unseen Adventures*, Rider & Co., Ltd., 1951, p. 45.

[6] Frieda Hohenner-Parker, *A Crusader Here and There*, A. I. Stockwell, 1952, p. 67.

and the reactions of our ideas and desires produce forms in the etheric atmosphere. *Thus we may create our seeming environments.* It is Hades, the underworld of classical mythology, where pale shadows flit aimlessly about, sometimes in pitch darkness and utter loneliness. *This 'transitional' plane is not a stable, material world but a temporary, and avoidable psychopathological condition, a period of psychological and astral-sensory adjustment, with the environment self-centred through earth-time memory—though it is seemingly as real as our present dream-experiences.*"[1]

(2) "These poor lads, whose physical lives are suddenly blotted out in the heat of action, pass into the astral [here = 'Hades']. They feel exactly as they did a moment before; they have (apparently) the same bodies and the same clothing. Can you wonder if they fail to realise what has happened to them? They can generally still see and hear people who are yet in the flesh, though *they cannot make themselves seen or heard.* On the other hand, they are unable *to see the Helpers or Messengers or their relations who have come to meet them. Often their sensations are those of wandering in a grey mist, aimlessly waiting for the fog to clear.*"[2]

(3) 'Lancelot', who died aged eight, like Mr. Potter's communicator (p. 22) and a 'Guide' (p. 31) contrasted natural with enforced death. He said, "Those who want to take their bodies with them" [adding that this applies to "people who are suddenly killed when they are quite well", as well as to those who have lived "earthly lives"] tend to become "earth-spirits" immediately after death—"they can't get away from the body". He explained, "People give out a sort of fluid-stuff called ectoplasm [from the 'vehicle of vitality'] and they make a shape of it that is like their earth-form; they don't want it when they learn to do without it, so they often leave it off almost at once [=they shed the vehicle of vitality] and it goes on in the place where they left it [='Hades'], going on, doing over and over again what they last did with it: it isn't anything to matter because it is only ectoplasm, a sort of matter-thing [a 'ghost', 'wraith', or 'astral shell'] and not anything of mind in it at all." 'Lancelot' then contrasted this 'earthbound', or 'Hades', state with that produced by natural death: he said, "They just go to sleep [i.e. Experience No. 4];

---

[1] Roy Dixon-Smith, *New Light on Survival*, Rider & Co. Ltd., 1952.
[2] Alice Gilbert, *Philip in Two Worlds*, Andrew Dakers Ltd., 1948.

they are so glad to be free when they awake" [in 'Paradise' conditions].[1]

(4) The Christian mystic Sadhu Sundar Singh received communications identical with those exemplified above. He was told: "Sometimes, after accident, the spirit departs while the body is still unconscious. Then, those spirits who have lived without thought of entering the Spiritual World . . . are *extremely bewildered. . . .* So they have to remain for a considerable period in *the lower and darker planes of the intermediate state* [='Hades' conditions]."[2]

(5) The airman son of Mrs. Rhys Davids, whose plane was hit, communicated and assured her that he had had no pain in dying. On the basis of numerous communications which she subsequently received from those who suffered enforced transition, Mrs. Davids said: "*Even when death has been apparently less instantaneous, as in drowning, in hanging, in burning, etc., I have been told the same: they felt no struggle nor any pain.*" She added, "It would appear that, *when the summons has come, the 'man' is not left in the body to wrestle for life but is emerging from it, leaving the struggle a purely mechanical one. The struggle by the 'man' takes place only when the period of death is to be warded off.*" (The information received by Mrs. Davids agrees with individual descriptions of death by drowning, etc., examined by the present writer and exemplified in the Third Part of this book: one person said, "I had no feeling of distress *once I had given up the struggle. . . .*")[3]

The communicator of S. Bedford stated: "To understand what occurs to people suddenly killed by an accident, one must realise two things. First, that at the actual moment of death everything happens at terrific speed, because the soul is passing on to a world in which we move on a much higher vibration. Secondly, that our soul-consciousness is very much ahead of our physical-consciousness. So, when instant death occurs through an accident, *the soul is aware of what is about to happen a split second before the impact occurs, and leaves the body. The soul having left, no pain is felt.* In the case of sudden death we do not lose consciousness because the soul has already left the body. *A soldier, for example, receiving a bullet in the brain,*

[1] *Letters from Lancelot*, Dunstan, 1931, p. 75.
[2] Sadhu Sundar Singh, *Visions of the Spiritual World*, Macmillan, 1926, p. 6.
[3] Mrs. Rhys Davids, *What is Your Will?*, Rider & Co., p. 169.

would feel nothing, but would find himself looking at what a split second or so ago was his body. These sudden transitions appear tragic and ghastly to the onlooker, but to the person who has just died, death is always wonderful." Again (speaking of natural, as well as of enforced, death): "The convulsive movements of the body often seen at death in no way touch the soul; they are merely the outward reflections of the nervous reaction as the Spirit leaves the body. Even though the body be convulsive, *our real self* [*the soul*] *has already left the body and so we feel nothing.*" He considered that "This simple fact should be understood."[1]

(B) ENFORCED DEATH BY EXPLOSION

It has been well said that the (apparent) exception 'proves' (i.e. tests) the rule (i.e. shows how far a generalisation holds good—for, outside those of the physical sciences, few, if any, generalisations are absolute). When the present writer was collecting the 'communications' of people who had suffered enforced death he soon found an exception, namely, a case of death by explosion. As he proceeded, he found that all cases of this type differed from those by blows, falls, bullets, drowning, etc. This is highly significant and should interest the modern world. The following are examples of such descriptions. Several of them offer an eminently reasonable cause for the difference described.

(1) "With those who die by explosion, the Astral [here= vehicle of vitality] Body, as well as the Physical Body, is shattered. It will take some time before the attractive power of the life-principle can draw the astral atoms round it and reconstruct the bodily form. *During this period the soul remains unconscious.*"[2]

(2) When 'Nigel' was killed by an explosion, the communicator said his etheric [here=vehicle of vitality], as well as his Physical, Body was 'hurt' and that he required special attention. Recovery took a few weeks of our time.[3]

(3) "When a Physical Body is blown to pieces, the Etheric Body gets a shock and it takes longer [than normally] to

[1] *Death—an Interesting Journey*, Alcuin Press, pp. 66, 144.
[2] The Rev. C. L. Tweedale, *Man's Survival After Death*, Grant Richards, Ltd., and ed., 1920.
[3] Geraldine Cummins, *Travellers in Eternity*, Psychic Press Ltd., 1948, p. 66.

gather itself together. But after a while it takes the form of the physical, and departs."[1]

(4) 'Raymond' said that he, newly-dead, was told that "when anybody has been blown to pieces *it takes some time for the spirit-body to gather itself all in and to be complete*. It [the explosion] dissipated a certain amount of the etheric substance which has to be concentrated again." He insisted: "The spirit is not blown apart, of course, but it has an effect on the spirit."[2]

(5) A deceased soldier communicated, telling his brother how he had died (*Light*, vol. lii, 1932, pp. 561-2): "There was a horrible explosion and then I remember no more [=the momentary coma, due to shedding the body, i.e. Experience No. 3B]. By and by I began to wonder why everything was so quiet. . . . Then I thought of mother and father and how I should like to see them and almost in the same moment I found myself in their bedroom. *I seemed to settle asleep again*."

A 'Guide' explained the above (p. 595) and incidentally contrasted natural with enforced transitions. He said: "Essentially all 'passings' are more or less alike. *In the case of a soldier, killed instantly, the conditions differ somewhat*. But in the main they are the same. [In *natural* death], as the moment of death draws nigh, the inner body, which is enclosed in the body of matter, begins gradually to leave it. Vitality is at a low ebb. During its vigorous life, the material body has held the inner organism in place. It had sufficient power to do so. . . . As the life and energy of the material body wane, the inner body rises to the surface, rises to and through the surface, becomes an entity, and casts off its worn-out case. Who has not seen a butterfly evolve itself from a chrysalis? Some sort of similar process takes place. . . . Once free of the material body, spirit-aid is given. It is a new birth. . . . In many cases he believes he is in a dream. First we have to convince him that he is dead. Very often a relative [=a 'deliverer'] awaits his coming. . . ."

It must be borne in mind that 'Hades' conditions are said to be of only a temporary nature and that they apply only to those men of average (or sub-average) spirituality who pass out of the body in an abnormal manner, namely, suddenly while still in the prime of life. No 'punishment' is involved:

---

[1] G. Vivian, *Love Conquers Death*, L. S. Publications, p. 117.
[2] Sir Oliver J. Lodge, *Raymond*, Methuen & Co. Ltd., 1916, p. 195.

it is a simple case of cause and effect. We are told that some knowledge of these matters, together with right thinking, right feeling and right living, can mitigate or obviate such experiences. Children, and adults who are markedly above-average, have no consciousness of 'Hades' conditions even if they 'pass on' suddenly, since the vehicle of vitality is not vitalised by gross desires, there are no grossly erroneous 'fixed ideas' and their attention is not earth-wards: they awaken in 'Paradise' conditions (in the unenshrouded Soul Body). Thus, a youth of above-average type killed in battle, some months after his 'passing' said: "I am beginning to understand Myers's 'Plane of Illusion [='Hades']; having missed it myself, I could not get at what he meant. But in my work [among newly-dead soldiers temporarily in the 'Hades' state] I come up against it constantly."[1]

[1] Alice Gilbert, *Philip in Two Worlds*, Andrew Dakers Ltd., 1948, pp. 139, 162.

THE FOURTH EXPERIENCE: THE 'SLEEP'

ACCORDING to many communicators, the actual shedding of the Physical Body may be experienced as a momentary coma, 'darkness', 'blackout', etc. But it is not felt by men who die in their sleep (since, according to communicators, in those circumstances the Physical Body would be already shed). Moreover, the experience may be so slight and transient as to make no impression on consciousness. It would seem that, during the brief period in which the Soul Body is disengaging from the Physical Body, neither is available as an instrument of consciousness.

Apart from this momentary coma (which may be experienced in either natural and enforced death), the *natural* death of *average* people is followed by a definite period of 'sleep'. The nature of the sleep (i.e. whether it involves (*a*) complete unconsciousness, (*b*) a dream-state or (*c*) alternations of the two), and its duration, vary in accordance with several factors, including the following: (1) the natural degree of mental alertness and integration of dying persons, (2) their age at the time and (3) the amount of physical and mental suffering (and consequently exhaustion) undergone. The interplay of these factors produces two extreme conditions of the after-death 'sleep', with all intermediate gradations: there is a maximum tendency to a deep and prolonged 'sleep' with people of a sluggish and stupid type who died in extreme old age and after a long, exhausting illness; on the other hand, there is no tendency to 'sleep' with those of the energetic and alert type who passed on suddenly in the prime of life and without exhaustion—they are 'awake' at once. Average people who die naturally tend to 'sleep' (and 'dream') for *an average period of three to four days.*

Sir Arthur Conan Doyle published an article on the teachings of the great clairvoyant Swedenborg in *Light* (vol. XLVII, 1927, p. 235). Swedenborg's statements concerning the difference between natural and enforced death correspond with those of the communicators of Mr. Potter (p. 22), 'Lancelot' (p. 28) and a 'Guide' (p. 31)—and with the results of the present analyses. He said that those whose transition was natural "had an immediate period of complete rest" (i.e. underwent 'the sleep') and that they 'awoke' "*in a few days* of our time." But a man named Brake who had been killed at 10 a.m. spoke to Swedenborg at 10 p.m. on the same day: the seer said, "He was with me for several days." This man had had no immediate after-death sleep.

Apart from the following examples of communications regarding the after-death 'sleep', references are made to it incidentally under the other experiences described—two occur under No. 3 above, three will be found below under No. 5 and one under No. 7.

(1) "The term 'Hades' has significance, but, unless the individual has a nature of a very worldly kind, he should not have any unpleasant associations with Hades—it is merely a condition of rest. . . . *For a short time after death, the soul remains in a 'veil'*. It corresponds to the chrysalis. The soul eventually breaks through it like a butterfly. Certain immature [=markedly below-average] souls remain in the 'veil' after death and do not make any effort to go further; all their yearnings are for earth. So when the veil is finally broken for them, they face the scroll of their past lives [=the 'Judgment', i.e. Experience No. 6]."[1]

(2) "People brought up to hold orthodox—often only another way of saying vague and confused—views of the next world, sometimes use, of a newly-dead friend, such an expression as that he is now 'with God' or 'asleep in Jesus'. One hardly supposes that they attach any clear meaning so such phrases. Their friend, even in this life, was never outside the presence of God, and the Christ-mind is always and everywhere at hand. But that he would, on passing over, have at once come in contact with the personal Jesus is highly improbable, nor, supposing his to be the *average* type of human being, is it likely that he remains—except perhaps during the *short time* that immediately succeeds his passing—in any sense asleep."[2]

(3) "During the *three days* of sleep which usually follow transition, the spirit is unaware [so long as the 'silver cord',

---

[1] 'A.L.E.H.', *Fragments from My Messages*, Women's Printing Society, 1929, p. 26.

[2] Montgomery Smith, *Life and Work in the Spiritual Body*, Hillside Press, p. 57.

permitting 'dual' consciousness, has not been 'loosed'] that his
Physical Body has been cremated or removed to the cemetery,
and when he wakens he fails to comprehend the new situation,
since he still occupies a body and retains old habits, etc.
Being as alive as ever, it does not enter his mind that anything
unusual has happened."[1]

(4) "In the case of the open-minded, unbiased individual
there is no protracted death-sleep, for, as transition from the
physical draws near, he will often discern the presence of
waiting friends from the Unseen, bidding him welcome to the
new life. . . ."[2]

(5) "The only sleep there is after 'passing' is that given to
those who have passed through severe illness with much
weakness and pain, who cannot free their minds from thoughts
of sickness and weakness. . . . Many think that there is a long
interval between 'passing' and active life on this side. . . . If
we are suffering from some complaint that gave us weakness
and great pain, then we are taken to a home and tenderly
nursed . . . because, although we can't with our Spiritual
[here =Soul] Bodies feel pain or weakness, yet our minds
continue to think we are so suffering, unless we are, as our mind
thinks, brought back to health. . . . Then, when we have
recovered, we are taken where our lives, ill or well spent
[=the 'Judgment', i.e. Experience No. 6) entitle us to be
[=the Assignment, i.e. Experience No. 7]."[3]

(6) "Only yesterday she got right away from her body
[=although she had shed her Physical Body some days before,
'only yesterday' had the 'silver cord' and all the subsidiary
'threads' been 'loosed']. She will go on resting awhile, waking
up and sleeping, gradually getting used to her new [Soul]
body. It is rather strange getting used to a body which is very
strong and well when you have had to treat yourself [in the
Physical Body] very carefully for a long time."[4]

(7) "I hear that some people have a deep and long sleep;
that may be so—I think it must be. I had a period of what I
should call rest, but I don't think it was total unconsciousness.

[1] Carl. A. Wickland, M.D., *The Gateway of Understanding*, Psychic Book Club,
p. 65.
[2] *Ibid.*, p. 16.
[3] Constance Wiley, *A Star of Hope*, The C. W. Daniel Co. Ltd., 1938, pp. 7, 22.
[4] The Rev. C. Drayton Thomas, *In the Dawn Beyond Death*, Lectures Universal
Ltd., p. 64.

It was not long before I wanted to take an interest in things. I was aware of great joy and revelation, of new possibilities, and yet I was supposed to be asleep. That again comes to people who have lived in a particular way, who have clear minds and know what they want and think. The very stupid, unimaginative and dull people and those who have had some illness that has weakened them, need the heavy sleep from which they partly awaken when [discarnate] friends tell them some fact they can digest."[1]

(8) "*Long illness has a tiring effect upon the Spirit* [=Soul] *Body* . . . and when, at last, the Physical Body is cast off, the Spirit Body usually goes to one of the numerous halls of rest. . . . There the new resident sleeps, ultimately to wake fully refreshed. . . . With some, a short time serves; with others it takes months of earth-time. In my own case, I was ill for only a brief period on earth; I passed without losing consciousness. I was able to gaze upon my Physical Body. . . . A friend who had passed on before me came to me, at the instant of departure [in response to the 'Call'], and took me to my new home. After a brief survey of it he recommended a rest. I awoke in perfect health."[2]

(9) "The rest of newly-arrived persons is frequently necessary to allow of adjustment of the Spirit [=Soul] Body to its new condition of life. It has been accustomed to being very securely fastened to the Physical Body—where it has received whatever unpleasantnesses the Physical Body received. . . . An alert mind can quickly throw off these physical repercussions and adjust itself to the new life: other minds are slower. . . . The long and painful illness will be one of the unpleasantnesses, and although an alert mind can soon clear itself of recent experiences, still it may take a little time, and so a period of rest is undergone. In no sense is the Spirit Body impaired by earthly illness, but the latter acts upon the mind. . . . A period of rest will, therefore, restore the Spirit Body to its proper and natural tone."[3]

(10) "In some cases the spirit sleeps for a week or more, if the last illness has been of an exhausting nature, or perhaps only for two or three days, or even a few hours. . . ."[4]

[1] *In the Dawn Beyond Death*, p. 34.
[2] Anthony Borgia, *ABC of Life*, Feature Books, Ltd., p. 35.
[3] *Ibid.*, p. 38.
[4] Mrs. A. L. Fernie, *Not Silent, if Dead*, Fernie, 1890, p. 25.

ENFORCED DEATH

The statements concerning the shedding of the Physical Body made by those whose transition was enforced show that these people are typically 'awake' at once, soldiers trying to continue the battle, etc. (As already said, enforced death by explosion constituted a significant exception to this generalisation.) The following illustrate general statements from communications to the same effect.

1) "If the Physical Body is suddenly cast off, *consciousness never seems to be lost*. Those who die suddenly are sometimes even unaware that the change they feared has taken place. It is when the spirit has struggled and struggled to be free . . that rest is needed for awhile."[1]

(2) "As a rule, those who by accident or sudden illness pass into the other life are *awake at once, and in great confusion of mind as to what has happened*."[2]

(3) "Sudden death confines a man to the Borderland State [='Hades']."[3]

Similar statements are made through accredited psychics. For example, 'Myers', communicating through Mrs. Holland stated, "It may be that those who die suddenly suffer no prolonged obscuration of consciousness. . . ."[4] 'Raymond' (Lodge), communicating through Mrs. Osborn Leonard, said that "Those who are killed in battle even go on fighting—at least they want to. They don't believe they have passed on."[5]

[1] K. Wingfield, *More Guidance from Beyond*, Philip Allan & Co. Ltd., 1928, p. 41.
[2] F. Heslop, *Life Worth Living*, Charles Taylor, p. 28.
[3] F. W. Fitzsimmons, *Opening the Psychic Door*, Hutchinson & Co. Ltd., 1933, p. 57.
[4] *Proc. S.P.R.*, xxi.
[5] Sir Oliver Lodge, *Raymond*, Methuen, 1916, p. 127.

THE FIFTH EXPERIENCE: THE 'AWAKENING'

NATURAL DEATH

As might be expected, in view of the manner in which we often awaken from sleep, a number of the newly-dead describe experiencing an 'awakening' which, at first, was of a partial nature.

(1) "I was slow to comprehend that I had passed through the experience called death. . . . *I did not seem to be in any place.*"

(2) "*My first realisation was simply a feeling of myself. Gradually my powers increased until I perceived my body lying under me, I was floating in the air some three feet above it* [=Experience No. 3a]. Next I saw my physical surroundings, the friends about the body, weeping, etc. I tried to make them realise my presence, but could not do so. Next came the recognition of my friends in spirit. *Soon I came into full consciousness of my immediate surroundings.*"[2]

(3) Curtiss described the 'partial awakening' as applying to 'the majority' of average persons. He gave the reason for it: "At this stage, they have not yet learned to use their astral senses or to discriminate among the strange sights, sounds and feelings."[3]

(4) "Loss of consciousness [=Experience No. 3] gives way to *a self-awareness but not a consciousness of one's environment.* The new senses have not yet begun to function."[4]

(5) The communicator of G. Vivian said: "I was not able to think at first. *I merely felt things were happening.* It was like a dream in which I saw people and sometimes recognised them. Claude came several times. . . . Later he broke the news that I was not returning to you. I saw that you were very unhappy. I tried to comfort you but you couldn't see me. That was a terrible surprise: I thought, 'Am I dead?' Then I was back in Claude's room—I could talk to him, and when I touched him, he felt it. Then he told me that I had died."[5]

[1] Anon., *Christ in You*, Watkins, 1910, p. 79.
[2] F. W. Fitzsimmons, *Opening the Psychic Door*, Hutchinson & Co. Ltd., p. 89.
[3] A. C. and F. H. Curtiss, *Realms of the Living Dead*, San Francisco, 1917, p. 67.
[4] Jane Sherwood, *The Country Beyond*, Rider & Co. Ltd., p. 26.
[5] G. Vivian, *Love Conquers Death*, L. S. Publications, p. 91.

(6) In *Light* (vol. XLIV, 1924, p. 274) a communicator was cited as saying: "I knew I was wounded, and I knew I was 'going out'. I wasn't quite sure whether it was a dream . . . at first. . . . They had me in what seemed a hospital ward. . . . Then I woke up, I somehow knew it was the other world."

(7) A communication received in Nova Scotia (published in *Light,* vol. XLVII, 1927, p. 230) included the following: "I felt a strange sort of feeling as if I were waking from a deep sleep and *at first I did not know where I was.* Gradually I became aware of my surroundings and I saw myself [physical body] lying there so quiet and still: it gave me a shock, for I did not know yet that I was dead. After a while I became more fully awake and saw my wife. . . . She told me I had died. She said she had been near me for *some days* [=Experience No. 4]. . . . Gradually I became more alive as if my faculties had just recovered from being numb. It was a pleasant sensation, like waking up on a lovely spring morning."

The examples cited above are from 'popular' books. Here are two that were obtained through accredited mediums. A communicator told Hodson: "At first I spent most of my time in meditation. *I was not very much aware of my surroundings.*"[1] 'Myers' said: "Before I knew I was dead *I thought I had lost my way in a strange town and groped my way along the passage.*"[2]

The following are examples of communications regarding the 'awakening' which is described as occurring in natural transitions:

(1) "What impressed me most, after a period of rest [=Experience No. 4] was *the reality of all things.* My body [double] seemed as tangible as before the change . . . my senses were more acute. I saw running brooks, lakes, trees, grass and flowers [='Paradise' conditions]. I took long deep breaths of wonderfully vitalising air."[3]

(2) "There seemed to be a period of unconsciousness [=Experience No. 3B]. Then I awoke. . . . Death really is just a sleep and an awakening."[4]

(3) "I heard voices . . . that I recognised as those of loved ones I thought dead [=death-bed visions]. For a time I had no

[1] Geoffrey Hodson, *The Science of Seership,* Rider & Co. Ltd., p. 132.
[2] Sir Oliver Lodge, *The Survival of Man,* Methuen, 1909, p. 288.
[3] Edward C. Randall, *The Dead have Never Died,* George Allen & Unwin, Ltd., 1918, p. 54.
[4] Edward C. Randall, *Frontiers of the After Life,* Alfred A. Knopf, 1922, p. 43.

recollection [=Experience No. 3b]. Then I awoke. . . . I found myself, saw my [Soul] body which appeared as usual, except lighter and more ethereal. I was . . . in a beautiful room filled with flowers."[1]

(4) "I seemed to pass into a peaceful sleep. . . . I hear now that I must have slept for *three or four days* [=Experience No. 4]. . . . When I woke completely I felt so refreshed. . . . I knew I was not on earth, not only because of the long-lost people around me again, but because of the brilliancy of the atmosphere."[2]

(5) "The greatest humbug of all is death. . . . I had that terrible pain for a only a few moments, *the darkness—delicious, and afterwards, no pain, just waking up like a child.*"[3]

ENFORCED DEATH

Those whose death is enforced typically describe experiencing a (more or less brief) period of mental confusion and often say that, at first, their environment was enshrouded by 'mist', 'fog', or was even 'watery' (hence, doubtless, the conception of the 'river of death'). Those of average type seldom, at first, realise that they have permanently shed the Physical Body ('died'). Their consciousness is restricted to earth-scenes or 'Hades' conditions (dream-elements mingling with the realities that are represented by the 'doubles' of physical objects). This temporary abnormal phase, with 'sub-normal' consciousness, resulted from an abnormal 'passing'. It ends when the vehicle of vitality is shed (at the 'second death'). Consciousness then operates in the un-enshrouded Soul Body and therefore at 'super-normal' levels. The environment is represented by 'Paradise' conditions, i.e. the normal sequence of after-death experiences has been resumed: the person concerned is then in the same state as those who 'passed' naturally.

(1) A young man described "*a misty opaqueness which resembled a dense sea-fog.*" His environment was a "foggy flat area" with "shifting", "blurred" outlines. He could feel the emotions of mortals on earth.[4]

---

[1] *Frontiers of the After Life*, p. 31.

[2] The Rev. C. Drayton Thomas, *In the Dawn Beyond Death*, Lectures Universal, Ltd., p. 67.

[3] Geraldine Cummins, *Mind in Life and Death*, Aquarian Press Ltd., 1956.

[4] Jane Sherwood, *The Psychic Bridge*, Rider & Co. Ltd., pp. 26, 27.

(2) Another said that, for a time, he "hung *between two worlds* [='Hades' conditions, between earth and 'Paradise']".[1]

(3) "Those who pass out of the body suddenly are often unaware that they have died and cannot understand what is the matter with them."[2]

(4) Lord Dowding described many cases of the awakening after enforced death. The state of three airmen was given as follows: "They are awake, but don't know that they are dead. *They have created their own surroundings.* Crowds are waiting to help them, but the three can't see them. They are talking: 'Have you noticed anything funny about these cigarettes?' 'Yes, but I didn't know what. . . .' 'It's so quiet.' 'Yes—no sound of firing.' [They were noting incongruities between the physical environment they had left—without realising the fact—and the new, 'Hades', environment].[3]

(5) "All I know is that one minute we were blasting away and then I was in the most beautiful and peaceful garden. . . . I asked the Padre where we were. *The place was familiar yet not familiar.*"[4]

(6) "I didn't realise at first that I had got mine. I woke up in a hospital. . . . One day I realised that, although my dressings were regularly done, I had no pain, there was no blood on the bandages. I wriggled my leg: it felt fine. So next time my nurse came along, I tackled her, and suddenly realised I had not seen a doctor. The nurse laughed and said I had been cured [from imaginary injury to the Soul Body]; for a long time but I wouldn't face up to it."[5]

The above are mainly from 'popular' books. Here are examples of similar communications which came through accredited mediums (Mrs. Osborn Leonard and Mrs. Piper respectively).

"For a second or two, as you count time", 'Raymond Lodge', killed in war, thought he was in a *"shadowy vague place, everything vapoury and vague."*[6] 'George Pelham', killed in an accident, at first found everything *"dark"*. He *"could not distinguish anything at first"* [=the 'partial awakening']. *This caused him to be "puzzled" and "confused".*

[1] M. E. Longley, *The Spirit World*, 1918.
[2] Yogi Ramacharka, *The Life Beyond Death*, L. N. Fowler, & Co. Ltd.
[3] Lord Dowding, *Lychgate*, Rider & Co. Ltd., p. 35.   [4] *Ibid.*, p. 37.
[5] *Ibid.*, p. 67.   [6] Sir Oliver Lodge, *Raymond*, Methuen, 1916.
[7] *Proc. S.P.R.*, iii, 301.

THE SIXTH EXPERIENCE: THE 'JUDGMENT'

NATURAL DEATH

An after-death experience which is known as the 'Judgment' is envisaged in every religion. According to 'communications', it is essentially an emotional and a personally-responsible review of the past earth-life which, with *average* people who die *natural* deaths, occurs within a few months (reckoned in our time) of 'passing'. (With men who are markedly above-average in the spiritual and moral sense, it may occur earlier, while with those who are markedly below-average it may be delayed. The latter include men who are excessively sensual or evil, who are 'earthbound', i.e. delayed in 'Hades' (not 'hell') conditions, because unable or unwilling to face the truth about their characters and earthly lives.) The 'Judgment' takes place after the 'second death' (which occurs, with average men who 'pass' naturally, some three or four days after their transition). Two examples of the 'Judgment' are mentioned incidentally under Experience No. 4, above. Here are others.

(1) 'E.K.' said: "The events of one's past life come back into consciousness. Each incident brings with it the feelings not only of oneself alone but of all those others who were affected by the events."[1]

(2) The Rev. C. L. Tweedale's communicator similarly said that soon after the 'second death', when 'Hades' conditions are left and 'Paradise' conditions entered, "We have to face a Judgment: we are shown our mistakes and given a chance to alter and atone for wrongs. It is an immediate Judgment, not a hypothetical one at 'the last day'!"[2]

(3) "The Judgment consists in being able to see ourselves as we are, and by no stretch of imagination being able to avoid seeing it. It is a Judgment of God on us [lesser selves] through our Higher Selves. On earth, even the best are subconsciously avoiding things, or trying to think things are

---

[1] Jane Sherwood, *The Country Beyond*, Rider & Co. Ltd., p. 73.
[2] The Rev. C. L. Tweedale, *Man's Survival After Death*, Grant Richards Ltd., 1909, p. 39.

slightly other than they are. . . . No other person could be so just a Judge as we ourselves can be when facing the truth. For many it is a terrible hour. . . . Directly one has realised how, where and why one was wrong, there is an instinctive feeling that one must work it out. And this way of recovery is in helping others who have exactly similar limitations, difficulties or vices."[1]

(4) "The Day of Judgment does not take place on our immediate arrival here. The word 'day' is incorrect, for the trial is not limited to twenty-four hours. It is not possible to talk of it in terms of earth-time. But there is a special period when we enter the Gallery of Memory and the pictures of our earth-life pass before us. Then our Spirit [=Greater Self] is our Judge. We face this time when we are fit for it."[2]

(5) "I saw my life unfold before me in a procession of images. One is faced with the effects emotionally of all one's actions. . . ."[3]

(6) The communicator of *Christ in You* (Watkins, 1918, p. 90) said: "The judgment-bar is the innermost of yourself. It is the judgment-bar of God, and when our actions are tested there, the Voice will cast into outer darkness that which is not of itself."

(7) "My past deeds crowded before me. Oh, the anguish as deeds long-forgotten rose up. Little or great, nothing was forgotten. At last, an inspiration seemed to seize me and I prayed. I had not done so for years, but now I prayed and, as I did so, the chaos began to sort itself out. It took chronological order. . . . Among the visions I saw some which came as a relief to my tired soul—little acts of kindness which I had long forgotten. . . . So I found my location [=Experience No. 7]."[4]

(8) "Like everyone who passes over, he had been through the whole of his past life, re-living his past actions in every detail. All the pain he had given to people he experienced himself, and all the pleasure he had given he received back again."[5]

[1] The Rev. C. Drayton Thomas, *Beyond Life's Sunset*, Psychic Press Ltd., p. 48.
[2] Geraldine Cummins, *Travellers in Eternity*, Psychic Press Ltd., 1948, p. 20.
[3] 'A.L.E.H.', *Fragments from My Messages*, Women's Printing Society Ltd., 1929, p. 198.
[4] J. S. M. Ward, *Gone West*, Rider & Co. Ltd., 1917, p. 31.
[5] Olive C. B. Pixley, *Listening In*, L.S.A. Publications Ltd., 1928.

(9) "The angel told me I had a process to go through—hard, but good for me to follow out. This, popularly, is supposed to come at the Last Day . . . the General Judgment. . . . All my earth-life came before me—naked, no disguises."[1]

(10) "We cannot escape this. And not only sad things, but, I thank God, kindness and things rightly done. . . I could see the earth-life brought before me in a picture with the smallest details. . . . I am thankful for all I have gone through."[2]

(11) "Now all the strength of this faculty [of memory] arose, far beyond my control. Scene after scene, long forgotten or skilfully smothered, rose before me. . . . I seemed to stand aside as a spectator, and, in those pictures, watch myself as I formerly watched and judged the actions of others."[3]

(12) Soon after Mildred H. Collyer began to receive communications from supposed discarnates by automatic writing, the latter said that they were "making memories". She did not understand this phrase. Later, having received fuller information, she stated that the process "appears to consist partly of a revival of actual earth-memories, and partly of the fulfilment of unrealised desires brought over". Still later she was told that it consisted in "a re-valuation of life". It was said to be "a prelude to even greater experiences."[1] [=Experience No. 7].

(13) The communicator of S. Bedford (op. cit., p. 40), having mentioned the first review [Experience No. 2] as occurring "just prior to the moment of passing", also described the second review, or 'Judgment'. He said, "It is necessary for us to see this picture again, when we arrive in the spirit world [here ='Paradise'], for then memory is complete; we know the full purpose of our life on earth. . . the whole picture has a much deeper meaning".

(14) A communicator told 'M.A.' (Oxon.) (From Worlds Unseen, Rider & Co. Ltd., 1927, pp. 67-8) of the 'passing' of his friend, 'A.L.' He said that the latter saw his 'departed' friends and then "had to go through his earth-life". He "was shown the real meaning of many things he never understood, was taught what he ought to have done or left undone, and

[1] E.L.B.S., *Realities of the Future Life*, Holywell Press Ltd., Oxford, 1908.
[2] *Ibid.*
[3] Harold Bayley, *The Undiscovered Country*, Cassell, 1918, p. 68.
[4] *Light*, LV, 1935, p. 191.

what he must do to make amends for unkind words or injuries to other people".

The statements cited above are from more or less 'popular' accounts, but communicators who used accredited mediums make identical ones. For example, 'Myers' said: "In the life-after-death man enters an intermediate stage and, in that time, his soul perceives, at intervals, the episodes in the past existence. . . . He becomes aware of all the emotions aroused in his victims by his acts. . . . He becomes purified through his identification with the sufferings of his victims."[1]

'Myers' made another reference to the 'Judgment' in a script of Miss Cummins that was published by Miss E. B. Gibbes in *Light*, vol. LV, 1935, p. 100. An elderly friend of Miss Gibbes, one who had led "a somewhat selfish life", communicated. After mentioning her transition, she said that she had been "looking back" over her life [i.e. that she had been engaged in the first, non-emotional, review, Experience No. 2]. Two years later, she communicated and described her 'Judgment' [Experience No. 6], thus: "I have had the most disturbing experiences. I don't really know how I lived through them. . . . One of the tasks set me was that of looking back. I have been shown the effects of all my acts upon other people's minds. Their thoughts were shown to me. It was the most humiliating and awful experience. . . . I have seen what is called 'the emotional reactions' to my own acts. . . . On the whole, I deserved what I got. . . . I am changed. I am a much softer person now."

Similar statements concerning the 'Judgment'-experience that are of a more general nature are illustrated below.

(1) "The events of the life just closed pass before his mind's eye . . . causes and effects are correlated, successes and their results, failures and their outworkings. This process of review is very important, for from it is distilled a certain wisdom, the fruitage of the life just closed."[2]

(2) "The soul begins to remember vividly . . . the emotional life. Not the small details of every day [=the first detailed review, i.e. Experience No. 2], but love and hate, anger, joy and sorrow, and the periods at which these were experienced

[1] Geraldine Cummins, *Beyond Human Personality*, Ivor Nicholson and Watson, 1935, pp. 29, 44.

[2] Geoffrey Hodson, *Clairvoyant Research and the Life After Death*, Theosophical Publishing House, 1935.

also come back. The human relationship which produced these reactions became more explicable, the meaning of life a little clearer."[1]

(3) "The whole mental condition becomes sensitive, each feeling more intense, whether it be love or regret for failure in life. That is why it is all-important to those still in the flesh to lead good, clean, honest, unselfish lives—lives of which they will not be ashamed when they see all their acts, after passing on, in a clearer way—see the real motives behind all they did, see whether those acts of kindness they might have done were done. . . . It is the motive that counts, no matter how small the deed. All will see and know these truths and will thus be able to know and judge themselves and their actions during earth-life."[2]

(4) "Every thought, being material, creates a condition about us and is retained in the brain. When, therefore, anyone goes out of this life and enters the etheric [here = 'Paradise' conditions], where everything, the good and the bad, is intensified beyond measure, the storehouse of the brain is opened and he is confronted with the record made. Nothing is forgotten."[3]

(5) "After a time of rest [=the 'sleep', i.e. Experience No. 4] we learn how to use the powers of the Spirit [here = Soul] Body and receive teaching from Higher Intelligences. But as the instruction proceeds we become conscious of the many defects of character. This self-revelation, which is, often painful, is the real 'Judgment'."[4]

ENFORCED DEATH

Whereas the 'Judgment'-experience of average people is described, in communications from 'beyond', as being under-gone fairly soon after natural death, where death is enforced in the prime of life (as with markedly sub-average people who die naturally), it is delayed (and this, in turn, delays the next experience, i.e. the assignment). This is because the 'Judgment' normally follows the 'second death': the process is

[1] 'A.B.', One Step Higher, The C. W. Daniel Co. Ltd., 1937, p. 100.
[2] Olive C. B. Pixley, Listening In, L.S.A. Publications Ltd., 1928.
[3] Edward C. Randall, The Dead Have Never Died, George Allen and Unwin Ltd., 1918, p. 160.
[4] F. Heslop, Life Worth Living, Charles Taylor, p. 29.

retarded with men who are excessively sensual or who are killed in their prime. Hence, many communicators who claim to have 'passed' normally also describe having undergone the 'Judgment'-experience fairly soon after death, but I have not seen one case in which a communicator claims that he was killed in the prime of life and who also said that his Judgment-experience followed soon after.

THE SEVENTH EXPERIENCE: THE ASSIGNMENT

NATURAL AND ENFORCED DEATH

ON the basis of the 'Judgment', each man 'goes to his own place': the 'sheep' are separated from the 'goats' and the 'wheat' from the 'tares'. Seven immediate 'spheres', 'planes', 'realms', conditions, 'mansions' or environments, are usually described but communicators insist that they are not sharply marked off from each other and that there are others, whose nature is indescribable, 'beyond'. Subdivisions are made for convenience of discussion only, so that the 'First', 'Second', 'Third', etc., 'sphere' of one account may not exactly correspond to those so-named in another. This is not surprising, since hard and fast classifications are impossible in our natural sciences. The *general* succession of 'spheres' or 'conditions' in numerous independent accounts shows remarkable similarity. ('Hades', it should be noted, is a temporary *abnormal* condition.) The following summarises numerous independent communications:

The First 'Sphere' closely resembles the earth: it is a place of adjustment for its inhabitants. The Second 'Sphere' (which interpenetrates the First) is only a slight advance on it. The Third 'Sphere' ('Paradise', 'Summerland', 'Elysium', 'The Garden of Eden', etc.) is a 'glorified earth' that interpenetrates those two already mentioned. The 'Judgment'-experience occurs soon after it is entered. Thereafter the tendency is to become more and more aware of the existence and needs of others. There is, however, no loss of individuality: true individuality is developed within groups of people who have similar interests. These form 'Group Souls', the experiences, wisdom and strength of each member of a Group being more or less available to all the others.[1] Development is due to the use of the intuitive and imaginative faculties rather than by the exercise of the intellect. 'Time' is largely subjective, depending partly on the intensity of thought and feeling and partly on

---

[1] Compare 'Gurney' (*Proc. S.P.R.*, vol. 52, 1960, p. 136: "To put on immortality is not to put off personality", and W. H. Salter (*Journ. S.P.R.*, vol. 40, 1960, p. 285): "They [the communicators] continue as constituents of a fusion. . . ."

rhythm: 'space' is also largely subjective, affinity of thought and feeling constituting 'nearness' and dissimilarity of ideas and emotions representing 'distance'. Descriptions of 'conditions' that obtain in the Third 'Sphere' are necessarily more or less symbolical. Higher 'spheres' are indescribable (I Cor. ii. 9).

Communicators agree that there is a duality of 'Spirit' (mind, consciousness, etc.) and 'matter' (environment) throughout the 'spheres', but the emphasis varies. During earth-life the emphasis is so strong on objective things (physical matter) that men may doubt the existence of the subjective, the 'Spirit'. As the earth is left behind and the 'spheres' are 'ascended' the importance of the objective aspect progressively diminishes and that of the subjective aspect progressively increases—but even in the 'highest', subtlest 'Sphere' of *human* evolution there is still an objective environment. Only the Absolute, Transcendent, Unmanifested, Infinite 'Father' is 'pure Spirit', 'purely subjective'.

'Death', the supreme adventure as seen by us mortals, is merely the *first* of a series of three unveilings, or births, into 'higher' and therefore more harmonious conditions or environments. After physical death the double consists of the Soul Body *plus* the vehicle of vitality, so that consciousness, if any, is more or less dreamy ('sub-normal') and the environment of the 'Hades' or illusory type. This usually brief phase ends with the '*second death*', the shedding of the vehicle of vitality from the Soul Body: 'Paradise' conditions are then entered and consciousness is of the 'super-normal' type (with telepathy, clairvoyance, foreknowledge, etc.)

We have been concerned with the *first and second* 'deaths' (actually births) and the *immediate* after-life. But there is a third 'death'—that transition in which the Soul Body itself is discarded. After this event, consciousness operates at Spiritual 'levels' in the Spiritual or Celestial Body, with the indescribable true 'Heavens' as the environment. The third 'death', more properly described as the third unveiling of the Greater Self, leaves no 'corpse', 'husk' or 'shell' (as do the first and second): in this process the body undergoes a progressive refinement and purification and consequently an increase in responsiveness. It is mentioned here only to complete the correspondence envisaged between the succession of bodies, 'levels' of consciousness and environments.

SECOND PART

"Nothing really matters except the answer to the burning question, 'Am I going to live, or shall I vanish like a bubble?' What is the aim and issue of all this strife and suffering?"—*Malinowski*.

"I am unaware of anything that has a right to the title of an impossibility, except a contradiction in terms."—*T. H. Huxley*.

"It is because of the Divine Spirit *within us* that we seek Truth: it is because of the Divine Spirit *without us* that there is Truth to discover."—*Lily Dougall*.

"If only one per cent. of the money spent upon the physical and biological sciences could be spent upon investigations of religious experience and psychical research, it might not be long before a new age of faith dawned upon the world."—*Professor A. C. Hardy*.

In the First Part of this book we deal predominantly with the experiences of people (of average spiritual status) in the course of transition and in the immediate after-life. Besides describing a succession of experiences, however, communicators offer causes for and explanations of those experiences, etc., and we now itemise these, preparatory to considering their coherence and probability (in the Third Part). The various statements are followed by the correlation that is implied between the bodily, mental and environmental factors involved.

I

ITEMISED STATEMENTS AS TO THE TOTAL DEATH-EXPERIENCE

INTRODUCTORY

Statement No. 1a.—Experiences in the immediate hereafter may be affected by dominant or habitual thoughts and feelings, and by strong expectations or fixed ideas developed during earth-life.

Statement No. 1b.—Communications agree with the teaching of St. Paul (I Cor. xv. 35, 44) that, in addition to his Physical Body, man possesses a 'body' that cannot be seen by the physical eye or touched by the physical hand. This is composite in nature. St. Paul called the Physical Body the *'carnal* body' and in addition, recognised first a *Psychical or Soul* (unfortunately translated 'natural') Body and secondly a *'Spiritual'* or *'Celestial'* Body. He said that those of the 'dead' who are 'seen' by the 'living' are recognised: this can only be because their Soul Bodies have the same shape as their Phyiscal Bodies had —the latter is the 'double' of the former.

Communicators give innumerable statements that are essentially similar to St. Paul's, using such terms as 'astral' (star-like, luminous) and 'etheric', 'ethereal' (light, airy, subtle, fine, unearthly) body.

They also say that the total Physical Body includes an 'ultra-gaseous' portion, a 'magnetic field', the vehicle of vitality, which is intermediate in nature between the Physical and the Soul Bodies. Since, we are told, it lacks 'sense organs', the term 'body' is inapplicable: nevertheless it has been called 'the vital body'. But it is not a vehicle (or instrument) of consciousness (as are the Physical, Soul and Spiritual Bodies). Though possessing the outer form of the Physical Body, it has nothing corresponding to our inner tissues or internal organs. Its chief functions are (*a*) to receive the vital energies that are collected, after the manner of a condenser, by the Soul Body, and to transmit them to the Physical Body (compare Gen. ii. 7) and (*b*) to bear impressions, or 'traces', of the events in the life of the mortal concerned (compare Matt. x. 26). It is thus a transmitter of vitality and a memory-record.

There is great confusion in the use of such terms as 'astral' and 'etheric' body, and they should be dropped.

The vehicle of vitality, (the 'etheric double' of the Theosophists and the 'vital body' of the Rosicrucians) is 'semi-physical' in nature. It interpenetrates the Physical Body and extends about $\frac{1}{4}$ inch beyond it. The accounts given of it by psychics agree with those given by communicators. It contains 'nervous force' or 'vitality', can give out 'ectoplasm' under suitable conditions, and is usually shed from the total double soon after death. It then remains as an 'astral corpse' or 'shell' (which disintegrates *pari passu* with the Physical Body). If any part of the vehicle of vitality separates from the Physical Body during life, the two remain united by an extension called a 'silver cord' at the solar plexus.

The Soul Body, which is 'semi-spiritual' in nature, is less immersed in the Physical Body. Whenever the two are separated during life (i.e. in sleep, trance, anaesthesia, etc.) they remain united by a 'silver cord' at the heads. Like the vehicle of vitality, it has the form and outline of the Physical Body but, in addition, the two correspond cell for cell and tissue for tissue. Like the Physical Body, it has 'sense organs' and is an instrument of consciousness. This is of the 'super-normal' type (with telepathy, etc.). The Soul Body is the primary body: the Physical Body is a 'condensation' of it.

Clairvoyants agree with communicators in many matters of importance, including that at present under consideration, i.e., that the Soul Body is primary and 'more real' than the physical body. For example, Phoebe (Payne) Bendit (with Dr. Laurence J. Bendit), *Man Incarnate*, Theosophical Publishing House Ltd., 1957, p. 14, said: "The (physical) body can be looked upon as a consolidation of dense matter inside the auric field."

The Soul Body interpenetrates the Physical Body (and its vehicle of vitality) and extends well beyond them. 'Vibrating' more rapidly than its physical 'condensation', the Soul Body is more sensitive and responsive: it receives impressions that are undetected by the physical senses, i.e. psychical impressions. One communicator described the Soul Body as "a magnetic area of creative thought—a vibrating, always-circulating system of electric currents which flow up from the solar plexus, cross behind the neck and emerge at the feet—a glowing whorl."

Another, insisted that the Soul Body is 'material' not 'vapourish' to those discarnates whose outermost body it is.

The Spiritual Body interpenetrates and 'extends' beyond the Soul Body. It is not immersed in the slightest degree in the Physical Body, but is 'above', 'beyond' or 'within' it—transcendent and not immanent. It 'vibrates' the most rapidly of all (when in operation). It is 'super-physical', or 'spiritual', in nature. Being concerned with the awareness of all that is good, beautiful and true, this body is relatively little organised in average people. It permits the receipt of inspirations and intuitions and these occasionally enter the 'normal' consciousness. The corresponding 'level' of consciousness, distinguished as 'mystical', 'spiritual' or 'cosmic' consciousness, includes the knowledge of our unity with the Supreme Being and with our fellows and, indeed, with all living creatures.[1]

Some of our most eminent psychical researchers consider that, whether we are aware of it or not, we are all receiving (presumably *via* the Soul Body) psychical impressions (telepathy, etc.) at all times, and the Church similarly teaches that, whether we are aware of it or not, we are all receiving Spiritual inspirations and impulses from the Supreme Being at all times: "Surely," exclaimed Jacob, "*The Lord* is in this place —and *I knew it not*" (Gen. xxviii. 16). "I am persuaded", said St. Paul, "that neither death nor life, nor angels, nor principalities, nor powers, nor things present, nor things to come, nor height, nor depth, nor any other creature, shall be able to separate us from the love of God which is in Christ Jesus our Lord" (Rom. viii. 38, 39). Many independent communicators agree with both of these important statements which most mortals would deny: it is their *awareness* that is obscured.

A 'loose' vehicle of vitality predisposes to mediumship. Persons in whom the vehicle of vitality is very loosely associated with the Physical Body—and they are extremely rare—are potential 'physical' mediums; ectoplasm can be exteriorized and can produce 'raps', 'levitations', 'direct voice', supernormal 'lights', 'materialisations' and other 'physical' phenomena. (These may occur apart from, though they are facilitated by, séances: in the latter the medium becomes particularly passive in trance and his ectoplasmic output is supplemented

[1] See *e.g.*, Dr. R. M. Bucke, *Cosmic Consciousness*, Dutton, 1942, Dr. Raynor C. Johnson, *Watcher on the Hills*, Hodder and Stoughton, 1959.

by that of the sitters.) Looseness of the vehicle of vitality may be natural (and the tendency is hereditary), but it may also be induced, or increased, by unusually debilitating illness, excessive fatigue, prolonged fasting, severe shock or the abuse of drugs (including alcohol).

In some people the junction between the Soul and the Physical Bodies is relatively 'loose': they are less immersed in matter and tend to be 'mental' mediums with telepathic, clairvoyant and pre-cognitive faculties, i.e. they have flashes of 'super-normal' consciousness and glimpses of the 'next' world. Whereas those who possess a loose vehicle of vitality may, or may not, be of high moral type, people with loose Soul Bodies are often (though not always) spiritually inclined. A truly religious person tends to be a 'mental' medium, though there is no warrant for reversing the proposition and saying that a 'mental' medium is necessarily religious—the 'looseness' may be a purely bodily characteristic.

A true mystic has a relatively highly organised Spiritual Body so that 'intimations of immortality', eternal truths, a conviction of the unity of all consciousness and an assurance that "underneath are the everlasting arms" tend to enter his 'normal consciousness', He is in touch with 'spiritual' influences (and may, or may not, in addition, receive psychical impressions). This 'level' of consciousness is beyond all limits of time, space and form.

The Theosophists have teachings much like those which many communicators give through 'mediums' who can never have heard of that sect. Although Geraldine Cummins had made no study of Theosophy, she obtained communications, from 'Myers'[1] that included identical teachings: the terminology differed from that of the Theosophists and resembled that used by Myers during his life-time.

According to communicators, Theosophists, Rosicrucians, etc., the 'Spirit', 'Higher Mind', 'Ego', 'Over-soul', Greater or Eternal Self assumes a series of progressively denser (and therefore less responsive) bodies; these are its instruments in corresponding environments. The subtlest body (with the 'highest vibrations') has been given many names: we call it the Spiritual Body. The next is the Soul Body and the densest

---

[1] Geraldine Cummins, *The Road to Immortality*, Ivor Nicholson and Watson, 1932.

(with the 'lowest vibrations') is the Physical Body. This assumption of a series of bodies constitutes the 'fall' (of 'Spirit' into 'matter'). *The Greater Self is a 'Cosmic' and 'Spiritual' Being.* 'He' is beyond time and space and is not of this earth. 'He' uses the three bodies for purposes of development and expression: they are his tools or instruments. Their assumption enables the Greater Self to learn his own Nature but it involves the payment of a price since they necessarily act, each in its own degree, like insulators, sphincters, or 'blinkers', limiting the 'level' of consciousness to that which is appropriate to a given stage of development. *The Physical Body of man is a highly-evolved animal-body.* The Greater Self 'descends' and 'borrows' it from the 'ascending' creatures, the animals. This facilitates the individualisation of 'Spirit', or Greater Self. With the formation of a self-conscious personality, or lesser self, the latter, if he will, can 'co-operate' with the Divine plan. As was pointed out by the Master, the destruction of *bodies* (in war, etc.) is much less terrible than the decay and eventual dissolution of *souls* (Matt. x, 28).

"The Soul (Greater Self)", declared Dr. Inge, "is a Spiritual Being, with its home in Heaven—the Heaven that is within us even while we are in the body." The communicator of *Christ in You* (Watkins, 1910, p. 134) similarly said: "You are greater than your form (physical body): *you have no limit*; you take limitations for purposes at present hidden from you. True personality . . . by reason of its greatness, is best manifested in part."

When the Soul Body leaves the Physical Body (whether during life or at death), it does so by all the pores, but generally chiefly by the head. In some few cases, however, there is a "weak place" in the body and it may then leave chiefly by the side, the breast, the solar plexus region or even the feet. (In such exceptional cases the 'silver cord' may seem to have an abnormal point of attachment.)

In the light sleep of average people (whose vehicle of vitality is closely knit to the Physical Body) the Soul Body is partially disengaged from (or 'out of gear' with) the Physical Body. In this condition the Physical Body ceases to transmit stimuli from, or act upon, the physical world. In somewhat deeper sleep, and especially with that of potential 'physical' mediums with 'loose' vehicles of vitality), a significant portion of the vehicle of vitality, may accompany the exteriorized Soul Body: hence during their sleep there may be some consciousness in 'Hades' conditions and some of the experiences may be 'remembered' as 'dreams'.

In deep sleep the Soul Body is almost completely disengaged from the Physical Body. At first it lies at a distance of from a few inches to a few feet above its physical 'condensation'. Many men spend much of the night with the Soul Body lying over the vacated Physical Body. The latter is not only being allowed a respite from physical activities; it is also being re-charged with 'vitality' that is absorbed, from cosmic 'currents', by the Soul Body. The 'vitality' is passed, *via* the cord-like extension that appears to be mentioned in the Bible (Eccles. xii. 6) as the 'silver cord'. It enters the vehicle of vitality and then the Physical Body. (We are told that the term 'cord' is symbolic; the feature has no definite thickness and it can stretch indefinitely.)

During sleep the exteriorised (or 'projected') Soul Body may move along horizontally over the physical feet, eventually standing erect. It is unaffected by gravity and can pass through walls, etc. The person who is thus out of the body in the Soul Body may, at times, be more or less conscious of the corresponding environment, i.e. 'Summerland', the 'Third Sphere', 'Elysium', or 'Paradise' conditions. Occasionally, if they 'get through' the physical brain, fragments of experiences in that environment are 'remembered' on awakening. They are usually dismissed as exceptionally vivid 'dreams', especially since they may suffer distortion in the course of transmission through the vehicle of vitality [='Hades' ='illusion'], to the brain.

In natural sleep and natural 'astral projection' the whole of the vehicle of vitality remains with the Physical Body—unless a person is 'mediumistic', i.e. with a more or less 'loose' vehicle of vitality, when part of the latter may leave the Physical Body along with the Soul Body. The latter also applies to exteriorisations (of both mediumistic and non-mediumistic men) that are enforced by anaesthetics, etc.—there is a tendency to force out part of the vehicle of vitality along with the Soul Body. (If all is ejected, then the man dies.) These enforced cases are, as it were, half-way to death, when the whole of the vehicle of vitality leaves the Physical Body and, with the Soul Body, forms the immediate after-death 'double'.

NATURAL DEATH

Statement No. 2.—This represents Experience No. 1. As a man, having attained a ripe old age, approaches death, his thoughts go out instinctively, if not consciously, to friends who have 'gone before'. The latter receive such thoughts telepathically: to them they represent a 'Call' they 'come' to aid, welcome and instruct him. The stronger the affection between the 'living' and the 'dead', the stronger is this 'Call'. Other features, besides our thoughts, warn our discarnate friends of an impending 'passing'. (Apart from any specific 'Call', all who die are 'met' by someone.)

Statement No. 3.—This is the converse of No. 2: excessively self-centred men, on dying, are not 'met' by particular 'departed' friends—they failed to 'call' them. Nevertheless, they are 'met' by certain discarnate helpers who voluntarily undertake such services and are specially trained in such duties. These helpers are appropriately called 'deliverers'.

Statement No. 4.—A fixed idea that there is no after-life, that death 'ends all', acts like a post-hypnotic suggestion: no 'Call' is sent to departed friends. Although men who die under this disadvantage are 'met', their mental condition necessarily delays their acceptance of instruction.

Statement No. 5.—This is Experience No. 2. There is *a review of the past earth-life.* It is of an impersonal, non-emotional and non-responsible nature (in which respects it differs from the Second 'Review'—No. 34).

Statement No. 6.—About an hour before 'visible death' (that is, before the cessation of breathing and heart-beat,) a dying man has often almost completely vacated his Physical Body and stands nearby, perfectly conscious and happy. To watchers at the bedside he is in a pre-death coma. He may still, for a short time—seldom for more than a few minutes or hours—be attached to his body by the extension that is likened to a silver cord. If this is the case he will continue to be more or less aware of his Physical Body and its surroundings (e.g. relatives in the room). His exteriorised double is often seen by mortals at about this time. (Its density is then at the maximum.)

Statement No. 7.—Natural death involves neither physical pain nor fear. Many communicators describe the act of dying as '*easy*', '*natural*', and even '*delightful*'. (Conan Doyle said: "The departed all agree that *passing is usually both easy and painless.*"

Statement No. 8.—This is the converse of No. 7. Being brought back to the body from the verge of death, by stimulants, etc., does involve pain and fear. *Those who thus 'return' from the brink of death to earth-life do so with reluctance.*

Statement No. 9.—This is experience No. 3. Some of those who were conscious of vacating the body had *a sensation of 'falling' or of 'rising'; others described a momentary 'coma', 'darkness', 'blackout' or 'passing through a dark tunnel'.* A communicator of Geraldine Cummins, killed in a 'plane crash, thought he had travelled through a "dark tunnel" while leaving the Physical Body. Another spoke of "travelling down a tunnel". One communicator[1] said: "I saw in front of me a dark tunnel. I stepped out of the tunnel into a new world." Brunton, describing a man in the process of shedding the Physical Body, said: "Irresistible forces have taken hold of him and are drawing him as through a long tenebrous tunnel."[2]

Statement No. 10.—Many of the newly-dead do not, for a time, realise that they have shed their Physical Bodies. Men of average morality and spirituality who die *naturally* may not, on awakening, at first realise that their transition has taken place—transition was 'gentle' and 'natural' and *their* 'next' world [='Paradise' conditions] is earth-like.

Most *average* men whose death is *enforced* in the prime of life at first fail to realise the fact of their transition: *they* have still to shed the vehicle of vitality and *their* 'next' world (='Hades') is even 'nearer' earth than 'Paradise'; again, they do not at first realise that the substance composing their environment resembles ectoplasm in being ideo-plastic and responding automatically to their thoughts, feelings, expectations, hopes and fears; thirdly, since the vehicle of vitality has no 'sense organs' and is not an instrument of consciousness, it enveils the Soul Body: consciousness is reduced to 'subnormal' (dreamy) 'levels'.

Those who die naturally, on awakening, feel 'well', 'light', 'free', 'serene', 'peaceful', 'secure', 'alert', etc., and find their environment 'natural' and 'bright'.

[1] Mrs. C. A. Dawson Scott, *From Four Who are Dead*, Arrowsmith, 1926.
[2] Dr. Paul Brunton, *The Wisdom of the Overself*, Rider & Co. Ltd.

Those whose death is enforced tend at first to be 'confused'. They are 'bewildered' by the dream-like quality of consciousness and they find their environment 'indistinct', 'unreal', 'misty', 'foggy' (even watery—hence the 'river' of death). Teachable and adaptable men, however, soon leave this temporary abnormal state. In any case, it ends when the vehicle of vitality is shed (at the 'second death'); consciousness, thus released, seems to 'expand' as it operates through the now un-enshrouded Soul Body.

Statement No. 11.—Death was "not what was expected": the process seemed 'natural', there was 'no abrupt change' in the self; the new environment was 'familiar', 'earth-like', 'substantial' and 'real'; the new body, superficially at least, resembled the physical body.

Statement No. 12.—Although several who died thought, at first, that they might be dreaming, most knew that they were not (once any 'partial awakening' was over—see No. 25).

Statement No. 13.—The double that leaves the Physical Body at death consists of the whole of the vehicle of vitality *plus* that portion of the Soul Body that was immersed in it. *It usually leaves the Physical Body chiefly by way of the head.* The vehicle of vitality takes longer to exteriorise than the Soul Body.

Statement No. 14.—A cloud-like mass first collects above the dying man. It usually floats horizontally over the recumbent body and is variously described as 'luminous', 'grey', 'smoke-like', 'steam-like', 'vaporous', 'cloudy', 'shadowy', 'misty' and 'hazy'.

Statement No. 15.—This exteriorised mist gradually assumes definite shape and finally resembles the vacated Physical Body (though it looks younger and brighter).

Statement No. 16.—In the majority of cases the distance of the exteriorised double above the vacated Physical Body varies from directly above to about four feet.

Statement No. 17.—*Many communicators describe how, immediately after death, they saw both their own Physical Bodies and the self-luminous 'double' in which they stood.* (Many saw the mourners round the death-bed and heard what was said. Some eventually attended their own funerals and observed the disposal of the discarded body.) Other communicators did not describe seeing these things. The difference is explained in communications as follows. *There may be some awareness of physical matter so long as the double of the newly-dead person includes the vehicle of vitality and especially so long as the 'silver cord', uniting it to the Physical Body, remains intact.* (Conan Doyle stated, "*The spirit-body is standing or floating beside the old body and conscious both of it and of the surrounding people* [=*'dual consciousness'*]. *At this moment the dead man is nearer to matter than he will ever be again* [because the total double includes the vehicle of vitality, the 'semi-physical' portion of the total Physical Body]. Hence it is that at that moment the greater part of those cases occur where, his thoughts having turned to someone in the distance, his spirit-body went with the thoughts and was manifest to the person.")

Statement No. 18.—Many of the newly-dead also saw and heard friends who had 'gone before'. They especially saw those whom they had 'Called' (=No. 2). Statements Nos. 17 and 18 mean that *a man who dies naturally may have glimpses of two worlds— namely, the physical world and the 'next' (in this case, 'Paradise' conditions), i.e. he may have 'dual' (or 'alternate') consciousness. But once the 'silver cord' becomes extremely thin, or is actually severed, consciousness is normally restricted to the 'next' world.*

*Statement No. 19.—*Many say that the newly-discarded Physical Body at first remained attached to the vehicle of vitality (and the latter to the Soul Body) by *something resembling a 'cord'* (as well as by numerous 'threads', such as intertwine to form the 'cord').

Statement No. 20.—Until the 'silver cord' snaps decomposition does not commence in the Physical Body. Until then (providing it is, in fact, re-habitable), the body can be reanimated. But once the 'cord' is broken (or, in the words of Eccles. xii. 6, is 'loosed') 'return' is impossible. It is said that the delay in the onset of decomposition until the severance of the 'cord' is due to the fact that it transmits vitality. Another function is the transmission of physical impressions from the physical body (via the Soul Body) to consciousness. In the latter connection it is noteworthy that a number of communicators issue warnings against the burial or cremation of a corpse *before* the 'cord' is 'loosed' (an event which, as already said, is indicated by the onset of decomposition—see John xi. 39). They say that— in extremely rare instances, as apparently in the case of Lazarus—there may be difficulty in distinguishing between the irreversible process of death and the theoretically reversible trance or suspended animation.

Statement No. 21.—In the natural death of *average* men the 'cord' may break immediately after, or within a few minutes or hours of, 'visible death'. (A definitely below-average man would have a relatively coarse double and a relatively strong 'cord': the period between shedding the Physical Body and 'loosing' the 'cord' may then be longer, extending, in extreme cases, to three or four days. As already said, 'dual consciousness' is possible until the 'cord' is 'loosed'.)

Statement No. 22.—This is Experience No. 3. After the 'cord is 'loosed', *the average man who dies naturally enjoys a recuperative sleep (often with dreams) lasting for three or four days (of our time).* A man who is killed in the prime of life, on the other hand, tends to be awake at once.

Statement No. 23.—The *post-mortem* sleep of the aged is due to mental fatigue and to a vehicle of vitality which is depleted of vital force. The newly-dead man is described as being in 'a veil' and his condition as resembling the chrysalis state of insects. Once the 'veil' (or vehicle of vitality) has been shed from the total double, the former, an 'astral shell', a partial corpse, gravitates to the Physical Body—from which it has seldom been far distant. The two decompose simultaneously.

Statement No. 24.—The after-death 'sleep' may be lengthened, and the 'sleep' may be deepened, by certain features: (*a*) a prolonged and severe last illness (causing mental exhaustion); (*b*) an exceptionally difficult and strenuous earth-life (also causing mental exhaustion); (*c*) excessive grief on the part of 'living' friends (depressing the newly-dead man =No. 27); (*d*) the fixed idea that there is no after-life (=No. 4), and (*e*) exceptional unteachability. The opposite conditions tend to shorten and lighten the 'sleep'. Thus, an above-average man who dies without exhausting illness, and whose wise friends replace selfish grief by quiet prayer, may have little or no sleep, while a below-average man who dies under certain conditions may sleep for weeks or months of earth-time.

Statement No. 25.—This corresponds to Experience No. 5. *Those who had a post-mortem sleep may have a brief partial awakening.* The newly-awakened man, and especially one who is relatively unevolved, may be conscious of his existence and identity, but not of his surroundings and environment. One communicator said: "The spiritual senses have not yet begun to function." Some of the newly-dead, on awakening, wondered if they were dreaming: several spoke of a short period of 'incertitude' while one described "a mere sense of identity, a point of self-awareness growing out of nothingness".

Statement No. 26.—Many do not describe a 'partial awakening': their awareness of a stable environment emerged simultaneously with their assurance of personal identity, and of having survived the death of the body. In such accounts the first feeling described is one of 'peace', 'security', 'well-being', 'expansion', 'release', 'intense reality', etc. Many declare that they were 'astonished' that death had not been what had been expected (No. 11): on the contrary, it had been 'natural' and the new environment was 'real', 'familiar', 'pleasant', 'beautiful' and 'earth-like'.

Statement No. 27.—Many communicators complained that *the excessive grief of still-embodied friends depressed and hurt the newly-dead.* It hindered their progress into happier conditions. Several offer an explanation of the fact: they say that the newly-dead are particularly sensitive to the thoughts and feelings of the physically-embodied (No. 2).

Statement No. 28.—*The first wish of many of the newly-dead was to assure their still-embodied friends of their survival and well-being.* Many tried to put this into effect soon after 'passing', but few succeeded. *Unless their friends were clairvoyant, they found themselves unseen and unheard by mortals.*

Statement No. 29.—The newly-dead greatly benefit by the prayers of 'living' friends.

Statement No. 30.—Related to Statements Nos. 27 and 29 is one according to which *suitable mortals, and especially potential psychics* (usually unconsciously)'co-operate' with certain discarnate souls ('ministering angels'—Heb. i. 14) in helping other mortals, the dying, the newly-dead and those long-dead who are delayed in 'Hades' conditions (i.e. the 'earth-bound' or 'spirits in prison'—I Pet. iii. 19). This is related to No. 38.

Statement No. 31.—As already said (No. 10) many of the newly-dead (of average type) do not at first realise that they have 'passed on'. *Where a man's transition was natural, certain experiences may aid him to realise the fact.* They are as follows: (*a*) the sight of his own vacated body (in addition to that of the 'double' from which he sees it), i.e., No. 17; (*b*) the sight of those whom he knows pre-deceased him (Nos. 2 and 18);

(c) the loss of his ability to make himself seen or heard by mortal friends (No. 28) and (d) the acquirement of new abilities, i.e. to defy gravity, pass through walls, etc. If these teachings are true, then certain orthodox teachings regarding death and the after-life may hinder the realisation of what has happened (Nos. 4 and 24d).

Statement No. 32.—The 'next' world (of average men), the 'new' environment ('sphere', 'plane', 'realm', 'world', 'state' or 'condition') is not, as is usually taught in Protestant churches, of a 'Spiritual' or 'super physical' nature; it is not the 'Heaven' of the Bible: on the contrary, *the 'next' world (of average men) is 'semi-physical' in nature; it is intermediate between our earth and the 'Heaven' of the Scriptures.* Terms in communications which embody this idea conclude: 'the threshold of' and 'the ante-chamber' to the Spiritual World, 'the transitional state', the 'semi-spiritual sphere', the 'semi-material sphere', the 'inner earth-plane', the 'astral plane', the 'borderland', the 'in-between land', the 'between land' and the 'preliminary sphere'.

Statement No. 33.—The immediate 'next' world of average men is 'earth-like' and 'familiar'.

Statement No. 34.—Early in the total death-experience there was a non-emotional review of the past earth-life (No. 5). The subsequent shedding of the vehicle of vitality that bore these memory-traces, permitted an 'expansion' of conscious-ness, an 'awakening'—the Soul Body became unenshrouded. During the period that follows, *the newly-dead man experiences a second review of the past earth-life, one that is of an emotional, selective and responsible nature. This, our Experience No. 6, clearly corresponds to the 'Judgment'.*

Statement No. 35.—On the basis of the 'Judgment', after a period of adjustment in 'Paradise' eventually, each person 'goes to his own place' in the 'Spiritual' ('super-physical') 'Heavens'. Although, we are told, these 'Heaven' conditions are beyond time, space and form and are indescribable except in poetic and symbolical language, they are far from being 'unreal': on the contrary, they are more 'real' than the physical world: communicators agree with St. Paul: "The things which are seen are temporal, but the things which are not seen are eternal". (II Cor. iv. 18.)

ENFORCED DEATH

Statement No. 36.—In unexpected death in the prime of life there is no time to 'call' friends who have 'gone before'. The double is not increasing in luminosity and discarnate friends may not know, for some time, of the 'passing'—they may not come to the aid of a man who dies unexpectedly. (They do come later, being brought by others—see below.)

Statement No. 37.—In enforced death the 'silver cord' between the Physical Body and the vehicle of vitality, may be 'loosed' at once, or rather, is not formed at all (see No. 41).

Statement No. 38.—It is significant that, whereas accounts of gradual and natural transition typically include descriptions of the person concerned (either just before or just after finally leaving the body) seeing friends whom he knew to be 'dead' (No. 18) accounts of sudden and enforced transition give no references whatever to such experiences just before the 'passing' and relatively few immediately after—*it often takes some little time before a man who dies suddenly in his prime sees discarnate helpers who, nevertheless, are 'there'* (Nos. 30 and 36).

Statement No. 39.—A man whose 'passing' is enforced tends to be 'awake' at once (apart from the 'momentary coma' caused by the shedding of the physical Body): he is mentally alert at the time of transition and his vehicle of vitality is charged with nervous energy. But persons who 'pass' on in old age, being exhausted (both mentally and physically) and having little vitality in the vehicle of vitality, 'sleep'. Transition must involve some shock, due to the changed 'vibration-rate'. The 'sleep' stage aids adjustment: its absence is a disadvantage. Again, the 'sleep' is, in part, due to the enveiling action, on the Soul Body, of the unshed vehicle of vitality and the person who dies *naturally* 'awakens' *after* the vehicle of vitality has been shed, but one whose transition is *enforced* is 'awake' *before* that event. Thus, whereas those who die naturally awake in the un-enveiled Soul Body to 'supernormal' consciousness (with telepathy, clairvoyance, etc.) in 'Paradise' conditions, those whose death is enforced are 'veiled'—their consciousness is confused (by their own dreamcreations) and 'sub-normal'; they are in 'Hades', i.e. illusory conditions. The disadvantage is largely neutralised if people understand these matters and especially if they were also aware that transition was a possibility (as in war).

Statement No. 40.—Since enforced death means that the Soul Body is at first enveiled, communicators from such conditions (and they are the most common) tend to give dream-like accounts, e.g. Raymond's 'cigars' and various opinions.

Statement No. 41.—Where, in enforced death, the 'silver cord' was 'loosed' at once (No. 37), the man concerned is also deprived of any clear view of the *physical* world. He tends to regard the 'doubles' or counterparts of physical objects as the objects themselves, seeing the latter only through a *fog or mist*. His accounts of the early environment often include those features. (Descriptions of 'fog' and 'mist' seldom occur in the accounts of people who died naturally.) Again the man who dies suddenly in his prime may, or may not, have the advantage of seeing his own Physical Body. Further, the very fact that he is 'bewildered' by the shock of sudden transition tends to prevent him from realising that he has 'died'. Still again, he may not have the opportunity of discovering that he is invisible and inaudible to (non-psychic) mortals. All these possibilities make enforced death disadvantageous as compared with natural death. Well does the Prayer Book say, "From sudden death, good Lord, deliver us".

Statement No. 42.—The man who dies (*a*) suddenly, (*b*) unexpectedly and (*c*) ignorant of after-death conditions does so under several disadvantages. Death involves more shock and it is particularly difficult for him to realise what has happened. He is liable to suffer bewilderment. In extreme cases it may be weeks (of earth-time) before realisation, and, therefore, peace, comes. *He knows that he is 'alive' (conscious), but does not know that he is 'dead' [=out of normal contact with the physical world]. Nor does he know that he has yet to make satisfactory contact with the normal 'next' world [='Paradise' conditions].* His religious 'teaching' on these matters may increase, rather than diminish, his confusion—the 'blind' had been led by the 'blind'. (Luke vi. 39.) Realising that he is neither in the orthodox 'Hell', nor the orthodox 'Heaven', and having been assured by his 'teachers' that the Scriptures mention these two states only and that no others exist, he is utterly bewildered. That which might have been envisaged calmly and assimilated over a period of time during earth-life is presented suddenly to a dis-ordered mind after death.

These disadvantages are much less disturbing than they may sound. Any bewilderment experienced by the *average* (or above-average) man is of brief duration. But it may be pro-longed for a definitely evil or grossly sensual man, for one who seeks revenge or who has certain fixed erroneous ideas and refuses to receive instruction (Mark x. 15). Such people may be 'earthbound', corresponding to the 'spirits in prison' (of sensuality, deliberate evil, false conceptions, etc.) to whom Jesus took the opportunity of ministering during His three-day period in the 'Hades' state (I Pet. iii. 19). His 'preaching' doubtless took the form of explaining the processes by which they had forged their own prison-bars and indicating how they might be broken.

Again, although the man whose death is enforced may not have time to 'call' friends who have 'gone before', he is not without aid; as already said, there are experts who under-take such special duties (No. 3). Although it may be some little time before he is aware of their presence, these 'deliverers' soon take him in charge and in this work they may have the 'co-operation' of mortals who are psychic (Nos. 30, 38). The newly-dead man thus comes to realise what has happened—that a transition of an abnormal nature has caused a temporary abnormal state. Discarnate friends whom he himself was unable to 'call' are then brought by the 'deliverers': as in the case of those who passed on naturally, he recognises them and knows that they are 'dead'. He realises what has happened to himself. He then enjoys a period of rest under special conditions. This prepares the Soul Body to operate at a rate higher than that of the Physical Body. The effect of any shock, due to his sudden transition, is eliminated and the newly-dead man enters upon the normal sequence of after-death experi-ences, shedding the vehicle of vitality, awakening in 'Paradise' conditions, passing through his 'Judgment', and thereafter going to 'his own place'.

II

CORRELATION BETWEEN BODILY CONSTITUTION, CONSCIOUSNESS AND ENVIRONMENT

Communications indicate various 'levels' of consciousness and imply that they can be correlated with (since they are determined by) the prevailing bodily constitution. The bodily constitution is clearly related to the environmental conditions. The following is a résumé of this important correlation.

That 'level' of consciousness that is due to all the three bodies (Spiritual, Soul and Physical) i.e. the 'normal' 'level' of consciousness, with reason as the 'highest' faculty, naturally seems to us mortals as the maximum possible. But discarnate communicators, St. Paul and many mystics and poets, assert that when consciousness is released from the governor-like, insulator-like, blanket-like, damper-like, sphincter-like, or 'blinkers'-like effect of the Physical Body, the 'level' of awareness is so 'high' that 'normal' consciousness resembles a mere dream. "Awake, thou that sleepest!" urged the great Apostle "Christ shall give thee light" (through the Greater Self). He spoke from personal experience. Shelley insisted that his 'dead' friend had "awakened from the dream of life". Some people take drugs or practise concentration and meditation in their endeavours to escape from 'normal' to 'supernormal' consciousness.

The Physical Body being shed at death, the 'outermost' component of the total double, namely, the vehicle of vitality, 'lowers' the 'level' of consciousness since it has no 'sense organs' and is not an instrument of consciousness but part of the total Physical Body.

So long as it forms part of the total after-death double and enshrouds the Soul Body, the vehicle of vitality reduces consciousness to a lower 'level' than that which obtains when it formed part of the Physical Body, during earth-life. This is especially the case when the vehicle of vitality is flaccid and depleted of vital force (i.e. when death occurs in extreme old age). People who die in extreme old age are also usually greatly fatigued and need rest from a mental point of view.

These two factors, one of a bodily and the other of a mental nature, cause the average man who dies in old age to *sleep and dream* for some three or four days: this 'sub-normal' 'level' of consciousness is the 'astral' of the Theosophists, and the 'hypnagogic state' of psychologists.

When a man is forced to die suddenly in the prime of life circumstances are different. This man is usually awake, alert and active at the time of transition and (apart from cases of death by explosion) he tends to remain awake for a period. But, since the Soul Body is enveiled by the vehicle of vitality (which in this case is charged with energy) his consciousness tends to be 'sub-normal' in the sense of being *between waking and dreaming*. During this waking-dream, the environment of the newly-dead man includes two different kinds of 'objects': the first consists of the 'doubles' (or 'etheric duplicates') of physical objects. (The Physical Body could not have a 'double' if all physical objects did not also have 'doubles'.) The second group of elements in his environment consists of mental images (such as we see nightly in dreams). Thus, the total environment in this, the (abnormal) 'Hades' state, consists of (*a*) things which are objective and common to everyone in that state (namely, the 'doubles' of physical objects) and (*b*) 'thought forms', i.e. mental images (some created collectively but others individually and therefore more or less private to their creators). Just as the substance of the vehicle of vitality (which is related to the 'ectoplasm' that is moulded automatically to form 'materialisations') is ideo-plastic, automatically assuming forms that correspond to people's mental images, so the substance of the 'Hades' environment (from which the vehicle of vitality is drawn and to which it is eventually returned) is ideo-plastic. Men whose transition was enforced may at first find it difficult to distinguish between 'reality' (the common and objective environment) and 'hallucination', 'illusion' or 'dreams', i.e. mental images): they may, for instance, 'think' (dream) that they smoke cigars.

This type of environment is clearly the 'Amenta' of the Egyptians, the 'Hades' of the Greeks (and Romans), the 'Sheol' of the Jews, 'Kama Loca' of the Hindus (and, following them, of the Theosophists), 'Bardo' of the Tibetans, 'Limbo' of the Scholastic theologians and the 'Lower Borderlands', 'Lower Astral', 'Plane of Illusion', 'Greyworlds', etc., of various communicators. (It is not 'hell', i.e. Gehenna, the place of torment. Average men do not enter 'hell'.)

These people who died suddenly in the prime of life may take longer than three or four days to shed the vehicle of vitality and leave 'Hades' conditions since it was charged with 'vitality' at the time of transition: indeed it may be 'super-charged' with vital force and, in dissipating this, 'physical' phenomena may be produced—hence 'physical' phenomena are observed to be much more frequent with enforced than with natural death.

The Soul Body has 'sense organs' (though they differ, both in form and function, from the physical sense organs). They are said to be wheel-like, the 'chakras' of the Hindus. The Soul Body is an instrument of consciousness at 'super-normal' levels (with the exercise of such facilities as telepathy, clair-voyance and pre-cognition). The corresponding environment is variously described as 'the Psychic World' (communicators), 'Paradise' (Persians, and, from them, the Jews and our Scrip-tures). 'Summerland' (Spiritualists) the 'Third Sphere' (St. Paul, II Cor. xii. 2), the upper 'Astral Plane' (the Theosophists), Elysium (Greeks), etc. In 'Paradise' conditions, earthly space and time are transcended, though there is something analogous to each: a certain rhythm of mental operations corresponds to earthly time, and great difference in thought and feeling corresponds to great separation in space.

Our analyses are concerned with the *immediate* hereafter and do not go beyond the 'Paradise' state intermediate between earth and the Christian 'Heaven' (=the 'Swarga' of the Hindus, the 'Sukhavate' of the Buddhists and the Mental Plane—Devachan—of the Theosophists). But a case could be made out that the 'level' of consciousness that corresponds to the Spiritual Body is that which is called 'Mystical', 'Spiritual' or 'Cosmic'.[1] It is characterised by selfless love (goodwill), the immediate apprehension of Truth and Beauty, and a realisation of the unity of all forms of life in God the 'Father' of all life: As St. Paul said, "In Him we live and move and have our being" (Acts xvii. 28). The 'environments' cor-responding to the Spiritual Body are the true 'Heavens'. They are beyond time, form and space and even symbolic descrip-tion, since "Eye hath not seen, nor ear heard, neither hath it

[1] See page 55.

entered into the heart of man, the things which God hath prepared for them that love Him" (Isa. lxiv. 4; I Cor. ii. 9).

The correlation envisaged above is summarised in Fig. 2. The basic idea is that the 'level' of consciousness—whether 'normal' (or, temporarily, 'sub-normal'), 'super-normal' or 'Spiritual'—is determined by the prevailing bodily constitution, that the 'higher' (Soul and Spiritual) bodies (by analogy with the Physical Body) are drawn from (and eventually returned to) 'environments', 'realms', 'worlds', 'spheres', 'planes', or 'conditions' which are progressively more subjective (or mental) and less objective (or material). Only the 'Father', the Divine, is 'Pure Spirit', outside material manifestation. He is the 'One God', the 'Alpha' and the 'Omega', the Source and the End of all.

These are stupendous conceptions. Yet in the Third Part of this book we hope to show that there is every reason to believe that they correspond to the truth!

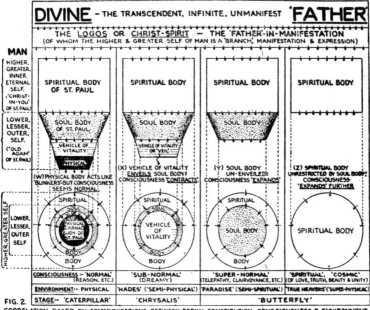

FIG. 2. CORRELATION, BASED ON COMMUNICATIONS, BETWEEN BODILY CONSTITUTION, CONSCIOUSNESS & ENVIRONMENT.

THIRD PART

"Professor Bergson . . . urged that statements about life on the other side, properly studied, like travellers' tales, might ultimately furnish proof more logically cogent than was possible from mere access to earth-memories. . . . I am inclined to think that the time is getting ripe now for the production and discussion of material of this technically unverifiable kind; to be *scrutinised and tested by internal consistency and inherent probability*, in the same sort of way as travellers' tales have to be scrutinised and tested. . . ."—*Sir Oliver Lodge, F.R.S.* (1916).

"What does 'proof' mean?" *A proof means destroying the isolation of an observed fact . . . the bringing it into its place in the system of knowledge.*"—*Sir Oliver Lodge, F.R.S.*

"When many coincide in their testimony (where no previous concert can have taken place), the probability resulting from this concurrence does not rest upon the supposed veracity of each considered separately, but on the improbability of such an agreement taking place by chance. For . . . *the chances would be infinite against their all agreeing in the same falsehood.*"—*Archbishop Whateley.*

"The terror which shaped primitive theologies still tinges for the populace every hint of communication with disembodied souls. The transmutation of savage fear into scientific curiosity is of the essence of civilisation. Towards that transmutation each separate fragment of our evidence, *with undesigned concordance*, indisputably tends."—*F. W. H. Myers.*

"Scientific caution and humility are not enough. A certain boldness also is required, a readiness to grasp *a vast range of converging evidence*, each item of which, standing alone, can lead us nowhere."—*Professor Wm. McDougall.*

"*Single facts can never be 'proved' except by their coherence in a system.* But, as all facts come singly, anyone who dismisses them one by one is destroying the conditions under which the conviction of new truth could arise in his mind."—*Professor F. C. S. Schiller.*

THE STATEMENTS SCRUTINISED AND TESTED

(a) *Internal consistency or coherence of communications*

Statement No. 1a.—This refers to the possible effect of 'fixed ideas', etc. on the early after-life.

The following communication, published in 1876, Anon., *Life Beyond the Grave*, E. W. Allen, p. 55, shows essential similarity to many others, e.g. those recently obtained by Geraldine Cummins (who had not studied psychic matters) from 'Myers', and published in *The Road to Immortality* and *Beyond Human Personality*: "Nearly all persons who are imperfect have *hallucinations* in the spirit world which cause them to see their surroundings in a distorted light—that is, their minds are influenced by their own thoughts. Thus, the miser sees nothing but bags of gold, the drunkard nothing but drink, the man of the world nothing but worldly pleasures. . . . They never see their friends and kin, because none such ever occupied their thoughts. They must, therefore, be lonely and find themselves *to all intents and purposes* in a bleak cheerless waste that is as objective *to them* as the Sahara."

The communicator added, "After all, they are not in a very different condition from what they were when in the body: their whole thoughts were then engrossed with such subjects. It is therefore natural that after death the same subjects should occupy their minds, since *the mind . . . becomes more vivid. . . . The subjects of which they think . . . take the appearance of living objective realities.* They must live for some time on the 'earth-plane' [='Hades', with self-created hallucinations] before they can see things as they really are" [i.e. before they can see the objective environment which is common to all who are in 'Paradise' conditions].

The people to whom the description given above applies are described as 'earthbound' by fixed ideas which were self-created during earth-life. A similar temporary state is said to follow sudden death in the prime of life—'Raymond' (Lodge), for example, communicated to say that some of the newly-dead soldiers smoked cigars. The communication would have been true had he said that they *dreamed or imagined*, that they smoked cigars—just as a miser, who died naturally in old age, might dream or imagine he possessed hoards of gold. If certain communications from beyond, that purport to describe conditions on 'the other side' are read with these possibilities in mind, i.e. that those newly-dead who suffer from obsessive ideas (and especially if they died suddenly in their prime) may temporarily have (*a*) a dream environment which partly or entirely obscures (*b*) the common, objective and 'real' environment, the descriptions received will be seen to be perfectly understandable. They will be seen to *indicate surviving personalities who are as yet only half awake.*

(*b*) *Inherent probability, support from psychic science, etc.*

In view of such phenomena among mortals as psychological blindness and post-hypnotic suggestion it is highly probable that fixed ideas and strong expectations do affect a man's immediate after-death experiences. His expectation that he will sleep "until the end of the world" (or 'Age)' may, it is said, prolong the sleep-stage (Statement No. 22).

Statement No. 1b.—The double, in the sense of the total after-death non-physical 'body', comprises (*a*) the vehicle of vitality (by means of which the physical body was vitalised during earth-life, (*b*) the Soul Body and (*c*) the Spiritual Body.

Flammarion, in his Presidential Address before the S.P.R., 1923, maintained, "There is such a thing as the double", while both Dr. Nandor Fodor and Dr. C. Raynor Johnson have gone further and insisted (as is indicated above) that it is composite in nature.

With the average man the Spiritual Body is so little organised or used (in the search for and the expression of, Truth, Beauty and Goodness), that it does not enter the present discussion.

The evidence in favour of this total bodily constitution is not here considered: it is to be dealt with in two further books.

Statements Nos. 2-4.—These are inter-related and will be considered together.

(a) Causes of the 'Call'

According to communications, discarnates know when their mortal friends are in course of transition. They often know this because a dying man, either consciously or instinctively, thinks of them. For example, 'J.V.H.'s' communicator stated: "As the hour of death approaches, the soul . . . sends out a wordless cry."[1]

A second source of this knowledge by discarnates is that the double of a dying person gradually becomes more or less visible to them—the natural brilliance of the Soul Body is returning, since it is no longer quenched by the close association with the Physical Body which obtains with young and healthy people. 'Judge Hatch', communicating, said: "I knew he was about to die—his body had become surrounded by a peculiar light."[2] The communicator of 'A.L.E.H.' promised, "I shall watch for your 'Call' to me. It will come as your spirit is leaving your body."[3] 'J.V.H.' was told, "The lamp of life burns low on your side and bright on ours. Then we see the earth-flame flicker, and know it will soon be out."[4]

Discarnates who are said to respond to the 'Call' and to assist those in process of transition are often compared with earthly midwives and called '*deliverers*'. 'Lancelot', who died aged nine, described being 'met' when he 'passed over'. He said, "Michael was waiting for me". He added (speaking to his incarnate mother): "If I couldn't be there when you come into this life, angels would be there to tell you why." Then he made a typical general statement: "Clouds of angels are round the earth to tell everyone what to do as soon as they leave their bodies. No one is alone. No one is left not guided."[5]

[1] *Death's Door Ajar*, Rider & Co. Ltd., 1934, p. 105.
[2] Elsa Barker, *Letters from a Living Dead Man*, Rider & Co. Ltd., 1914, p. 184.
[3] *Fragments from My Messages*, Women's Printing Society, Ltd., 1929, p. 14.
[4] *Death's Door Ajar*, Rider & Co. Ltd., 1934, p. 100.
[5] *Letters from Lancelot*, Dunstan, 1931, p. 35.

(b) Inherent probability, support from psychical science, etc.

In the first place, telepathic communication between 'living' people undoubtedly occurs and we may suppose that, if survival is a fact, it may also occur between those of the 'living' who are on the point of transition and their 'dead' friends.

There is, in fact, evidence on the files of the S.P.R. as to the existence of the 'Call': Myers[1] mentioned "a considerable number of cases where a spirit seems to be aware of the impending death of a survivor."

Thirdly, many death-compacts have been fulfilled (often in most unexpected circumstances): these clearly represent 'Calls' in reverse—they are from the 'dead' to the 'living'. Myers[2] pointed out that Gurney, struck by successful cases of death-compacts, considered that they have "a certain efficacy".

(c) Converse communications

Communicators' assertions that a 'Call' is not sent out by excessively self-centred persons are understandable, as is their claim that fixed ideas of non-survival also inhibits the 'Call'. These statements are given independently (in different terms and in different settings, by different communicators) yet the underlying idea in all is identical.

(d) Conditions that affect the 'Call'

Communicators say that telepathy occurs very readily between two discarnate persons (whose Soul Bodies are not 'blanketed', 'screened', 'insulated' or 'blinkered' from each other by corresponding Physical Bodies), but that telepathic impressions pass still more readily from a 'living' to a 'dead' person (because the Physical Body of the 'living' acts after the manner of a resistant base, comparable to a gun-emplacement, for the thoughts and feelings sent out—see also Statement No. 27). These latter statements accord with three others: (a) that undue grief by embodied friends injures the newly-dead (No. 27), (b) that prayers help them (No. 29) and (c) that psychics may 'co-operate' with discarnates (No. 30).

The statement that, in cases of natural death, many people

---

[1] F. W. H. Myers, *loc. cit.*, *Proc. S.P.R.*, VI, 20, xi, 429 and *Phantasms of the Living*, p. 428.

[2] F. W. H. Myers, *Human Personality and its Survival of Bodily Death*, Longmans, Green & Co. Ltd., 1916, p. 232.

are already outside the Physical Body an hour or so before the heart stops beating, etc. (No. 6) agrees with (a) the 'Call' (No. 2) and (b) No. 18, concerning dying persons often seeing 'departed' friends, i.e. enjoying death-bed visions. Conversely, it is an established fact that whereas *pre*-death apparitions are not uncommonly seen in cases of natural death, they are unknown in cases of enforced death in the prime of life. In natural death we may suppose that the dying person's double, 'loosened' from the Physical Body, obeyed his 'Call' and appeared to an incarnate friend. When death occurs suddenly in the prime of life (since the double is not in process of loosening from the body) a 'Call' of this type is not 'sent out'.

(e) The 'Call' in a wider setting

The incidence of the telepathic 'Call' is not, of course, confined to the process of transition. On the contrary, the latter is only a special case of a process that has universal application. We are told (and the gun-emplacement analogy lends support to the statement) that when any mortal thinks definitely and emotionally of discarnate souls, the latter are immediately aware of it: they *receive* a 'Call' and that independently of whether the thinker is, or is not, *aware* of the fact. The following are examples of this statement.

'Phillip'[1] assured his incarnate mother: "You can always attract my attention by a strong act of thought". 'Judge Hatch', having told Elsa Barker[2] that the newly-dead can hear earthly music, etc., added: "Most of all they feel the power of the *thought directed to them*." 'A.B.'[3] was informed: "When you seek us we know, for we can read your thoughts." Again, "It is not impossible to reach any of us if the *desire* of the sitter is strong." André[4] was assured: "You have only to *direct your thoughts*, impelled by *earnest desire*, to your risen friends . . . to gain their attention. Hence, this form of communication—mind-impression—is attainable by all." Mrs. Sewall[5] was told: "The returned (excarnate) friend is instantly conscious when be becomes the subject of reflection" (by an incarnate friend). Again, "Your thoughts are more powerful in the spirit world than your physical acts are in yours."[6]

---

[1] Alice Gilbert, *op. cit.*, 1948, p. 201.   [2] *Ibid.*, p. 266.
[3] *Ibid.*, 1937, pp. 52, 54.   [4] *Ibid.*, 1926, p. 16.
[5] *Ibid.*, 1921, p. 306.   [6] Anon., *Life Beyond the Grave*, E. W. Allen, 1876, p. 105.

Mrs. Heslop's (deceased) husband assured her: "Your Spirit, when directed towards me, draws me to you." 'Stead'[1] soon after his 'passing', said that he was told that, when mortals *think "intensely"* of their discarnate friends, the latter 'see' them. Jane Sherwood's communicator in Great Britain made a statement identical with that of Elsa Barker's in America. The latter said, "When man is excited, exalted or in any way intensified in his emotional life, the spirits draw near to him."[2] The former observed, "In times of excitement or heightened being you glowed into clear view and your thought came strongly to me. . . . You were lit up for me." [He had reasoned to himself thus: "Your thought reached me, so mine must reach you, even though you were unaware of its source."] Jane Sherwood[3] was also told: "Urgent thought of the personality you want often attracts his attention and then 'contact' can be made. The same idea was communicated in France. A communicator of Allan Kardec (L. H. D. Rival, 1804-69)[4] was told: "All spirits receive the thought you desire to communicate to them, simply by *directing the thought towards them.*" The communicator of Mrs. Dawson-Smith[5] said that the ability to reach her was due to "your affection" and "my love". According to a communicator of *Spirit Teachings* (by 'M.A., Oxon', p. 270), thought that was *"directed strongly towards him"* operated as a *'Call'.*

(f) Converse communications

The converse of the idea that we can, and do, 'call' the dead is also communicated. 'Judge Hatch' (in Elsa Barker's *Letters from a Living Dead Man*, Rider & Co. Ltd., 1914, p. 74), after saying, "Your thought of us can make us happy," continued: "Your *forgetfulness* of us can throw us back entirely upon ourselves." 'Myers', communicating through Geraldine Cummins said, "Only in *forgetfulness*, in the fading of love, is there negation of life" (compare the communication cited from *Light*, vol. XLII, 1922, under No. 27, p. 156). Myers appealed to mortals to think of their 'departed' loved ones, and to think of them as living.[6] Many who 'come through' urge their

---

[1] *Blue Island*, Hutchinson & Co., 1922, p. 94.   [2] *Op. cit.*, 1914, p. 243.
[3] *Op. cit.*, p. 76.   [4] *Book on Mediums*, Paris, p. 92.
[5] Mrs. C. A. Dawson-Smith, *From Four Who are Dead*, Arrowsmith, 1927, p. 4.
[6] *Beyond Human Personality*, Ivor Nicholson and Watson, 1935, p. 89.

mortal friends and relatives to keep their memories 'green' by carefully observing special occasions, such as birthdays and anniversaries.

Again, Professor Hornell Hart (*Proc. S.P.R.*, vol. 50, p. 167) in his important paper entitled 'Six Theories About Apparitions', pointed out that in about a half of the numerous cases of conscious apparitions of the *living* which he had studied, the appearer's attention was specially directed towards the percipient: he considered that this supports the idea that many apparitions of the *dead* are caused by surviving personalities directing their thoughts to the living.

(g) Communication is facilitated by the 'Call'

Many people (with no real knowledge of these matters) have categorically declared that it is wrong to 'call up' the dead, that we should not 'disturb' them. 'Raymond' (Lodge) communicating, on the other hand, made a typical statement: "If you people only knew how we long to come to you, you would *call* us."[1]

The most moving 'Call'—that of affection and goodwill— is often described by communicators as the chief prerequisite to significant and successful communication. Such being the case, the rarity of deep and true affection might, in part, explain the scarcity of really convincing 'messages'. 'Myers' said that only those mortals who are actuated by love and faith "obtain convincing evidence of the survival of their loved ones".[2] 'Judge Hatch'[3] pointed out that a discarnate soul is "very sensitive to *the call* of those he loved on earth".

The communicator of Mrs. Dawson-Smith stated: "There is no doubt as to your thoughts reaching us. Thoughts are . . . the chief realities in this world."[4] Frieda Hohenner-Parker was told: "It is easy to come back to you because you create an atmosphere of love and harmony about you."[5] 'Claude'[6] told his mother that "love makes the most satisfactory *link*". An anonymous communicator from 'high' 'Paradise' levels

[1] Sir Oliver Lodge, *The Survival of Man*, Methuen & Co. Ltd., 1909, p. 69.

[2] Geraldine Cummins, *The Road to Immortality*, Ivor Nicholson and Watson, 1932.

[3] Elsa Barker, *Letters from a Living Dead Man*, Rider & Co. Ltd., 1914, p. 194.

[4] Mrs. C. A. Dawson-Smith, *From Four Who are Dead*, Arrowsmith, 1926, p. 153.

[5] *A Crusader Here and There*, A. J. Stockwell, 1952, p. 84.

[6] Mrs. L. Kelway Bamber, *Claude's Book*, Psychic Book Club, 1918.

declared: "An atmosphere of love is the one we can most readily enter."[1] 'A.B.' said: "You must be a brother to all before you can be greatly helped by us", and he indicated the reason—"for we are linked together in one mighty whole".[2] Stead's communicator[3] ('Julia') insisted: "It will make all the difference to your results . . . if you pursue the investigation from a love motive and not from mere cold curiosity." Again, "The communion between the quick and the dead can only persist when the Borderland [='Hades'] is bridged by love. And unless there be self-sacrificing love and the desire for service on both sides, there will not, and cannot, be more than a brief, intermittent, and not altogether pleasant, intercourse between the two worlds."

The communicator of 'A.B.'[4] having said that spirits who inhabit "high" spheres, or conditions, in the after-life, find it "difficult to penetrate" the spheres intermediate between theirs and earth, stated, "Love has a cleansing effect on the psychic atmosphere, and where that is the path to earth is purified and made clearer". André[5] was informed by his communicator: "Your spirit-helpers are ready at your call when the call is made in faith and love. *Loving thought is your call to one out of the body.* When you hold that one steadily in thought you have provided a way of communication."

(h) Inherent probability, support from psychical science, etc.

These statements, by 'communicators', are supported by the findings of psychical researchers. Myers[6] said, "Love is a kind of exalted, but specialised, telepathy". Gabriel Marcel[7] maintained, "A . . . meaningful theory of survival cannot be carried out except in a connection with a philosophy of love." Colonel Reginald M. Lester's[8] great experience in communication led him to say, "The strongest bridge of communication is love."

J. Middleton Murry (*The Betrayal of Christ by the Churches,*

[1] Anon., *Christ in You*, Watkins, 1919, p. 82.
[2] Mary Bruce Wallace, *The Coming Light*, Watkins, 1924, pp. 69, 141.
[3] W. T. Stead, *After Death*, Stead's Publishing House, 1897, p. 87.
[4] 'A.B.', *One Step Higher*, The C. W. Daniel Co. Ltd., 1937, p. 162.
[5] G. G. André, *Morning Talks with Spirit Friends*, Watkins, 1926, p. 17.
[6] F. W. H. Myers, *op. cit.*
[7] Gabriel Marcel, *F. W. H. Myers, Memorial Lecture*, 1955.
[8] Colonel Reginald M. Lester, *Towards the Hereafter*, George Harrap, 1956, p. 183.

Andrew Dakers, 1940, p. 172) mentioned "moments of imaginative communion with the great dead" and continued: "But always the condition of these moments is one and the same: the motion of love must have possessed our hearts."

(i) *Converse communications*

The converse of this statement also comes from 'beyond', and is also supported by the experience of psychical researchers: the investigator or the sitter who entertains strong suspicion and antagonism either fails to get phenomena, or they are unsatisfactory: he has sent out an inhibiting 'call'—'you *can't* do this!' The two effects, the production of worth-while communications, under certain conditions and their absence under the opposite ones are accentuated by the fact that, since both the communicator and the medium are temporarily in a highly suggestible condition, they tend automatically to respond to the thoughts and feelings (exactly as they would to verbal suggestions) of investigators and sitters.

(j) *Scriptural support for the 'Call'*

Biblical texts afford support to Statements 2-4. Just as the newly-dead 'Private Dowding'[1] stressed the importance of our making earthly friends (so that those who pre-decease us will eventually 'hear', and answer our 'Call'), so Jesus (Luke xvi. 9) counselled, "Make to yourselves friends even of the mammon of unrighteousness [=even of irreligious people], that when ye fail, they may receive you into everlasting tabernacles". (N.B. These 'friends' were not, as some theologians think, 'sleeping' until 'the end of the Age'—compare remarks under Statements 22, 23, and 34-5.)

The idea of 'deliverers' which occurs in so many independent communications, was also given by the Master (in the Parable of the rich man and Lazarus—Luke xvi. 22) when He said that when Lazarus died he was 'carried by the angels' into 'Abraham's bosom'. (The latter phrase refers to the happy conditions of 'Paradise', in contrast with the boredom of 'Hades': it was taken from the custom of reclining at meals, a position in which, the head leaning back will rest on the bosom of one's neighbour. The favoured guest occupied the seat next to the host and his head would, therefore, be on

---

[1] W. T. Pole, *Private Dowding*, Watkins, 1917, pp. 22, 33, 88.

the latter's bosom. Thus, the beloved disciple leaned on Jesus' bosom (John xiii. 23), while Jesus Himself 'is in the bosom of the Father' (John i. 18). To the Israelites the reward for a good earth-life was entrance into the society of Abraham, Isaac and Jacob, in which case they could 'lean on Abraham's bosom'. The Master's phrase, "carried by the angels" (='messengers'), clearly refers to the work of delivery from the Physical Body (which may include the severance of any unduly resistant 'cords' or 'threads', i.e. still unseparated portions of the Physical and Soul Bodies—see Statements 19-21).

(k) Internal consistency or coherence of communication

It will be seen that Statements 2-4 are concordant with six others, i.e. Nos. 1b, 6, 18, 27, 29 and 30.

Statement No. 5.—communicators claim that early in the total death-experience they had a panoramic non-emotional review of the earth-life which had just closed.

(a) Inherent probability, support from psychical science, etc.

This common statement by the dead (made through mediums) is supported by two facts: first, that psychologists agree that no memory is ever really "lost" to us, and secondly, that many who *nearly* died, by drowning, etc., described undergoing a review of their past lives. The latter descriptions were *not* made through mediums. Professor William Brown (*King's College Lectures on Immortality*, p. 154) said: "There is no such thing as a real loss of memory resulting from brain lesions. A pathological change in the brain simply prevents the memories from actualising themselves. Memories are unconscious, but if the motor mechanism of the brain is excited, they may come to the mind as conscious memory. If the mechanism is out of order, then the memories cannot come to the surface. This does not mean that they are lost, but simply that they are in abeyance."

(1) Professor Heirn fell sixty feet in the Alps. On regaining physical consciousness [=re-entering the body] he said that he had reviewed his past life. He felt no pain on striking the ground. Heirn interviewed many who had had similar experiences: all described a review of the past life and said they had been unafraid and had suffered no pain.[1]

(2) Professor Pastor recorded that, during the crisis of an illness in which he almost died, he had reviewed his entire life. He also claimed to have seen the dead: *"My mother, who died four years previously, met me"*.[1]

(3) Leslie Grant Scott said, "Dying is really not such a terrifying experience. I died and came back. *I found death one of the easiest things in life. [Statement No. 7]: but not the returning: that was difficult and full of fear*—[No. 8]. The will to live had left me and so I died. . . . *Suddenly my whole life began to unroll before me.* . . . I seemed to view it all impersonally. . . ." After telling of his doctor's attempts at bringing him back to the body, Scott continued: *"My consciousness was growing more and more acute. It seemed to have expanded beyond the limits of the physical brain.* . . ." [No. 26.] I was dead, yet I could think, hear and see more widely than ever before. *From the next room came great engulfing waves of emotion, the sadness of a childhood companion [No. 27.] My increased sensitiveness made me feel and understand these things with an intensity hitherto unknown to me. The effort to return to my body was accompanied by an almost unimaginable sensation of horror and terror.* I had left without the slightest struggle: I returned by an almost super-human effort of will."[2]

(4) After Johann Schwerzeger almost died but recovered, he said that he had seen "his whole life".[3]

(5) S. Bedford said that when he was twelve years old he had a school boy friend of the same age. The latter fell from a tree that overhung a pond. He was rescued. Bedford said: "As soon as he was able to speak he gasped out excitedly, 'What do you think happened? As I touched the water I seemed to leave my body and, in a flash saw everything I had done in my life.'" Bedford commented: "He was so enormously impressed by this incident that he completely forgot he was covered with slime and drenched to the skin. The most important statement about the whole incident was the fact that *he felt himself leave his body and, strangely enough, did not feel afraid.* This accident was the sole topic of our conversation for a long time afterwards, but naturally at that age we were completely baffled as to its real meaning. Now . . . the meaning of the incident is clear. The sudden shock caused my friend's soul

---

[1] *Ann. Psychic Science*, February, 1906.   [2] *Psychical Research*, March, 1931.
[3] Catherine Crowe, *The Night Side of Nature*, 1848; Routledge ed., 1904, p. 133.

[-body] to be ejected from his [physical] body into that intermediate state of divided consciousness on the threshold of the life beyond. He *remembered* because in this state of divided consciousness *the brain is partly active.* Had he been unconscious, the brain would have been inactive, and he would have remembered nothing." This case, concerning a quite young boy, shows that similar narratives which come from adults were not (as has been suggested) copied from each other.[1]

(6) Samuel Warren contributed an article to *Blackwood's Magazine* (December, 1854) in which he mentioned a man who was almost drowned, but had "a sense of freedom from pain and a sudden recollection of all his past life."

(7) A contributor to *Notes and Queries*, 1st Series, vol. xii, p. 500, quoted the following from his own diary: "How intense and how rapid the thoughts which rush through the mind of a drowning man!" He added: "Of corporeal sufferings I have no recollection."

(8) *The Progressive Age*, 1865, related the case of a businessman, 'A', who held a bond against another, 'B', which was not payable for some time. Before the period expired, however, 'A' mislaid the document. He eventually wrote, telling 'B' of the fact and hoping he would honour his agreement. On the contrary, 'B' repudiated the contract. Some time later 'A' was almost drowned. The narrative continues: "As soon as he gained sufficient strength, he went to his bookcase, took out a book . . . and extracted the bond. . . . While drowning . . . *there suddenly stood out before him, as it were in a picture, every act of his life. . . .*"

(9) Epes Sargent (1813-80), an American research worker (and Editor of *The Boston Transcript*), after mentioning this type of experience, said that it had occurred to him when he had "anticipated instant death from an accident".[2]

(10) Sir John Heron Maxwell[3] was almost drowned when fifteen years of age. He said that he "felt just as if he were sitting quietly suspended in the air with everything beautifully green around him" (Statement No. 32). He had no fear (No. 7). "Things rushed through his memory—little things, little untruths. . . . " Then he felt a sudden tug at his collar. . . .

---

[1] *Death—An Interesting Journey*, The Alcuin Press, pp. 41-2.
[2] *Planchette, the Despair of Science*, Boston, 1869, p. 377.
[3] Sir John Heron, *The Spiritualist*, June 18, 1875, p. 292.

(11) S. W. Cozzens[1] described how he fell down an almost perpendicular slope. His speed increased until he gave himself up for lost. The narrative continued: *"Convinced that death was inevitable, I became perfectly reconciled to the thought. My mind comprehended in a moment the acts of a lifetime.* Transactions of the most trivial character . . . stood before me in bold relief. . . . I seemed to be gliding swiftly and surely out of the world, but *felt no fear* . . . ; on the contrary, rejoiced that I was so soon to see with my own eyes the great mystery concealed behind the veil; that I was to cross the deep waters and be at rest. . . ." He was, however, saved by a projecting rock.

(12) The Rev. Wm. Stainton Moses[2] described having undergone this experience. He said: "A strange peacefulness took the place of my previous feeling of confusion. *I recognised fully that I was drowning, but had no fear.* . . . I recollected my life. . . . *Objective pictures of events seemed to float before me.* . . . The events were all scenes in which I had been an actor and no very trivial and unimportant ones were depicted. . . . *I was an interested spectator; little more.* This peaceful state was interrupted by a series of most unpleasant sensations which were attendant on resuscitation."

(13) Fr. John Gerard published an experience of this type.[3] When skating with a friend, the latter fell through the ice. Gerard lay down and gave him his hand, but was himself pulled under the ice. He said: *"There flashed across me, along with the realisation that death was, apparently, immediately inevitable, a perfect picture of my past life in every detail.* . . . Everything seemed to be included, however trivial. . . . *Conscience appeared to play no part in the matter.* I can remember nothing in the way of recognition of good and evil in my past actions. . . ."

(14) Fr. Herbert Thurston, S.J., in an article entitled "Memory at Death" referred to some of the cases mentioned above in *The Month*, vol. clxv, 1935, pp. 49-60. He was interested in them because his father had the experience when he was almost drowned. His father had said: *"Everything that I had ever done in my life passed before me in a flash."* Thurston made the following wise comment on such cases: "In almost every

[1] S. W. Cozzens, *The Marvellous Country: or Three Years in Arizona and New Mexico*, 2nd ed., 1875, pp. 235-7.
[2] The Rev. Wm. Stainton Moses, *The Spiritualist*, June 4, 1875, p. 267.
[3] Fr. John Gerard, *The Month*, 1913, p. 126.

case, the range, the minute detail and the incredible rapidity of the vision came as a complete surprise. Nothing in their previous knowledge of their mental processes had prepared them to believe that such a lightning flash of illumination was possible in their case." This 'illumination', is well described by Leslie Grant Scott (Example No. 3).

(15) Dr. G. Stretton recorded the case of a man whose aircraft fell 4,000 feet before he regained control: during the fall he experienced a panoramic survey of his past life.[1]

(16) Professor Flammarion also told of a man who, having fallen into a ravine, said that he had reviewed his entire life: the review occupied only a second or two; the life covered many years.[2]

(17) Thomas de Quincey[3] said that, in his opium-induced dreams, "The minutest details of childhood, or forgotten scenes of later years, were often reviewed." He also mentioned a relative who had been nearly drowned when a child and who declared that all her previous life had passed "in an instant", like a picture, before the mind's eye—"not successively, but simultaneously". De Quincey concluded, "There is no such thing as forgetting; traces once impressed upon the mind are indestructible", a conclusion that is endorsed by psychoanalysts, hypnotists, etc. He stated that he had twice found similar cases in modern books, "accompanied by a remark which is probably true, viz. that the dread Book of Account, of which the Scriptures speak, is, in fact, the mind itself of every individual". In his *Sequel to the Confessions* (*Works*, vol. xvi, 1871, pp. 19-20) de Quincey noted that, though his former account had been treated with scepticism by certain critics, similar experiences had been reported by people "who had never heard of each other".

(18) Flight Lieutenant J. P. Wynton wrote (June 27, 1957) and told the present writer that when he crashed in a 'plane and was almost burned to death, he experienced "a timeless review" of his past life. A 'voice' or 'thought' then commanded him to "pull himself together", and he struggled free.

(19) The following cases from Germany and Central Europe were cited by Dr. Carl du Prel. (*The Philosophy of Mysticism*, Redway, 1889). A lady developed a violent *headache*:

[1] C. Flammarion, *Death and Its Mystery*, T. Fisher Unwin, Ltd., 1923.   [2] *Ibid.*
[3] *Confessions of an English Opium-Eater*, in *Works* (1862 ed.) vol. i, pp. 259-60.

when the pain was at its worst, it suddenly ceased (presumably because the Soul Body had vacated the Physical Body). *She found herself in very pleasant conditions (Statements Nos. 25 and 32 regarding 'Paradise' conditions, and note that, according to No. 13 the Soul Body typically leaves the Physical Body chiefly by way of the head).* Then her memory "reached back to her earliest years". Dr. du Prel reported that two men and a women, when dying, said that they had reviewed their past lives, 'living' the incidents over again.

(20) Edmund Whymper,[1] who fell 200 feet in a succession of bounds, said: "I was perfectly conscious of what was happening and felt each blow. *But I felt no pain* [No. 7]. *I thought, 'Well, if the next blow is harder than the last, that will be the end'. . . . The recollection of a multitude of things rushed through my head.* Many of them were trivialities which had long been forgotten. More remarkable, this bounding through space was not disagreeable."

(21) George Sandwith[2] when a boy, was nearly drowned. He said: "It was as if I were at a magic lantern show: a series of pictures showed me the happy events of my past life."

(22) A. W. Osborn[3] had a friend who was nearly drowned and who said: "*All the events of my life seemed to whirl around me. . . .* The memory of events became so clear that they were re-experienced."

(23) Dr. Nandor Fodor[4] had a patient, a man who cleaned vats in a chemical factory. One day, believing a vat to be empty, he vaulted over the brim. It was, however, full of boiling, poisonous chemicals. The narrative continues: "*The moment he let go, the realisation that he would die came to him. In a flash his whole life spread out before his mind. . . .*" (He was saved by a plank which spanned the vat.)

(24) Dr. Fodor (*loc. cit*) said that another patient, who had nearly drowned as a child said: "*I saw my whole life rolling by.*"

(25) According to J. G. Williams (*Light*, LXIX, 1949, p. 98) three cases were published in *The Listener* (November 6, 13, 1947; October 21, 1948) describing falls when climbing. In all three cases "The individuals were surprised that *fear*

[1] Edmund Whymper, *Scrambles Among the Alps*, 1871.

[2] George Sandwith, *Magical Session*, Omega Press, 1955.

[3] A. W. Osborn, *The Expansion of Awareness*, Omega Press, 1955.

[4] Dr. Nandor Fodor, *International Record of Medicine and General Practice Clinics*, vol. 169, 1956, p. 529.

was entirely absent; and also the sense of *pain was absent* in the two cases where collisions during the fall produced bodily injuries". The writers had no explanation of the surprising phenomena, and Mr. Williams pointed out: "It is not due to any dimming of the mind, for there is evidence to the contrary."

(26) Dr. H. Carrington and J. R. Meader quoted the experience of a man who fell from "a tremendous height" and who stated: "I experienced none of the anxiety which occasionally attacks us in dreams at supposed falling accidents." While falling he never lost consciousness. He said: "When my body finally bounded against the rocks . . . I became unconscious *without experiencing any pain whatever.*" Moreover, he declared: "The moments when I stood at the brink of the life were *the happiest I ever experienced.*"[1]

(27) Carrington and Meader (*op. cit.*, p. 315-16) also quoted (from *The Encyclopaedia of Death*, vol. ii, pp. 384-5) the case of Dr. Heim, who fell "at least 100 feet, to finally land against a snow wall." He heard "the dull noise" when his head struck various corners of rocks, "But," he stated, "in all this *I felt no pain.*" He added: "Pain only manifested itself at the end of an hour or so." [When, because falling, he was out of the body, he could not feel the injuries inflicted upon it—and had he 'died' and subsequently communicated, like many other communicators, he would have declared that he had suffered no pain during transition—but when he re-entered the body he became aware of the damage done to it.]

(28) Mrs. Mary Marks, who was so ill that she nearly died, on recovering, stated that she had reviewed the whole of her life up to that time.[2]

(29) Anita Kohsen (*Journ. S.P.R.*, 39, 1958, p. 324) reviewed a book by Professor W. H. C. Tenhaeff entitled *Telepathie en Helderzienheid* (Telepathy and Clairvoyance), published by W. de Haan, Antwerp, 1958. She described the book as containing a number of examples of the 'review' of the past life in face of death. One lady who experienced the review twice, on the second occasion included what had happened to her since the first occasion. According to the diary of Heinrich Zschokke, a Swiss educationist, the 'review' was not of his own

---

[1] *Death, Its Causes and Phenomena*, Rider & Co. Ltd., 1911, p. 315.

[2] Muldoon, J. Sylvan, and Dr. Hereward Carrington, *The Phenomena of Astral Projection*, Rider & Co. Ltd., 1951, p. 91.

life, but that of a neighbouring man at the dining table. Similarly, a lady social worker, on grasping the hand of a body 'reviewed' certain of his acts, i.e. has a partial review by proxy. [In the two latter cases the phenomenon is interpreted by the present writer, as a 'reading', by Zschokke and by the social worker, of the 'auras', or vehicles of vitality, which carry the memory record, of the diner and the boy respectively.]

(30) Dorothy Grenside referred to several other cases of the 'review'. Wexhull reviewed his life on three successive nights "in dream". Fechner quoted the experience as having occurred to a lady-friend, and she herself had met two similar cases, one of whom was "a man who nearly met his death by drowning".[1]

(31) Partial reviews of the past earth-life are also known. To those who observe the phenomenon they may seem more remarkable than apparently complete ones. Goethe related the case of a dying man who recited sentences in Greek, though he knew no Greek whatever. It transpired that he had learned the sentences by casually hearing someone speak. A similar case was reported by Dr. Steinbeck: he told of a clergyman who, called to the death-bed of a peasant, heard him uttering prayers in Greek and Hebrew. Enquiry showed that, when a boy, the peasant had heard his parish priest uttering those prayers. Writing of cryptomnesia (or unconscious memory), Lombroso[2] said, "Under certain circumstances (e.g. when I am at a great altitude, say seven thousand feet) I remember Italian, Latin and even Greek verses which had been forgotten for years. . . . Similarly during certain dreams in nights when I am afflicted with conditions showing intestinal poisonings, disagreeable moments of years previous (e.g. the examinations made in 1896) are reproduced with precision. . . . They are always fragmentary and incomplete recollections. . . ." He proceeded to give similar examples from the experience of others.

A most interesting and suggestive example of the partial 'review' is observed in connection with dental operations under nitrous oxide. *Borderland*, i, 1893-4, p. 564, carried an account, by a doctor, of a patient who had teeth extracted under gas, without feeling any pain or discomfort whatever. However, a few days later, "*while half awake*" (i.e. while the vehicle of

---

[1] *The Meaning of Dreams*, G. Bell & Sons Ltd., 1923, p. ii.
[2] Cesare Lombroso, *After Death—What?* T. Fisher Unwin, Ltd., 1909.

vitality, with its memory trances, was in loose association with the physical body) she 'reviewed' the whole experience. Another patient felt "every detail of the operation" *during the night* that followed it. The same experience occurred to the present writer, who during the night following a dental operation 'dreamed' that his teeth were being extracted, one by one. This 'review' occurred on two or three successive nights. Similar experiences are described in *Journ. S.P.R.*, vi., p. 209. Mrs. Gladys Osborn Leonard (*My Life in Two Worlds*, Cassell & Co. Ltd., 1931, p. 48) 'reviewed' a dental operation *just as she was falling asleep* ("the very second I lost consciousness"). The experience was repeated every night for two or three weeks and she feared going to sleep. It also occurred every time that she tried to leave the body *in trance*.

The statement made in these accounts of drowning, etc., to the effect that fear and pain ceased and that the 'review' of the past earth-life occurred *immediately the body was shed and when death was accepted as inevitable*, is particularly significant in view of communications from supposed discarnates to the effect that in both natural and enforced transition the body is vacated *before* actual death (and this presumably applies to all who 'pass' in their 'sleep', in a state of 'coma' or 'unconsciousness', etc., i.e. out of contact with the physical world because already out of the body): Mrs. Rhys Davids' discarnate communicators, for example (pp. 14, 23) made this statement. The accounts of the first 'review' include those of famous mountaineers and authors (e.g. Bedford, p. 87, Cozzens, p. 89, and Whymper, p. 91), a Roman Catholic priest (Gerrard, p. 89), a Church of England clergyman (Stainton Moses, p. 89) and a technician (cited by Dr. Fodor, p. 91), while an Admiral (Beaufort, p. 166) made the same statement when he described having experienced the second 'review'). We make the following points: First, it will be clear that no collusion was possible between these men. Secondly, their *bona fides* and reliability is beyond question. Thirdly, this statement occurs in no book on psychology, philosophy, theology, etc., that has come to my notice, and it cannot have been 'borrowed'. It occurs in several independent, reliable accounts of men who claimed to experience 'death': some of them, who managed to 'return' and complete their earth-lives, did not make it through mediums: others failed to 'return' but were able to report their experiences through mediums. This matter cannot be attributed to the mediums involved in the latter cases: it clearly concerns experiences of the still-living 'dead'.

(b) The cause of the first review

What might cause the first review? The Theosophists do not indicate any possible mechanism. Powell, having described the review, said, "How or why this occurs, and what is the mechanism by which it is brought about, has never, to the knowledge of the present writer, been explained."[1]

A number of independent communicators, however, say that the vehicle of vitality (the 'etheric double' of Theosophy) bears a detailed record of a man's earth experiences and that, immediately after the Physical Body is shed, this 'outermost' component of the total double loosens (preparatory to being shed in turn and the process causes a panoramic review of the past earth-life.

(1) 'Philip' said: "There is a sort of photographic mesh round every human being and all his life is printed on it: it is part of his aura."[2] In later communications he observed: "A newly-arrived person, still surrounded by his earth-aura [=vehicle of vitality] carries his "dossier" imprinted round him, to anyone skilled to read the thought-webs."[3]

(2) The American lawyer, Randall, on the basis of a number of communications, said: "Thoughts are things, and every act and thought functions around and about us in the aura. . . . Every act and thought is photographed in this psychic ether and, in dissolution, becomes visible."[4]

(3) Roy Dixon-Smith's communicator also connected the first review with the loosening of the 'etheric double' (vehicle of vitality). He added: "All the while, the etheric-double matter is gradually disintegrating from the astral [here =Soul Body], thereby clearing its clogged senses and bringing more and more into view the astral plane [here ='Paradise' conditions] to which it is naturally attuned."[5]

(4) Another communication reads as follows: "The thoughts

---

[1] Lieut.-Colonel A. E. Powell, *The After-death Life*, Besant & Co. Ltd., 1929.
[2] Alice Gilbert, *op. cit.*, 1948, p. 102.
[3] *Ibid.*, *Philip in the Spheres*, Aquarian Press Ltd., 1952, p. 35.
[4] Edward C. Randall, *Frontiers of the After-life*, Alfred A. Knopf, 1922.
[5] Roy Dixon-Smith, *op. cit.*, 1952.

and secrets of the heart create man's immediate environment; his imaginings are photographed in the mind-stuff emanating from the Physical Body."[1]

(5) "The etheric body [here = the vehicle of vitality] . . . has to be shed before we can enter the astral planes [here = 'Paradise']. . . . It is essentially the vehicle of the clear-cut, detailed earth-memory, and as the real being [in the Soul Body] draws away from it, the memory-record is exposed."[2]

(6) Max Heindel similarly said that "When a man is freed from the Physical Body he is able to read pictures in his vital body [=vehicle of vitality] which is the seat of sub-conscious memory. The whole of his past life passes before his sight like a panorama. . . . But he has no feeling about them at this time; that is reserved until the time that he enters the Desire World [='Paradise'], which is the world of feeling and emotion [i.e. until the 'Judgment'—Statement No. 34]. At present he is only in the etheric region of the Physical World [='Hades']."[3]

(7) Dr. Rudolf Steiner (*Occult Science*), another Rosicrucian, also ascribed the first review to the loosening of the 'etheric body' [here = vehicle of vitality] which, he said, is "the bearer of memory". The second review, or 'Judgment', he ascribed to the dissolution of the 'astral' [=Soul] body. Whereas (*a*) the first review takes place 'in a flash', the second occupies a period equal to about a third of the earth-life reviewed; (*b*) whereas the first review merely consists of *pictures*, the second consists of resurrected *experiences*, (*c*) whereas the first review concerns only one's own experiences, the second includes the experiences, feelings, etc. that were caused in other people. Only when the 'astral' (here = Soul) Body is shed (at the 'third death') is the true spiritual world entered (in the 'Higher Mental' or Causal, Body); thereafter, direct communication with mortals is impossible.

(8) E. C. Merry (*Spiritual Knowledge*, Anthroposophical Publishing Co. Ltd., 1936, p. 79) similarly said that "At death, the Ego, the astral body or soul [=Soul Body] and the etheric body [here = vehicle of vitality] leave the physical body. During the first three days the astral body, indwelt by

[1] Anon., *Spiritual Reconstruction*, Watkins, 1918.
[2] Jane Sherwood, *The Country Beyond*, Rider & Co. Ltd., p. 63.
[3] Max Heindel, *The Rosicrucian Cosmo-conception*, 1911.

the Spirit, perceives the separation from itself of the etheric body which has been the shaper and the life-giver to the physical and the vehicle of memory. As it leaves, it expands. . . . In expanding it presents that panorama of the life that is ended."

(9) Max Freedom Long (*The Secret Science at Work*, Huna Research Publications, 1953, p. 17) cited, among the teachings of the kahunas, or priests, of Polynesia: (an area which was completely cut off from civilisation until its discovery by Captain Cook): "At death the low self [the animal self] in its aka body [=the vehicle of vitality] leaves the physical body and takes with it the memories."

(10) Dion Fortune (*Sane Occultism*, Inner Light Publishing Society, 1938, p. 61) said: "The record of every action performed, or feeling felt, or thought conceived is preserved as an image in the reflecting ether, which is really the memory of the planetary spirit. . . ."

(11) Violet Burton (*My Larger Life*, Rider & Co. Ltd., p. xi) was told that " 'Masters' see . . . the map of life, forces used by the experience in the early life. The map of life-force is a record impressed on the ether-aura which immediately surrounds the physical body. . . . Man, by his activities and thoughts, makes his own records. . . ."

(12) "On these folds, or layers, of which it [the brain] is constituted, every act that has taken place, from the cradle to the grave, has been indelibly printed. . . . *Everything is inscribed on the spiritual counterpart of these layers.* . . . With a proper medium, we can read this many-leaved book. . . . It is just a big panoramic picture. "Will it be opened to us when we pass away?" "It will!"[1]

(13) "The floodgates of memory are swung open and the ego lives over . . . the entire panorama of existence back to the moment of birth. This, because the etheric body [here =vehicle of vitality] is . . . the reservoir of memory and, at the hour of death, the etheric body increasingly loosens its grip upon the physical body so that *the subtler vibrations can enter the brain* and precipitate there the . . . pictures of the past."[2]

(14) Greber, a German Roman Catholic priest who had read nothing about psychic matters, was told, through a farm-boy

[1] David Duguid, *Hafed, Prince of Persia*, May Nesbitt & Co. Ltd., 1893.
[2] Anon., *The Science of Initiates*, Lucis Pub. Co., 1934, p. 164.

I

medium: "The odic band [=vehicle of vitality] . . . reflects your entire existence; every act, every utterance, every thought of yours is reproduced by it as a film. It retains and reproduces everything."[1]

(15) Léon Dennis's French communicator said, "Every thought has a form, and this shape . . . is photographed in us. . . . Our fluidic envelope [=vehicle of vitality] reflects and preserves, like a register, all the facts of our existence. . . . At death it slowly opens."[2]

(16) The communicator of S. Bedford said that the past earth-life was reviewed *just prior to the moment of passing*", when the person concerned was "in a state of consciousness poised *between* two worlds", i.e., *between* earth and 'Paradise'. He described it as "a vivid picture of life . . . down to the final act", and made an important point: "The fact that we retain our memories after we have discarded the physical body proves that memory is not entirely a function of the brain. Throughout the whole of our lives every incident is recorded in our soul's memory."[3]

(17) *Light*, vol. XLII, 1922, pp. 595, 596, mentioned a communicator who stated: "During earth-life every deed we commit, every thought we think, is registered by the ether surrounding us [=the vehicle of vitality]. It is as a photograph. A lusty babe, as it kicks and crows, on its mother's knee, causes by its own vitality a certain ebb and flow in the surrounding atmosphere. It is a kind of magnet, to which the waves of ether respond. The baby's spirit-body is made up of ether . . . its vitality, acting as a magnetic rod, creates a thought-form of itself automatically. . . . As the baby grows, the creative photograph grows and changes with him, takes colour and shape from his actions. Everyone, as he goes through life, carries with him his life's record. . . ."

(18) A statement similar to those of the above-mentioned discarnate communicators was made by one of the greatest of modern seers, Thomas Lake Harris. His views in general were summarised in a book entitled *Three Famous Occultists*, (Rider & Co. Ltd.) and this particular matter was given on p. 165. Harris recognised that portion of the total physical

[1] Johannes Greber, *Communications with the Spirit World*, New York, 1932, p. 84.
[2] *Here and Hereafter*, Rider & Co. Ltd., 1910, p. 218.
[3] *Death—An Interesting Journey*, The Alcuin Press, pp. 32, 147.

body which we designate the vehicle of vitality: he called it 'the geist', 'the double', 'the shadow form', 'the astral image', described it as "a kind of *impersonal* animated photograph of the man". Since it holds "every thought, every act", indeed "the whole story" of a man's life, he also gave it the appropriate title of 'the memory form'. (Like many others, Harris claimed that "the picturings of events that are inscrolled into its layers" can be vivified by mediums, with the production of what may be called pseudo-communications—see (*c*) below.

(19) The above are from more or less 'popular' books. But 'Myers', communicating through Geraldine Cummins, said, that memory is not only imprinted on the brain-cells, but is also "graven on a very fine essence which accompanies the human being and . . . hangs about him like a cloud" [=the vehicle of vitality].[1]

(20) The American clairvoyant, Helen Rhodes, clearly refers to what we call the vehicle of vitality as a memory-record in teachings which she claimed to have received when out of the body: she likened the 'vehicle of vitality' to a sensitive plate upon which the physical life experience is recorded."[2]

(c) Psychical science supports a first review

The statement, by communicators, seers and others, that the first review is caused by the loosening of the (memory-trace-bearing) vehicle of vitality is supported by evidence which suggests that the separated vehicle of vitality (a partial corpse that is often called an 'astral shell') may, as Harris said, be re-vivified by mediums and thus produce pseudo-communications. (This is probably related to the 'psychic factor' theory of Professor C. D. Broad and the 'mindlet' theory of C. E. M. Joad. Other pseudo-communications are probably 'readings' of the living recipient's memory-records. Still others may, of course, be due to telepathy from the living.)

Again, once the vehicle of vitality has been shed, unimportant details of the past earth-life may be irrecoverable and this may be one of the reasons why communicators sometimes find it

[1] Geraldine Cummins, *The Road to Immortality*, Ivor Nicholson and Watson, 1932, p. 84.
[2] Helen Rhodes, *Psychoma*, Elizabeth Towne, Holyoke, Mass., U.S.A., 1913, p. 18.

difficult to give (what seem to mortals) obvious tests of identity. It would then be the significance, especially the emotional significance, of the events of the past life that was carried forward. (Questions to communicators from beyond 'Hades' conditions, i.e. from 'Paradise' conditions, should be framed with this in mind).

(d) Internal consistency or coherence of communications

A number of other statements of supposed discarnates (Statements Nos. 2, 7, 8, 13, 18, 27, 32 and 34) *transmitted through mediums* also occur in narratives, *not transmitted through mediums*, of what was experienced by those who were able to return from near-death to physical life. Moreover, they are also found in narratives (also *not transmitted through mediums*) of astral projectors.[1]

Statement No. 6.—A dying man has often vacated the Physical Body an hour or more before 'visible death'.

(a) Internal consistency or coherence of communications

With average men the 'silver cord' (which unites the Physical Body to the double during any time that they are separated) is said to be severed at, or very soon after, 'visible death' (i.e. the cessation of heart-beat, breathing, etc.). But, we are told, the cord is occasionally unusually 'strong', 'thick' or 'resistant' (corresponding to an unusually dense Soul Body), in which case it may persist for some hours and even, in extreme instances, up to three or four days. Since the 'cord' carries sensory stimuli from the Physical Body (via the Soul Body) to consciousness, an unsevered 'cord' would (as stated) afford the newly-dead person some awareness of his Physical Body and its surroundings. Again, since the Soul Body is practically released from the Physical, he would also have some awareness of the 'dead' and of their environment: i.e. during any period of transition in which the 'silver cord' is not 'loosed', there would, as communicators declare, be 'dual' (or 'alternate') consciousness (Nos. 17, 19 and 22).

Statement No. 6 is also concordant with (a) No. 7 (that natural death involves no pain—the double, which includes the Soul Body—the primary organ of consciousness—has left

[1] See *The Theory and Practice of Astral Projection* by the writer.

the body) and (*b*) No. 8 (that while natural exteriorisation is easy, painless and even pleasant, resuscitation is difficult and may involve fear and pain). It further agrees with the claims that the newly-dead man is aware of the thoughts and feelings of physically-embodied friends—once outside the body, he has telepathic, as well as clairvoyant, abilities. The latter statement, in turn, agrees with Statements Nos. 27 and 29 (regarding the newly-dead being depressed by the grief, and encouraged by the prayers, of mortals).

(b) *Inherent probability, support from psychical science, etc.*

The vacation of the body prior to death is clearly the cause of the frequent pre-death coma.

As already said, *pre*-death doubles are fairly often seen by mortals in cases of natural transition but are unrecorded in narratives descriptive of sudden, enforced death.

There is considerable evidence to support the statement that 'dual' (or 'alternate') consciousness may occur in the first few minutes, hours or days following transition. For example, many cases are on record in which newly-deceased women communicate complaining of the removal of rings from their hands soon after their 'passing'.

Statement No. 7.—The claim that natural death involves no physical pain or fear cannot be attributed to imagination or to suggestions: most people imagine the contrary.

(a) *Cause of absence of pain or fear*

The communicators of Mrs. Rhys Davids, Jane Sherwood, 'A.B.' and S. Bedford independently indicated the reason why transition involves no physical pain: it constitutes Statement No. 6.

An Englishwoman, 'Helen', also said: "All nervousness goes when one comes to the point [of dying]. All fear goes then *because the soul has disengaged itself sufficiently to realise the happiness and safety into which it is entering.*"[1] Father Greber's German communicator said: "At the time of death the soul [-body] is partially released from the body."[2]

---

[1] The Rev. C. Drayton Thomas, *From Life to Life*, Rider & Co. Ltd., p. 65.
[2] *Communion with the Spirit World*, John Felsberg, N.Y., 1932.

A sergeant who was drowned said he had "no feeling of distress *once he had given up the struggle.*"[1]

'Myers', communicating, similarly said that average men have no pain in dying because "*they have become so dissevered already from the body* that when the flesh seems to be in agony the soul actually merely feels drowsy".[2]

(b) Inherent probability, support from psychical science, etc.

There is evidence of the truth of this statement from people who were brought to the very verge of death and yet escaped. Some examples are given under Statement No. 5 above. Another concerns David Livingstone,[3] who was attacked by a lion. He said: "He *shook* me as a terrier does a rat. It caused a sort of dreaminess in which there was no sense of pain or feeling of terror, though I was conscious of all that happened." (In later life, asked what he was thinking of during those moments, he replied, "I was wondering what part of me he would eat first!" The wounds he received caused suffering for three months afterwards and thereafter it was always painful to him to raise the left arm to any position above the elbow). We suggest that the violent shaking caused an exteriorisation of the Soul Body and therefore a loss of physical sensation. (The violent dervish dances, ending in trance, produce a similar effect.) In natural death the 'silver cord' has usually become too thin to transmit sensations from the Physical Body to the Soul Body, though there are people with exceptionally 'thick' cords.

Many independent communicators say that convulsive movements of the Physical Body during the process of transition are not felt by the person concerned—that they are reflex movements. In this respect they would, as said, resemble the convulsive movements of entering trance—which are also presumably connected with vacating the Physical Body.

R. H. Ward said, "A car in which I was a passenger seemed to be on the point of . . . a head-on collision. . . . I felt myself to be actually shocked out of my body. I had the strange impression that one aspect of myself was several yards distant from the cars, and watching, quite calmly and objectively, all

---

[1] W. T. Pole, *Private Dowding*, Watkins, p. 87.
[2] Geraldine Cummins, *The Road to Immortality*, Ivor Nicholson and Watson, 1932, p. 81.
[3] J. I. Macnair, *Livingstone the Liberator*, Collins, p. 83.

that was happening to the bodily aspect of myself, which was still sitting in one of the cars. . . . It mattered not at all to my separate and usually conscious self that my body was likely . . . to be smashed to pieces; death was quite unimportant, and evidently something which might happen to a quite unimportant part of my total nature."[1]

A doctor[1] who realised that the 'plane in which he travelled was about to crash (and which did crash, nearly killing him) said: "The moment it became obvious that a crash was inevitable , . . . one lost all apprehension." On the contrary, he was in a state of "pleasant awareness", looked down at his body on the ground some 200 feet below. He was reluctant to return, wondering why the rescuers were "bothering" to pay attention to his body: he "wished they would leave it alone" (Statement No. 8).[2]

A. C. Benson, the author, observed the absence of both pain and fear when near death. When climbing the Alps he fell into a crevasse. He said, "My first feeling was amusement. . . . I hung over an immense depth. . . . They tried to haul me up, but could not. I was certain of death. I hung like this for twenty minutes and all that time I had no single thought of fear. I was being slowly strangled by the rope. At last the guide risked his life by coming to the edge of the crevasse. He cut the ice away and they drew me up. *And for a few minutes I was not wholly pleased.* . . ." (Statement No. 8.)

At a meeting of the British Medical Association on July 19, 1957, Dr. Grant, a family doctor for over thirty years, dealt with the subject of transition. He said: "Few patients are aware that they are dying: those who are aware accept the end peacefully."

Statement No. 8.—This also cannot be due to the imagination of mediums, to suggestion or to reasonable expectation—no one thinks that, on the one hand, it is easy and painless to die, and, on the other hand, that 'return' may involve pain and fear and that it is normally undertaken only with reluctance.

(a) *Inherent probability or support from psychic science*

These communications, which came to us through mediums, are matched by the experiences of many people who did not

[1] R. H. Ward, *A Drug-taker's Notes*, Victor Gollancz Ltd., 1957, p. 15.
[2] *Journ.* S.P.R., 39, No. 692, 1957, p. 92.

consult mediums, but who were brought to the point of death by drowning, etc. (See Statement No. 5.)

Statement No. 9.—This concerns what is said, by communicators, to be experienced when the Physical Body was shed (a sensation of rising or of falling, a momentary coma or 'blackout', a feeling of passing through a 'doorway' or 'tunnel') and the effects of that process (an expansion of consciousness, glimpses of discarnate friends, and occasionally the sight of the 'silver cord').

(a) Causes of the experiences

While a few communicators say that shedding (or vacating) the body involves a feeling of falling (sinking, fainting, etc.), many describe the reverse experience, namely, a sensation of rising. The difference doubtless depends on the direction of the attention at the critical time: as the double separated from the Physical Body, those whose attention was body-wards would have a sensation of falling, while those whose attention was double-wards would have one of rising.

A momentary coma or 'blackout' would, presumably, be due to a brief non-alignment of the separating bodies (the Physical Body and the Soul Body) precluding the use of either and therefore of awareness of *either* the physical world *or* the 'next' world. There would be a momentary blank. The sensation of passing through a tunnel would have the same origin but would indicate that, in these cases, the process took slightly longer.

(b) Internal consistency of coherence of communications
(i) A sensation of rising or falling

It is reasonable to suppose that those whose consciousness was earth- or body-wards at the time of 'passing' would feel *a sensation of falling*. This would particularly apply to men who died in the prime or who were of an exceptionally sensual type. Those whose consciousness was mainly in the Soul Body would have a *sensation of rising*. Our explanation receives some support from the fact that (where the shedding of the body was experienced as either of those sensations) communicators who claimed to have died in old age frequently described a sensation of rising, while those whose transition was enforced in the prime of life (as well as particularly sensual men) very often mentioned one of falling.

This view is also supported by the fact that those who experienced *temporary* excursions from the body in a natural, unforced, manner (which—apart from certain special circumstances—indicates a relatively high degree of 'evolution', and, therefore, a 'loose' Soul Body) almost always described *rising* out of the body.

On the other hand, as might be expected, 'physical' mediums (who are characterized by a 'loose' vehicle of vitality) describe the reverse, i.e. the sensation of *falling*. Mrs. J. B. Mellon (Annie Fairlamb), the 'materialising' medium, described "a feeling as if I were *sinking* down into the earth" when going into trance (i.e. shedding the Physical Body). The 'death' of a 'materialised' form is similarly felt as a *falling-away* by the medium who provided the ectoplasm (and who remained throughout connected with the materialised form by a 'silver cord', or 'cords', so that she had 'dual' consciousness.) Thus, after 'Yoland', a 'materialisation' of Mme. d'Esperance (seized by a 'sitter') began to disintegrate, the medium said, "I felt I was *sinking down*." The same sensation is reported[1] in connection with another 'physical' phenomenon, that of transportation.

The (Italian) Marquise Centurione Scotto described having some 'dual' consciousness, i.e. awareness, of both the Soul Body and the Physical Body (see No. 17): he said, "I could not feel my legs any more, having the impression of going into trance. . . . I felt myself light, light, but *such lightness*! [=consciousness in the Soul Body]. . . . I felt myself as if *fainting* [=consciousness in Physical Body]."

The description of a falling sensation by certain of the 'dead' is also concordant with what occurs at 'Rescue Circles' where 'earthbound' men (who have shed the Physical Body without being aware of the fact, and whose Soul Body is still enveiled by the vehicle of vitality) are made to realise their condition—that they have 'died'. Such men are said to be so near to earth 'conditions' that they are either unable to see discarnate 'deliverers' who wish to assist them, or seeing them, regard them as 'ghosts' (compare 'Myers' communication cited under Statement No. 10; also Statement No. 30). The 'earthbound' men are allowed to enter the Physical Body of a medium (which is vacated in trance), when a third person, a mortal,

[1] Dr. Nandor Fodor, *op. cit.*, 1933, p. 394.

speaks to them and explains their condition, its cause and its cure. Conversations of this nature may enable 'earthbound' persons—'spirits in prison'—to shed the vehicle of vitality and thus leave 'Hades' for 'Paradise' conditions. The point of interest in the present connection (lending support to our statement that men who die in full bodily consciousness, and especially men of sensual type, tend to experience a sensation of falling when shedding the Physical Body), is that an 'earth-bound' man also typically described *a falling sensation* when, eventually, he vacated the Body of the medium. In these circumstances the experience of 'falling' was produced not by the shedding of his own body, but that of the medium! It was 'death' by proxy! This is highly significant.

(*ii*) *A momentary coma, passing through a 'doorway', 'tunnel', etc.*

A common symbol used in describing the act of shedding (or vacating) the Physical Body is that of passing through a 'tunnel' (or a 'door', 'passage', 'tube', 'shaft', 'hole', 'funnel', etc.): this is clearly related to the 'momentary coma', though lasting somewhat longer and, perhaps, with some dim consciousness, of existence if not of environment. There are many considerations which strongly suggest that in this symbol a genuine experience of a surviving soul is indicated. *The following are statements by people who left the body other than by death and who used identical symbols: they were not transmitted through mediums.*

(1) The tunnel symbol is very common with those who left the body naturally but temporarily, i.e. 'astral projectors'. Mrs. Leslie[1] said: "I seemed to float in a *long tunnel*. It appeared very narrow at first but gradually expanded into unlimited space." The experience of Miss I. V. Yeomans, who declared that she knew nothing of psychic matters, was described by William Oliver Stevens:[2] "Suddenly there appeared an opening, *like a tunnel*, and, at the far end, a light. I moved nearer to it and was drawn up the passage. . . ." Frank Lind[3] who has had the advantage, as Editor of *Prediction*, of seeing many accounts of astral projections, said: "A constant preliminary to the loss of consciousness is the symbolic passing through a *pitch-black tunnel*."

[1] Mrs. Leslie, *Prediction*, December, 1952.
[2] W. O. Stevens, *The Mystery of Dreams*, George Allen and Unwin, Ltd., 1950.
[3] Frank Lind, *My Occult Case-book*, Rider & Co. Ltd., 1953.

Oliver Fox[1] described leaving his body thus: "I was falling . . . down a dark, *narrow tunnel or shaft*. . . ." Later he said: "Sometimes the speed is so tremendous that one gets the effect of tumbling through *a hole* into a new sphere." Miss L. M. Bazett[2] also said that leaving the body was "like going through a *tunnel*". Hermione P. Okeden was cited by the Hon. Ralph Shirley[3] as saying that she declared that she could leave the body: "I find myself going down *a long dim tunnel*. . . . At the far end is a tiny speck of light which grows, as I approach, into a large square, and I am there!"

Mrs. E. Bounds,[4] who almost died, said: "I was rushing along through *a pitch-black tunnel*. . . ." Muldoon and Carrington[5] cited the case of Mrs. D. Parker, who found herself leaving the body. She said: "Soon I encountered *a tunnel or passageway* through dark clouds, at the end of which I could see light." Mrs. C. A. Dawson Scott[6] relaxed and closed her eyes. She said: "I saw in front of me *a dark tunnel*. Curiosity took me through it. I stepped out of the tunnel into an unknown country. . . ." Among the things she saw was Mr. Craven, who had 'passed on', with his wife, who had not, but who was exteriorised. The latter (or, rather, her Soul Body) was connected with her Physical Body by "a twisted rope of white material" (i.e. the 'silver cord'—Statement No. 19). Dr. J. H. M. Whiteman (*Proc. S.P.R.*, vol. 50, 1956, p. 254) said: "In one of my own experiences I seemed to pass through *a tunnel* in a dream-like state and emerged through the opening at the end into a scene of bright sunlight [='Paradise' conditions]."

Miss Zoila C. M. Stables, B.A., an Australian, told the present writer (*in litt.*): "I had not heard, nor read, nor had the slightest inkling of projection, or any other psychic subject" before having a projection. She described as "a very frequent sensation", "that of going down *a long tunnel . . . a creek with high banks, or a long pergola*". She insisted: "It is too frequent a happening not to have some correspondence with reality." Mrs. Tarsikes also told the writer that she had had

1 Oliver Fox, *Astral Projection*, Rider & Co. Ltd., p. 106.

2 Miss L. M. Bazett, *Beyond the Five Senses*, Basil Blackwell, 1946.

3 Ralph Shirley, *The Mystery of the Human Double*, Rider & Co. Ltd.

4 Mrs. E. Bounds, *Psychic News*, October 2, 1954.

5 Sylvan J. Muldoon and Dr. Hereward Carrington, *The Phenomena of Astral Projection*, Rider & Co. Ltd., 1951.

6 Mrs. C. A. Dawson Scott, *From Four Who are Dead*, Arrowsmith, 1926, p. 13.

'projections' before she had heard of such things and described leaving the body as "like passing through a thick, dark wall of cloud, with an opening about one-inch in diameter". Dr. B. Kirkwood,[1] who had been given up as dead: said, "I was hurried off at great speed. Have you ever looked through a very long tunnel and seen the tiny speck of light at the far end? . . . Well, I found myself . . . hurrying along just such *a tunnel or passage.*"

(2) The tunnel symbol for shedding the body is also used by people who are aware of that process (which most of us are not) when they "fall" asleep. Muldoon and Carrington[2] quoted the following from Dr. Walsh: "Many people, on going to sleep, experience the feeling of *sliding down a hole, or an incline.* . . ."

(3) As might be expected, the symbol is also commonly used by people whose exteriorisation from the body was enforced by anaesthetics. In *Light,* vol. LV, 1935, p. 249, Nurse Mary Osborn described what 'most' patients told her: it included the phrase, "I was in *a long tunnel* with a light at the end. . . . I knew that if I could only get to the light at the end I should understand everything." (Compare the saying attributed to both Cleanthes and Democritos the Derider, "Truth is found at the bottom of *a well*".) Ralph Shirley[3] said: "The symbolical passing through a *tunnel* will be familiar to many, as indeed it is to myself, as a preliminary to the loss of consciousness under anaesthetics." He added: "The subconscious self tends to think in terms of symbology. . . ."

Mrs. E. Hatfield, given an anaesthetic, told the present writer: "I seemed to float down *a dark tunnel,* moving towards a half-moon of light that was miles away. . . ." Mrs. G. E. Mullick told the writer the following: "On being given ether I was moving, at a terrific rate, through what seemed to be *a tunnel.*" *Prediction,* March, 1955, carried an account from 'W.E.H.', who was given gas: "I found myself in *an avenue of trees,* slowly moving farther and farther from my body." He added: "I continued to advance along the avenue towards a brilliant light at the end of it". *Borderland,* vol. i, 1893-4, p. 564,

---

[1] Dr. B. Kirkwood, *Light,* LV, 1935, p. 226.
[2] Sylvan J. Muldoon and Dr. Hereward Carrington, *The Projection of the Astral Body,* Rider & Co. Ltd., 1929, p. 38.
[3] Ralph Shirley, *op. cit.,* p. 33.

noted the case of Mrs. Asa L'Orme, who, given an anaesthetic, said: "I found myself proceeding along *a straight black
tube* with hardly any room to move."

(4) The tunnel symbol is used by people who vacated the
body as they fell from great heights, as by Douglas Bader
(*Follow the Stars*).

(5) It is used by mediums to indicate leaving the body. For
example, one evening, after Dr. Hodgson died, Mrs. Piper
'dreamed' that she tried to enter *a dark tunnel* in which was a
bearded man, but the latter stopped her by raising his hand.
The hand was like Hodgson's. Mrs. Piper told her daughters
of this experience at 7.30 a.m.: news of Hodgson's sudden
death came at 8.30.[1]

(6) The tunnel also occurs in psycho-analytical literature
as a symbol for shedding the Physical Body. Dr. Nandor
Fodor[2] had a patient who dreamed that, sentenced to death,
he "was to die by being hurled down *a dark ramp-like incline*
backwards while sitting in a chair".

(7) Still more significant, the tunnel symbol is used not only
to describe the shedding of the Physical Body, but also (at a
later period of some 'projections') the shedding of the vehicle
of vitality from the Soul Body (corresponding to 'the second
death'). This is the phenomenon described above as occurring
at 'Rescue Circles'. 'Myers', quoted by Sir Oliver Lodge,[3]
used the symbol in describing this stage of his own 'passing':
"Before I knew I was dead, I thought I had lost my way in a
strange town [he was in the dream, or 'Hades', condition]
and groped my way along the *passage*." ('Myers' had a brief
awareness of 'Hades' conditions—he was possibly somewhat
mediumistic.) A communicator of Major Tudor Pole, O.B.E.,
described the shedding of the vehicle of vitality as
causing "a sleep." Miss Dorothy Peters[4] who had had out-of-
the-body experiences before she had heard of such things,
described the total double (the Soul Body *plus* part of the
vehicle of vitality) leaving the Physical Body, after which she
"stood at the entrance to *a dark tunnel*" (i.e. began to shed the
vehicle of vitality—to pass through 'the second death').

[1] Alta Piper, *The Life and Work of Mrs. Piper*, Kegan Paul, p. 118.
[2] Dr. Nandor Fodor, *Samiska*, vol. 9, pt. 1, 1955, p. 3.
[3] Sir Oliver Lodge, *The Survival of Man*, Methuen, 1909.
[4] Miss Dorothy Peters, *Two Worlds*, August, 1952.

Edmund Bentley[1] said: "Between the point of entry through the third eye and the point of departure from the Physical Body there is *a long tunnel*. This is a kind of no-man's land through which the traveller must venture. . . . Most of the experiences undergone through the tunnel are familiar to every occult student. . . . They are an accumulation of the sub-conscious storehouse of memory. . . ." (It should be remembered that communicators say that the vehicle of vitality bears memory-traces of all that happens to a man throughout his earth-life, and Mr. Bentley's statement therefore agrees with this conception—as well as that of 'Myers' who was in 'Shadow-land', or 'Hades', until the vehicle of vitality had been shed.)

Olive C. B. Pixley[2] also used the tunnel-symbol for shedding the vehicle of vitality: "If the natural flight of our Spirit in sleep wings its way to the Realms of Reality, the World of Light [= 'Paradise' conditions], we can pass through the corridor of hallucination [= 'Hades' conditions] so swiftly that no impression of unreality is retained by the waking brain. We all know that glimpses of unreal conditions . . . that wandering down *eternal corridors*. . . ."

Mrs. Alice Gilbert[3] was told by her discarnate son that, when entering sleep, she shed her vehicle of vitality (from the total double) so quickly that she had no experience of 'Hades' conditions: that she was not 'mediumistic'. 'Philip' told his mother that on one occasion she had been 'half asleep', adding, "half out of your body". He said: "It's like a rabbit, half in and half out of its hole—one part of you contacting the Light of the outer world, the other the earthly dark of *your burrow*."

(8) The tunnel symbol is also used in describing the shedding of the Soul Body, i.e. in passing through the 'third death' (or, rather, unveiling). A writer quoted in Warner Allen[4] described the preliminary stage of a mystical experience thus: "I closed my eyes and watched a silver glow which shaped itself into a circle with a central focus brighter than the rest. The circle became *a tunnel of light* proceeding from some distant sun in the heart of the Self. Swiftly and smoothly I

---

[1] Edmund Bentley, *Psychic News*, March, 1957.
[2] Olive C. B. Pixley, *The Trail*, The C. W. Daniel Co. Ltd., 1934, p. 48.
[3] Mrs. Alice Gilbert, *Philip in Two Worlds*, Andrew Dakers Ltd., 1948, p. 147.
[4] Warner Allen, *The Timeless Moment*, Faber and Faber, 1946 pp. 31-3.

was borne through the tunnel. . . ." (The present writer suggests that the Soul Body is concerned in psychical experiences and the Spiritual Body in mystical, or cosmic, experiences.)

(9) The experiences exemplified in Nos. 1-8, and symbolised as passing through a tunnel, are all concerned with *vacating* a denser, and therefore less responsive, body and operating in a subtler, and therefore more responsive, one. As might be expected if there is truth behind these statements, the symbol is also used for describing the experience of *re-entering* the Physical Body—this also is felt as a brief coma, 'blackout', or passage through a 'tunnel' (depending on the duration of the experience).

Mr. Percy Cole, author of a number of papers on psychology, etc. informed the present writer that, on coming round after having been given ether, "I turned away from the bright light . . . and entered *a gloomy tunnel*. I fought my way back to a tiny light in the distance. . . . When I got back to the light, I found myself back in bed." (N.B.—The 'light' mentioned in our examples Nos. 1-5 above became greater: that to which Mr. Coles 'returned' was 'tiny'—compare 'the *kenosis*'.) The return of Aridaeus of Soli (Asia Minor) to his body (from which he had been forcibly ejected by a severe fall) was described thus: "Then, as though he were suddenly sucked through *a tube* . . . he lit in his body." This case was written about A.D. 79! It was given in Plutarch's *On the Delay of Divine Justice*.

Dorothy Grenside (*The Meaning of Dreams*, G. Bell & Sons Ltd., 1923, p. 77) summarised a number of out-of-the-body experiences: she said that when people who are out of the body re-enter it, "there is always a moment of unconsciousness". This is shorter than the 'tunnel' experience and corresponds to the 'blackout' or 'momentary coma' described by the dead. (Miss Grenside said that this 'gap' in consciousness was one of the reasons that we seldom remember our out-of-the-body experiences.)

(10) Just as 'earthbound' souls (in 'Hades'conditions) felt themselves *leave the medium's body* at the close of a Rescue Circle (experiencing it as 'falling'), so a communicator from 'Paradise' conditions felt themselves *enter a medium's body*— and employed the tunnel analogy to describe the experience. The discarnate 'George Pelham', communicating through

Mrs. Piper, pleaded with the experimenter, Dr. Richard Hodgson: "Do not look at me too critically: to try to transmit through the organism of a medium is like trying to crawl through *a hollow log*."

Similarly the discarnate 'Philip'[1] described entering a medium's physical body (vacated in trance) as getting into "*a sort of funnel*". Florence Marryat[2] was told by a communicator that she, Florence, seemed a long way off, even when they were really quite near each other. She said, "You seem to me as if you were at the *bottom of a well*."

The following use of the symbol is particularly significant. The 'Control' (or 'door-keeper') told W. S. Montgomery-Smith and E. M. Taylor[3] about a would-be communicator who failed to 'get through' to earth: "He was able to see the light in the darkness of *a long funnel*. But he doubted so much that it went out. He was frightened for fear he would never find his way back."

It is significant that none of those who described death by explosion (see No. iii below) used the tunnel analogy.

All the considerations reviewed under these ten headings indicate that the tunnel analogy, used in communications from the 'dead', is descriptive of a real experience undergone by surviving personalities. These 'travellers' tales' were clearly true.

(iii) Death by explosion

The description of death by explosion given in a number of accounts is always the same. If, as is said, it does differ from other types of enforced death (by drowning, by falling, by a blow, etc.) in that the Soul Body (as well as the Physical Body) is shattered, the former would have to be reassembled before it could be available as an instrument of consciousness there would, presumably as communicators say, be a period of 'unconsciousness'. Hence, whereas in enforced death in general, the person concerned is 'awake' at once, death by explosion involves a 'sleep'—and a relatively long one. A communicator of Borgia's[4] said that such cases are treated in

---

[1] Alice Gilbert, *op. cit.*, 1948, p. 184.

[2] Florence Marryat, *The Spirit World*, F. V. White, 1894.

[3] W. S. Montgomery-Smith and E. M. Taylor, *Light in Our Darkness*, Psychic Press Ltd., 1936, p. 99.

[4] Anthony Borgia, *ABC of Life*, Feature Books Ltd., p. 40.

special 'rest-houses' in the period between the partial dis-integration of the Soul Body and its re-constitution. The interesting point is this: the period of unconsciousness in cases of *enforced death by explosion* clearly corresponds in its origin to the momentary coma which is caused by the shedding of the Physical Body in *natural death*. In the latter, for a brief time, both of the instruments of consciousness, the Physical Body and the Soul Body, are 'out of gear' and neither is available to perform its function. This brief coma, it should be noted is distinguished from the three-day after-death 'sleep' of the aged (Statement No. 22), being called a 'coma', 'uncon-sciousness', 'darkness' or 'blackout', but never 'sleep' or 'semi-consciousness'. Franchezzo[1] who, like many others, said that mankind possesses a series of several non-physical bodies that are shed successively, described the process, in his own experi-ence, as "more like paralysis of the brain than sleep". It may also be observed that whereas 'dreams' are often described as occurring in the natural after-death 'sleep', none is men-tioned in connection with the coma that follows death by explosion.

(iv) Glimpses of discarnate friends

If communications are essentially true, i.e. if the Physical Body, 'blinkers'-like, shuts out our awareness of the 'next' world and its inhabitants (Statement 1*b*), then the removal of the body will permit us to see the 'next' world and dis-carnate friends (see Statements Nos. 2-4).

(v) An expansion of consciousness

The statements, by communicators, that they saw discarnate friends, during, or soon after, transition (the former often known to us as 'death-bed visions') is only part of a more general statement, namely, that they experienced a great expansion of consciousness. The communicator of Mrs. C. A. Dawson Scott[2] said, "On earth we were as buds with our possi-bilities folded tight within us. . . . Now we are like flowers that have expanded from those buds—try to imagine that *expansion*."

[1] Franchezzo, *A Wanderer in the Spirit Land*, transl. by A. Farnese, The Progressive Thinker Publishing House, 1910, p. 76.
[2] Mrs. C. A. Dawson Scott, *From Four Who are Dead*, Arrowsmith, 1928.

K

What is the cause of the expansion of consciousness? Max Heindel (*op. cit.*, p. 73) said that it is due to the fact that the physical body (which, being in time and space, compels us to receive impressions in terms of time and space) has been shed; even the earliest stage, i.e. when the exteriorised double includes the "vital body", or vehicle of vitality, physical space ceases to exist for the person in course of transition. Hence Heindel said, the latter receives "many impressions from various sources, all seeming to be close at hand". The shedding of the vehicle of vitality from the total after-death double will necessarily cause a still greater expansion of awareness.

(c) *Inherent probability, support from psychical science, etc.*

The statement concerning an expansion of consciousness *which came through mediums*, is identical with the description, *which did not come through a medium*, of Leslie Grant Scott (cited as Example No. 3 of the 'review' under Statement No. 5): Scott's "consciousness seemed to have expanded beyond the limits of the physical brain". Similar statements are made by 'astral projectors'.

It is also instructive to note the similarity in the accounts of those who shed the body permanently (at 'death') and those who left it only temporarily. For example, the deceased 'Private Dowding', communicating to W. T. Pole, stated: "I am where I am, yet I am everywhere! I am a self that is far greater and vaster than what I thought myself to be." Mrs. Willett, leaving her body only temporarily (in trance) said: "I am going out of myself. . . . I want to be *enlarged*." Arthur J. Wills also described his out-of-the-body consciousness as "*enlarged*" (H. P. Prevost Battersby, *Man Outside Himself*, Rider & Co. Ltd., p. 58). Mr. G. Costa (*Di la della Vita*) declared that he experienced "*boundless liberation*", while another Italian, G. F. Anfiano, who had been released from the body on several occasions by anaesthetics considered that anaesthesia "cannot be far removed from the first stage of death", in which case, death is "*an expansion . . . a sensation of becoming infinite . . . a transformation of a unit into wholeness*" (*Luce e Ombra*, 1928). An American, Mrs. Cora L. V. Richmond, found that when she was in trance there was "a seeming *expansion of all the powers*" (H. D. Barrett, *The Life and Work of Mrs.*

Cora, L.V. Richmond, 1895). Dr. J. H. M. Whiteman, when out of the body, thought "*I have never been awake before!*" (*Proc. S.P.R.*, vol. 50, 1956, p. 250). The phrase is reminiscent of that used by Shelley about his newly-dead friend, Fitzgerald: "He hath awakened from the dream of life!"

Statement No. 10.—The statement which is made by numerous independent communicators in many countries to the effect that many people of average (and most people of sub-average) mental and moral development may not, at first, know that they have left the body permanently, seems incredible. After an event which we mortals think of as stupendous and cataclysmic, how, we ask, could the person affected be unaware that it has taken place? This idea could not have been obtained by mediums (or by fragments of their total personalities) from science, theology, philosophy or literature. On this account it has an important bearing on the view we are obliged to take as to the nature of 'communicators'. If fragments of personalities can tell us truths that are unknown to doctors of theology, of science, of philosophy and of literature, then we have something to learn indeed. Unless, we are told, they come to realise it through making certain observations themselves (see Statement No. 31), the news has to be 'broken' to these people by discarnate friends! Until the newly-dead person realises that he has made 'the great [*sic*] change' he is necessarily bewildered: he cannot 'progress' since his attention will remain directed towards mundane affairs. Orthodox teachings, so far from helping, sometimes hinder early realisation of that transition has occurred (see No. 1*a* above).

The statement is not made through little-known mediums only. It was, for example, made by 'Myers' through Mrs. Thompson, in his first communication after 'passing'. He said: "I groped my way, as if through passages, before I knew I was dead. . . . And even when I saw people that I knew were dead, *I thought they were only visions.*"[1] (Compare under Statements Nos. 9B and 30).

(a) Causes

The reasons which communicators give for many people failing, at first, to know that they have died—namely, that the process was so gentle, natural and painless, that substance

[1] Sir Oliver Lodge, *The Survival of Man*, Methuen, 1909, p. 288.

composing the 'next world' is so malleable to thought and imagination (see No. 1*a* above) and the immediate 'next world' is very earth-like (Statement No. 32)—are highly reasonable.

(b) Inherent probability, support from psychical science, etc.

The statement under consideration is supported by the statements (not transmitted through mediums) of people who left their bodies only temporarily ('astral projectors'): some of the latter do not *at first* realise the fact and only *later* 'awaken' to it, and they tell us that others, although also out of the body do 'awaken' to the fact—they remain 'unconscious', 'in a trance', 'in a dream', 'like sleepwalkers', etc. These considerations offer an explanation of cases such as that of Gordon Davis[1], who communicated through a medium and later, to the consternation of the recipient of the messages, proved to be still embodied and to have no knowledge of the communications. But it is pure assumption to suppose that only the 'dead' can communicate through mediums. Sir Lawrence J. Jones (Presidential Address to S.P.R., 1928) described how his daughter, out of the body during sleep, communicated through Kate Wingfield. W. T. Stead received communications from the 'living', as did Hester Dowden. Further, a man who is only temporarily out of the body may suppose his condition permanent.

Again, the status of the persons concerned in the statements under consideration corresponds. The 'dead' say that (apart from special considerations) those who fail, at first, to realise their 'passing' are people of average (and, even more, those of sub-average) spiritual development. The same is said, quite independently, by 'astral projectors' concerning those who leave the body temporarily: the spiritually-minded tend to 'awake' and realise that they have left the body (though subsequent memory may be fragmentary), while the sensualist and the gross materialist tend to remain unaware of anything. If, as life proceeds, these people turn their attention to the beautiful, the good and the true, and to the wants of others, they organise their 'higher' bodies and tend to develop consciousness while out of the body during sleep. This is a great help: discarnate aid, encouragement and advice can be received and, even if specific details fail to enter 'normal' consciousness, they receive "intimations of immortality" and

[1] Gordon Davis, *Proc. S.P.R.*, xxv, 560.

have an intuitive certainty, that "underneath are the ever-lasting arms". The unbelief and the insensitiveness of the materialistic in the flesh partly protects him from contacts with discarnate materialists; the faith and the sensitiveness of the spiritually-minded man is his reward; it permits more or less conscious association with spiritually-minded discarnates, and they both benefit. "To him that hath shall be given" (Matt. xiii. 12, 25, 29). The conditions under which this 'gift' is received are safe conditions. The Psalmist (Ps. cxxvi. 2) said: "He giveth his beloved *during* sleep."

All these, and other, considerations (which will be given in detail in the book to be published by the writer entitled *Experiences on the Threshold of the After-life*) show that there may not, as we mortals suppose, be a great difference *to the person concerned* between temporary and permanent exteriorisation from the body—between sleep, etc. and death—hence the asseveration that the newly-dead may not, for a time, know that they have died is reasonable.

Statement No. 11.—Death was not what was expected.

(a) Internal consistency or concordance of communications

This statement is clearly concordant with several others (often given independently of each other), i.e. Nos. 1*b*, 6, 7, 10 and 32.

(b) Inherent probability, support from physical science, etc.

We have noted several reasons for giving credence to the superficially unbelievable statement that many of the newly-dead fail, at first, to realise their transition. There are others. First, both the 'dead' and the 'astral projectors' who were in this condition ascribed their eventual enlightenment to the same sources, i.e. they began to observe discrepancies between the old (physical) and the new ('next-world') environments: they could pass through walls, etc.

Secondly, some who left the body temporarily at first wondered if they had died. (This applied, for example, to Muldoon.)

Thirdly, clairvoyants often find difficulty in determining whether the exteriorised Soul Body which they are observing is that of a 'living' or a 'dead' person: this, they say, is because there are only two differences and they may not be very obvious.

Although a man's Soul Body becomes brighter as a result of its release from association with its physical counterpart, this applies (though in a less degree) to temporary, as well as to permanent, releases, and relatively advanced men possess relatively luminous Soul Bodies. Again, the 'silver cord' though relatively thick (and therefore conspicuous) in average or sub-average men, may be so thin in spiritually advanced men as to escape observation. There are many accounts in communications, both from the dead and from clairvoyants on this matter. W. E. Butler, a clairvoyant (*Light*, vol. LXII, 1922, p. 475) observed: "The difference between the astral forms of the dead and the appearance of living people . . . is so slight that one may quite easily confuse them. . . . Practically the only differences to be noted are that they (the latter) are rather more easily seen [a statement, it should be noted, which agrees with a fact of psychic science, namely, that, according to the S.P.R. Census of 1889-90, no less than seven out of every ten doubles that were identified were of 'living' people], and that, in any case, a curious hair-like thread [the 'silver cord'—see Statement No. 19] seems to trail behind them."

St. Paul (II Cor. xii. 2) experienced the difficulty described by Mr. Butler. He said: "I knew a man in Christ [=a believer] . . . whether in the body, or whether out of the body, I cannot tell . . . such a one caught up to the Third Heaven [='Paradise']."

Fourthly, there is no distinction between an exteriorised 'living' man and a 'dead' one as regards communication with mortals: although Gordon Davis and Sir Lawrence Jones's daughter were 'alive', they nevertheless were able to communicate.

Fifthly, the analyses, by the present writer, of statements of (*a*) the 'dead' and (*b*) 'astral projectors' reveal the highly significant fact that *the differences in the experiences undergone are determined far more by the nature of the vacation of the body (whether it was natural or enforced) than by its duration (whether permanent or temporary).* Men who were forced out of the body—whether by bullet or by anaesthetic—described a certain set of experiences, while men who left the body naturally—whether permanently or temporarily—described another set of experiences.

Statement No. 12.—The remark that some discarnates, on awakening after transition, at first think that they might be dreaming is understandable. An example (by 'Myers') is cited under Statement No. 10.

Statements Nos. 13-16.—According to communicators, in the process of dying, the double (then consisting of the vehicle of vitality *plus* the Soul Body) leaves the Physical Body mainly by the head, and, at first, is an ill-defined, smoke-like mass. Gradually it takes the form of the Physical Body from which it emerged and was 'born'. If (as is usual) the person in course of transition is recumbent (in bed), the exteriorised double usually lies *horizontally* above the corpse, the distance between the two being remarkably small—varying in different accounts from a few inches to a few feet only. Then the double, representing the 'newly-born' non-physical body, stands erect, often looking down on the corpse.

(a) Inherent probability, support from physical science, etc.

These communications, which come to us from mediums differ essentially from the teachings of scientists, philosophers and theologians (as such), yet they have no inherent improbability.

In point of fact, many people who have been present at death-beds have described (quite independently of mediums) phenomena identical to those. Such accounts are numerous. They are, of course, complementary to death-bed visions. Two examples are here given, one by an American medical man and the other by an English journalist. There are also cases in which several people have simultaneously seen these phenomena—some published by the S.P.R.

Dr. R. B. Hout of Goshen, Indiana, U.S.A., a medical man, described his personal observations at the death-bed of his aunt in *Light*, vol. lv, 1935, p. 209. His narrative has increased value, since he was able to preface it with the assurance that *before then he had not read any similar accounts*. He said: "I had not read of the actual process of the soul leaving the body, and I had not known of the cord that connects the spirit-body with the earth-body." The following details are from Dr. Hout's account: "I suddenly became aware that there was much more in that room than the physical senses had been able previously to detect. For my attention was called, in some inexplicable way, to something immediately above the physical body, suspended in the atmosphere *about two feet above the bed*. "At first I could distinguish nothing more than *a vague outline of a hazy, fog-like substance*. There seemed to be only a mist held suspended, motionless. But as I looked, very gradually there grew into my sight a denser, more solid, condensation of this inexplicable vapour. Then I was astonished to see definite outlines present themselves, and soon I saw *this fog-like substance was assuming a human form.*

"Soon I knew that the body that I was seeing resembled that of the physical body of my aunt. . . . *This astral body hung suspended horizontally a few feet above the physical counterpart*: it was quiet, serene, and in repose. But the physical body was active in reflex movements and subconscious writhings of pain. I continually watched and . . . the spirit-body now seemed complete to my sight. I saw the features plainly. They were very similar to the physical face except that a glow of peace and vigour was expressed instead of age and pain. The eyes were closed as though in tranquil sleep, and a luminosity seemed to radiate from the spirit-body. . . .

"As I watched the suspended spirit-body, my attention was called, again intuitively, to a silver-like substance that was streaming from the head of the physical body to the head of the spirit double. Then I saw the connecting cord between the two bodies. As I watched, the thought, 'The Silver Cord', kept running through my mind. I knew, for the first time, the meaning of it. *This 'silver cord' was the connecting link between the physical and spirit bodies, even as the umbilical cord unites the child to its mother.* . . .

"*It was attached to each of the bodies at the occipital protuberance, immediately at the base of the skull.* Just where it met the physical body it spread out, fan-like, and numerous little strands separated and attached separately to the skull-base. But other than at the attachments, the cord was round, being perhaps about an inch in diameter. The colour was a translucent luminous silver radiance. The cord seemed alive with vibrant energy. I could see the pulsations of light stream along the course of it, from the direction of the physical body to the spirit double. . . . With each pulsation the spirit-body became more alive and denser, whereas the physical body became quieter and more nearly lifeless. . . .

"*My uncle, the deceased husband of my aunt, stood there beside the bed. Also her son, passed away many years previously* [='deliverers']. . . . By this time the features were very distinct. The life was all in the astral body and the physical body had entirely stopped the restless moving, was entirely oblivious to all reflexes and death seemed imminent. The pulsations of the cord had stopped. . . . I looked at the various strands of the cord as they spread out, fan-like, at the base of the skull. Each strand snapped and curled back as would a taut wire if it was suddenly cut. . . . The final severance was at hand. A twin process of death and birth was about to ensue. . . . *The last connecting strand of the silver cord snapped and the spirit-body was free.*

"*The spirit-body, which had been supine before, now rose and stood erect behind the bed*, where it paused momentarily before commencing its upward flight from the room. The closed eyes opened and a smile broke from the radiant features. *She gave a smile of farewell, then vanished from my sight.* The above phenomenon was witnessed by me as an entirely objective reality. The spirit-forms I saw with the aid of my physical eye. . . . The whole of this event covered twelve hours. I watched, commented, and moved about during the occurrence."

E. W. Oaten (*That Reminds Me*, Two Worlds Publishing Co. Ltd., 1938) described the passing of a friend named Daisy as follows: "I saw *a faint, smoke-like vapour* rise from the body. It rose some few feet above the bed and stayed there. It was full of motion and rolled over and over until it became a ball of greyish smoke, in a state of motion, with slight traces of opalescence in it here and there. It condensed and grew larger, supplied with a steady stream from the body, a stream of vapour some three inches in diameter.

"Slowly the ball assumed the size of about 5 ft. 6 in. in length by 18 in. in diameter. Condensation continued until it became to me, a semi-solid body, light-grey in colour, but still like a volume of smoke all in motion. Then, gradually, definition began to come. It assumed the form of a roughly-moulded dummy of the human form.

"*An umbilical cord united it with the physical body. I could see the flow of energy in the umbilical cord.* The etheric form began to assume the perfect shape. . . . Presently there was the exact duplicate of Daisy *floating face downwards in the air.* It was connected to the body by the silver cord through which her life slowly escaped. Then the form began to heave and rock. like a balloon tearing at its moorings. The silver cord began to stretch. It grew thinner and thinner at the middle until at last it snapped and the floating form assumed *an upright attitude*. It was the living duplicate of the sleeping form on the bed. She turned to me and smiled. She was thanking me for the hours I had spent in trying to help her. Then, from the corner of the room, near the ceiling, there came a rush. *Two white-robed figures, a man and a woman* [='deliverers'] *came to her, and, wrapping their robes around her, they floated away. . . .*"

Statements *Nos. 17, 18:*

(a) *Internal consistency or coherence of communications*

The claim that a dying man often sees his own exteriorised double (No. 17) is concordant with No. 6 (that an hour or so before 'visible death' the double is often already outside the body). The further claim that he also often sees his body on the bed is also acceptable in view of No. 21 (that the double may remain attached (by the 'silver cord') to the Physical Body for a period of time after death (from a few seconds to three or four days). The function of the 'cord' during earth-life was (*a*) to transmit impressions from the physical senses, via the Soul Body, to the mind and (*b*) to carry orders from the mind to the Physical Body: if in some cases the 'cord' does remain intact for a brief period after 'visible' death, an awareness of the corpse and of its immediate surroundings is to be expected.

Besides possible glimpses of his own vacated Physical Body, and the adjacent physical world (Statement No. 17) we are told that a dying man often gets glimpses of the 'next' world and its inhabitants, so that there may be 'dual' (or 'alternate') consciousness (Statement No. 18). Those glimpses of discarnates and their environment which may be obtained by men in course of transition, when known by mortals, are popularly called 'death-bed visions', and the discarnate souls who are claimed to be seen by the dying often include those whom he may have 'Called'—namely, personal friends and relatives (Statement No. 2). The knowledge that these people made their transition some time ago, would help the newly-dead man to realise his own condition (Statement No. 31). The claim is also in accord with No. 1*b*—it is because he is free from the 'blinkers'-like, sluggish, restricting Physical Body and is now partially using the more responsive, and sensitive, Soul Body that he is 'clairvoyant' and can see the 'dead'. And here enters an element of justice: during earth-life he had found it difficult, if possible, to credit invisible presences; he is now one of them and, we are told, it is his turn to experience disappointment.

There is a 'pointer' in connection with No. 18. Communicators who died naturally typically described seeing their discarnate friends either just before, or just after, vacating the body—and in some cases their claims are supported by clairvoyant observations. But those whose transitions was enforced do not typically make such claims: we have seen no case in which the latter claimed to see the 'dead' *before* their own transition (and very few in which they claimed to see them immediately after death).

(b) *Inherent probability, support from physical science, etc.*

The fact that the files of the S.P.R. contain well-authenticated cases of 'meeting cases' ('death-bed visions') which were not confined to the dying person but were also seen by others—'collectively-seen' cases—gives strong support to the statements of communicators that, just before 'passing', they did, in fact, see discarnate friends and relatives. One such case occurs in *Proc. S.P.R.*, vi. 20. A Miss Pearson, when dying, claimed to see her deceased sister Ann, who had "come to call her". Ann was also seen, independently, by two nieces and a housekeeper who were in the house at the time.

Again, a few death-bed visions have been corroborated. In a case noted by Dr. Hodgson, Mr. 'F' died. At a 'sitting' with Mrs. Piper, Mme. Elise, a supposed discarnate, communicated. She said that she had been present at 'F's' death-bed and had spoken to him. She repeated what she claimed to have said, and it was an unusual form of expression. Now, 'F's' nearest surviving relative had been at 'F's' death-bed. She spontaneously stated that, when dying, 'F' had claimed to see Mme. Elise and to hear her voice: he repeated what she was saying. The expression was identical with the unusual expression given by Mme. Elise through the entranced Mrs. Piper.[1]

If death-bed visions are due to the dying directing their

---

[1] *Proc. S.P.R.*, xiii, 378.

thoughts towards friends *in general* there should be approximately as many visions of the 'living' as of the 'dead'. Actually, there is a significant preponderance of the latter. Again, there seems to be no single case on record in which a dying person claimed to see a 'living' friend whom he erroneously thought to be 'dead'. On the other hand, there are many recorded cases of dying people who 'saw' friends whom they supposed to be 'living' and yet who were, in fact, 'dead': they say, "You didn't tell me that 'X' had died! Why didn't you tell me?" Cases of the latter type were collected by Miss Cobbe; others are given in *Proc. S.P.R.*, iii, 93, xiv, 288.

Supplementary evidence with regard to the reality of death-bed visions consist in the fact that those who have published their observations of the dying also state that *such visions occur at the very moment of transition*. Miss Cobbe[1] said: "The dying person is lying quietly, when suddenly, *in the very act of expiring*, he looks up—sometimes starts up in bed—and gazes on (what seems to be) vacancy, with an expression of astonishment, sometimes developing instantly into joy. . . . If the dying man were to see some utterly-unexpected but instantly-recognised vision . . . his face would not better reveal the fact. *The very instant this phenomenon occurs death is actually taking place. . . .*"

A. T. Baird[2] quoted the Rev. Dr. Worcester as saying that on several occasions he had seen dying persons brighten up as they appeared to see friends who had 'gone before'. He added: "*In every instance within my experience this has proved the immediate precursor to death.*" Dr. Worcester further said that this was the experience of "the old doctors" (who remained with patients until the end). *The old doctors expected death soon after the patients appeared to see friends who had pre-deceased them.*

Nurses make the same statements. Joy Snell,[3] who was a nurse for twenty years, said: "I notice that often, *just before the end* the dying would seem to recognise someone who was not of those at the bedside and was by the latter unseen. I have seen a woman who had been in a coma for hours suddenly open her eyes with a look of glad surprise, stretch forth her hands as though to grasp invisible hands outstretched

[1] Frances Power Cobbe, *The Peak in Darien.*
[2] A. T. Baird, *A Case Book for Survival*, Psychic Press Ltd., p. 140.
[3] Joy Snell, *The Ministry of Angels*, Greater World Association, 1950, p. 27.

towards her, and then, with a sigh of relief, expire." After describing several similar cases, Mrs. Snell said: "That at such moments as I have described the dying really see some spirit-form—someone who has come from the other world to welcome them—I have never doubted. And the time came when it was revealed to me that they really do see."

Professor C. Richet[1] who tried to explain all psychic phenomena without recourse to the hypothesis of survival, and who in pursuit of this purpose, credited psychics with a 'sixth sense' that amounted to potential omniscience, admitted that the facts of death-bed visions (and especially those seen by quite young children) were "much more explicable" on the hypothesis of survival than on that of the 'sixth sense' he envisaged.

Communications often include the statement that, just as an earthly midwife assists in the release of the newly-born body in physical birth, so discarnate souls often assist in the release, from the Physical Body, of the double. In each case there is a connecting 'cord' which may have to be severed, and in each case this 'cord' has conducted vitality from the original body to the one which is 'born' from it. It is reasonable to suppose that, just as some babies are born more easily than others, so some people are born into the 'next' world more easily than others. Those discarnates with special duties to help in the process of the birth which we call death are named 'deliverers' (Nos. 2-4); they are naturally often seen as death-bed visions, and they are sometimes seen by those present at a death-bed. A similar state of affairs is said often to obtain in the *temporary separation* of the double from the body ('astral projection'): discarnate helpers, obviously, corresponding to the 'deliverers' of communications from 'beyond', assist suitable persons to leave their bodies for various reasons. (While out of the body, and conscious, it is possible to be assured of survival and to obtain help, guidance and strength without recourse to a medium. Again, the temporarily exteriorised person can 'co-operate' with discarnates in assisting other mortals, the newly-dead and the 'earthbound'[2]—No. 30.) Many who claim to have left the body during earth-life say that they witnessed railway accidents, etc. during their 'sleep'. Although

---

[1] Dr. Charles Richet, *Thirty Years of Psychical Research*, W. Collins & Sons Ltd., 1923.
[2] See *The Theory and Practice of Astral Projection*, by the writer.

they may think such experiences are 'dreams', in some cases they correspond to reality. An example was given by Sir Oliver Lodge. A lawyer, H. W. Wack, seems to have been drawn to the scene of the accident telepathically—by the emotions of those present. During the 1914-18 War, a correspondent of Dr. Carrington[1] said: "I testify to that which I have seen. For I have often been liberated from my physical body, though not by death, and sometimes I have been transported to battlefields where I have seen angels—hosts of angels—ministering to the wounded and dying. . . ." (Compare No. 3 regarding 'deliverers'.)

Statements Nos. 19-21.—During earth-life the vehicle of vitality, if partially exteriorised for a time, remains connected with the Physical Body by a 'silver cord' (which is attached at the solar plexus). This feature is not a part of orthodox science, philosophy or religion. Ministers of several denominations, of whom I enquired, regarded it as a poetic fancy. Dr. E. H. Plumtree, Dean of Wells, does not mention it in his (otherwise excellent) treaty on eschatology,[2] although the 'cord' seems to be mentioned by Ecclesiastes (xii. 6). The present writer discusses this feature in detail in a book to be entitled *Events on the Threshold of the After-life*.

The 'cord' that unites the vehicle of vitality to the Physical Body is said to transmit vitality (collected by the exteriorised Soul Body during sleep) to the Physical Body. Whereas during sleep most, if not all, of the vehicle of vitality remains with the Physical Body, at death it entirely withdraws (along with the Soul Body). Again, whereas in sleep the 'cord' remains intact, at death (sooner or later) it is severed. When the body of an apparently dead man does not decompose it is, we are told, because the vehicle of vitality remains attached to it (by the 'cord'): in theory, he can 'return' (as, indeed, occasionally happens); in practice, however, this may be impossible because some vital organ has ceased to function and the body is not in a condition for re-habitation. Lazarus and the daughter of Jairus were presumably cases of suspended animation, of deep trance: Jesus, seeing (*a*) that the 'cord' was intact and (*b*) that the body was habitable, commanded their return.

[1] Dr. Hereward Carrington, *Psychical Phenomena and the War*, T. Werner Laurie, 1918, p. 254.
[2] *The Spirits in Prison*, Wm. Isbister Ltd., 1887.

(a) Inherent probability, support from psychical science, etc.

Fr. Herbert Thurston, S.J. (*The Month*, vol. clxv, 1935, p. 49) referred to an essay by the Spanish canonist, Fr. Ferreres, S.J., on the administration of the sacrament of Extreme Unction in cases of apparent death. "He did not set any definite terms to the possibilities of survival so long as putrefaction had not unmistakably set in." Thurston said that "nearly all moral theologians" agree that "actual death and apparent death cannot be identified", since "there is every reason to believe that life does not terminate at the moment when the action of heart or lungs ceases to be perceptible". In this, as in prayers for the dead, in the conception of a state intermediate between earth and 'Heaven', and in the rejection of cremation (p. 137), the Roman Church may, like the Moslems, show wisdom.

Recent research tends to support the general claims made in communications in connection with suspended animation. In 1955 Dr. Audrey Smith reported on her experiments with animals at the National Institute for Medical Research, London. She first caused suspended animation by suffocation, and then reanimated the animals. Golden hamsters were sealed in a glass jar: as they continued to breathe the 'same' air (with a constantly increasing proportion of carbon dioxide—as, it should be noted, in the dangerous Yoga exercise of Pranayama or "hold-breath") they became drowsy and fell asleep. They were then gently cooled and packed in ice. Neither breathing nor heart-beat could be detected. After an hour of this death-like state they were gently thawed out and were found to be quite normal. On the basis of these, and other, experiments, Dr. Smith suggested that many human beings who have been given up as dead after air and sea accidents in frozen areas might have been revived by suitable treatment.

The phenomena of 'materialisation', as well as those of death, 'astral projection' and sleep, resemble physical birth. Among the details which may be mentioned (one which is placed beyond doubt by photographic evidence) is the fact that a 'materialised' form may be united to the body which gave it 'birth' (i.e. the body of the 'physical' medium) by a 'nutriment'-conveying 'cord' (or 'cords'). Further (as is claimed by discarnate communicators concerning the after-death state), this 'cord' *undoubtedly* permits 'dual' (or 'alternate') consciousness as between the medium and the 'materialisation'. Henslow[1] quoted from a lecture given by the Ven. Archdeacon Colley in 1903 in which he described the 'materialisation' of a little 'girl' one wintry night. The 'girl' (materialisation) happened to be near the fire when it suddenly blazed out with great heat, causing 'her' to recoil. Colley said, "Did it burn you?" The *medium* replied, "Yes; for *I* felt it." Colley commented: "Yet he at the moment was standing at the far end of the room, away from the fire." Again, Mrs. Mellon said: "I feel as though I *were* that form and yet I know that I am not and that I am still seated on my chair." Mme. d'Espérance[2] made identical observations concerning the 'materialisations' which were produced on the basis of the ectoplasm exteriorised from her Physical Body: when someone put her arms around the *materialistic form*, the *medium* said: "I feel somebody's heart beating against *my* breast. . . . I begin to wonder which is I— Am I the white figure or am I the one in the chair?"

In these cases the ectoplasm (from the vehicle of vitality) released from immersion in the Physical Body during the passivity of trance (yet remaining attached to it by a cord-like connection or extension) permitted 'dual' consciousness. It is significant that almost identical words were used independently concerning the parallel phenomenon of sleep. A woman who was said to 'visit' her (deceased) husband while her Soul Body was released from immersion in the Physical Body during the passivity of natural sleep (yet presumably remaining attached to it by a cord-like connection or extension) said: "Which is I? For I see myself—I feel myself—back there [in the Physical Body] also, I seem to be in two places. Which I is really I?[3]"

Turning to cases of people who experienced 'astral projection', the phenomenon of 'dual' consciousness (made possible by the 'silver cord') is often described. Mr. Huntly[4] said: "I woke from sleep to find myself out of the body. I was conscious in two places—in a feeble degree in the body in bed and in a great degree away from the body. . . ." 'H.F.P.'[5]

[1] The Rev. Professor G. Henslow, *The Proofs of the Truths of Spiritualism*, Kegan Paul, Trench, Trubner & Co. Ltd., 1919, p. 237.

[2] Mme. d'Espérance, *Shadow Land*, Redway.

[3] Mrs. C. A. Dawson, *From Four Who are Dead*, Arrowsmith, 1926.

[4] J. Arthur Hill, *Man is a Spirit*, Cassell & Co. Ltd., 1918.

[5] *Light*, lxxiv, 1954.

made a very similar statement: "I was simultaneously conscious both of the numbness of my Physical Body and the 'aliveness' of the 'inner', and more vital, body."

Thus in all four possible, yet independently-described, conditions in which a hypothetical 'silver cord' *could* theoretically permit 'dual' consciousness—namely, (*a*) in some cases of the very early stages of transition, (*b*) in 'materialisations', (*c*) in sleep and (*d*) in 'astral projection',[1] the phenomenon has in fact, been described.

Our present point is that the above constitutes strong, though indirect, confirmation of the communication that the *newly-dead* may have 'dual' consciousness (during any period that the 'silver cord' remains unsevered).

Scientists in general have completely overlooked the 'silver cord'. Sir Oliver Lodge[2] has no reference to it in his Index, though in the text (p. 276) he cited Mrs. Piper, returning to her body from trance, as saying, "I came in on a cord, a silver cord" (compare Appendix I), while later in the book (pp. 297, 298, 300) a child 'control' clearly referred to the same feature in connection with Mrs. Thompson, describing it as a "stick" which "went right through" the medium's body. The communicator "seemed to have to talk through it" and when another would-be communicator "interfered" with it, communications became confused. It is not mentioned by Podmore.[3]

The Theosophist A. E. Powell[4] gave a résumé of the teachings contained in about forty of the best Theosophical books. He did not index the 'silver cord'. C. W. Leadbeater,[5] the greatest of the Theosophical clairvoyants, also did not index the feature in his numerous books. As already said, in addition to much indirect evidence, there is direct photographic evidence for the existence of the 'silver cord' in 'materialisation' and other physical phenomena.

It is significant that, while accounts of natural death typically describe the 'cord', extremely few narratives of enforced death mention it.

[1] Many examples of 'dual consciousness' during 'astral projection' are given in the writer's *The Study and Practice of Astral Projection*, Aquarian Press Ltd., 1959.
[2] Sir Oliver Lodge, *The Survival of Man*, Methuen, 1909.
[3] Frank Podmore, *Modern Spiritualism*, Methuen, 1902.
[4] Lieut.-Colonel A. E. Powell, *The Etheric Double* (1926); *The Astral Body* (1926); *The Mental Body* (1927); *The Causal Body* (1927), Theosophical Publishing House.
[5] C. W. Leadbeater, *Man Visible and Invisible* (1907); *The Other Side of Death* (1928), *ibid.*

(b) Internal consistency or coherence of communications

A communication from a discarnate lady through Geraldine Cummins (*Light*, vol. XLVI, 1926, p. 88) illustrates the internal consistency and coherence of communications in general concerning these and related matters. It was said that we mortals, beside the Physical Body, have *three invisible bodies* (compare Statement No. 1*b*): the "densest", the "almost semi-material" body, called the 'double' or 'image', is *seen at death-beds as "a mist"* by people who have "the inner sight" (Statement No. 14)—this clearly corresponds to the 'vital body' of the Rosicrucians, the 'etheric double' of the Theosophists and the 'vehicle of vitality' of the present writer; (2) 'the body of air' (=the Psychical, or Soul, Body of St. Paul) and (3) 'the body of light' (=the Spiritual, or Celestial Body of St. Paul), which is "the finest". At death, these three bodies leave the Physical Body "gradually", one (evidently the Soul Body) sometimes leaving first, in which case the person in course of transition will "seem to wander in his mind", since "the Spirit cannot make a proper connection with the body". The communicator continued, "*Gradually, these three parts gather above the Physical Body on the bed. They are still bound by . . . an important thread, the umbilical cord . . . and many invisible threads . . . which matter also. . . .* It depends a good deal on the human being how long he remains thus *looking down* [Statement No. 9] in a *kind of dreamy wonder* (compare 'the partial awakening', No. 25) at himself [Physical Body—Statement No. 17] not quite sure whether he is alive or not [Statement No. 10], but sensible of a wonderful freedom from pain [Statement No. 7] and of an exhilarating lightness you do not know in life. *Gradually these fine threads are snapped, and when the last is broken the Soul rises away* from the body" [Statement No. 20]. She further stated that souls who are little developed, i.e. who are 'earthbound' for a time after death, still retain 'the double' (vehicle of vitality) that she herself was using 'the body of air' [=Soul Body] and that "only high Spirits" can do without the latter. When "high Spirits" work 'here' [='Paradise' conditions] or 'near the earth' [='Hades' conditions] they must use a Soul Body: at other times they use the Spiritual Body in "the state far beyond".

Communications may describe *two* 'silver cords', one (which is attached to the solar plexus) conveying vitality, and the other (which joins the head of the Physical Body to that of the Soul Body), transmitting consciousness. (In a few cases *both* 'cords' have been seen: we suggest that this is where (*a*) the Physical Body, (*b*) the vehicle of vitality and (*c*) the Soul Body are separating simultaneously). Since most people leave the body via the head, the head-cord is most often described, but in a few cases when the physical head is unduly resistant, the feet may offer an easier exist, when the 'cord' is seen as joined to the feet. (It is evident that 'cords' are, in fact, temporary extensions of the various bodies.)

Statements Nos. 22-4

(a) Causes of an after-death 'sleep'

According to communications, people who are of sluggish type, those whose death ends a long and tiring life and those who have a long and exhausting illness tend to have a definite after-death sleep. These statements are reasonable.

Again, we are told that the vehicle of vitality vacates the Physical Body along with the Soul Body and tends to bedim, enshroud or enveil the Soul Body (and therefore markedly to 'lower' its natural 'level' of consciousness). The latter becomes available when it is shed (at 'the second death'). This accords with No. 1*b*—the vehicle of vitality is not an instrument of consciousness. Many communicators say that the unshed vehicle of vitality is a cause of an after-death sleep. The Frenchman, Allen Kardec[1] made the following generalisation: "Observation shows that, as a rule, the *semi-material perispirit* [=the vehicle of vitality] frees itself from the Physical Body only gradually—not all at once. The spirit recovers the full use of its faculties and full consciousness of itself only when this complete freedom has been attained [=when the vehicle of vitality has been shed from the total after-death double]. *Many take only three or four days for this liberating process.* Some take months." Individual statements, chiefly from Britons, of this kind were cited in the First Part of this book.

'Lancelot',[2] who died aged eight, gave an interesting description of his own 'second death' (which occurred twenty months after his transition). He began by saying: "I am able to see more than I did before." He added: "I thought I

[1] *Revue Spirite,* 1888.   [2] *Letters from Lancelot,* Dunstan, 1931, p. 53.

would always be like this . . . but *I sort of cast a skin like a butterfly coming out of its chrysalis. . . .* I felt a crack in me and it all came ever so clear like a chrysalis breaking open. I came out of my shell all beautiful like a butterfly. . . . I am an angel now. Angels are people who have changed and got beautiful like I did. . . . We come out of our earth-likenesses and get beautiful and then we are angels." 'Lancelot' (*ibid.*, p. 61) prefaced another significant observation concerning his 'second death' by saying "I must tell you another thing which is very curious: I don't know how to put it into words." (It was to the effect that, with the shedding of the vehicle of vitality, *his double had become luminous.*) It now consisted of the Soul Body only, an unenshrouded instrument of consciousness. (The various names that are applied to the unenshrouded Soul Body are instructive: they include the 'body of light', the 'radiant body', the 'luminous body' and the 'astral body'.) 'Lancelot' said: "I light dark places now when I go where it is dark. I don't know how I do it, but I seem to have a light in me which I didn't know I had before. . . . I love to go in the dark and see me shine like a candle-light all bright." *Corresponding with this increase in the luminosity of his double, this boy noted an increase in both the range and the depth of his consciousness.* He told his mother that, besides being able to see "more than before" he now had "a power of coming ever so much nearer than before". He continued, "*I can reach your mind on the inside when I come. . . .*" and added: "Do tell Dad about my getting out of my *shell. . . .*" [=vehicle of vitality].)

The causes of the after-death sleep which are advanced by supposed discarnates are at least reasonable. The Archbishop of Canterbury recently said, in the *Sunday Express*, that the idea of a 'sleep' until "a Final Day of Judgment" is an error. He stated, "If we sleep, it will only be to be refreshed after a tiring journey through this world."

(b) The duration of the after-death sleep in natural death

Spencer[1] was told that the period of 'sleep' is "rarely as much as seven and *generally two or three days*"; Swedenborg[2] claimed to speak with certain men who had 'passed on' naturally on *the third day* afterwards.

[1] M. K. Spencer, *The Other World*, Coimbatore.
[2] E. Swedenborg, *Heaven and Hell*, Swedenborg Society Inc., 1937.

The Communicators of 'A.L.E.H.',[1] Wickland,[2] Wood,[3] and Kardec[4] all mention *three days* as the common or average duration of the 'sleep'. Here are other communications to that effect.

Dr. J. Haddock, M.D., as early as 1851 (*Somnolism and Psycheism*, London), said: "The patient, Emma, while in a state of ecstasy made some revelations in which man is represented as a spirtual being, rising from what she calls 'the shell' of the dead material body immediately after death. It was sometimes *two or three days* after death, but not always alike; some were a longer, others a shorter time. During this time, they were like a person asleep and in a state [=the 'Hades' condition] between this [earth] world and the next ['Paradise']."

A girl communicator told R. H. Saunders: "We are told the spirits rest *three days* [after transition]." An adult communicator said: "It takes *three days* to get the spirit into proper form. At first it is in a comatose state. . . . On the third day cognisance of your surroundings begins and you know what has taken place" (*Light*, vol. XLIII, 1923, p. 627).

Grace Margerite Lady Drummond Hay 'returned' and communicated in fulfilment of a death-compact (*Light*, vol. LXVI, 1946, p. 229). She spoke of 'awakening' on the *third day* and said: "That was the birth of the spirit into the spirit-world" [=the shedding of the vehicle of vitality from the total after-death double]."

There must be significance in the fact that the *post mortem* period of three days has almost universal reference. Describing the beliefs of Australian aborigines, Ronald Rose (*Living Magic*, Chatto and Windus, 1958, p. 129) said: "There is also at least one secondary spirit (*mogwee*) . . . which is like a ghost. This survives usually for about *three days*, longer in the case of violent death, but then just disappears. . . . The secondary spirit, or ghost, is apparently seen quite frequently by relatives or close friends. They speak to the apparition, calling on it to leave them in peace."

Cesar de Vesme[5] said that primitive people "believe in the temporary survival of the 'larva', which is a corporeal phantom, though generally invisible, composed of a 'fluidic' substance having the form of the human body and all the

[1] 'A.L.E.H.'. *op. cit.*, 1929.   [2] Dr. Carl Wickland, *op. cit.*
[3] Dr. Frederick H. Wood, *After Thirty Centuries*, Rider & Co. Ltd., 1935.
[4] *Op. cit.*, 1888.
[5] Cesar de Vesme, *Primitive Man*, Rider & Co. Ltd., 1931, vol. i, p. 238.

animal instincts of the living creature, but only a rudiment of intelligence. . . ." This 'larva' clearly corresponds to the 'vehicle of vitality'. de Vesme also made this generalisation: "For many peoples, this 'larva' lasted about *three days*."

D'Assier[1] insisted on the reality of the human 'double' [here =the vehicle of vitality] which was animated by 'vital fluid'. He tried to explain all apparitions of the dead as representing nothing more than this.

John Denham Parsons[2] listed a number of religious teachings, including those of Hosea, the Zoroastrians, the ancient Phrygians, Syrians, Chinese and Tibetans, in which Resurrection (in this case meaning entrance into 'Paradise' conditions) took place on the *third day* and, in addition to correlating the period to certain aspects of sun-worship, said that experience showed that decomposition has generally begun in a corpse by the third day after death, indicating the departure of the soul (in, we would say, the Soul Body) from a Physical Body which could not be re-animated. He summed up: "The Spiritual Body of Jesus doubtless rose from His 'natural [here meaning carnal] body' upon '*the third day*' in accordance with the belief of the Zoroastrians, and many others, that it took the surviving Spiritual Body about *three days* to free itself from the dead body of flesh and blood." The fact that these teachings were not (as so many have supposed) meant to apply merely to mythical solar deities but also to *discarnate human beings* is shown by the reference (e.g. in the case of the Zoroastrians and ancient Egyptians) to the fact that *the three-day 'sleep' was followed by the 'Judgment' and the latter by the 'assignment'*. The Zoroastrians said that a man's good and evil works were weighed against each other; the Egyptians said that his deeds were weighed in the Scales of Osiris (see also under Statement No. 34). Moreover, the Zoroastrians and others taught that, after the 'Judgment', the righteous 'ascend' while the wicked 'descend' (Statement No. 35). *The Tibetan Book of the Dead*, edited by Dr. W. Y. Evans-Wentz (Oxford University Press Ltd., 1927), summarises ancient verbally-transmitted teachings concerning transition and the early after-life which correspond in essentials with those that are received, through mediums, in Europe,

---

[1] Adolph d'Assier, *Posthumous Humanity*, George Redway.

[2] J. D. Parsons, *The Nature and Purpose of the Universe*, T. Fisher Unwin, 1906, p. 147.

America, etc., at the present day. The priests taught that, when a man dies, his soul normally takes *from three and a half to four days* to completely separate from the body (i.e. from (*a*) the dense physical body and (*b*) the 'Bardo' Body, which corresponds to what we call the vehicle of vitality. The priest helps a dying man to avoid the 'Bardo' realm of dream and illusion (i.e. 'Hades') and to awaken in 'the Clear Light' (of 'Paradise').

According to Samuel S. Cohen, when Hosea (vi. 2) said, "After two days will he revive us and on *the third day* he will raise us up that we may live before him", although the immediate reference was to the nation, "*his imagery was borrowed from personal life*" (*Does Man Survive Death?*, a symposium edited by Eileen J. Garrett, 1957, p. 139).

In point of fact, Jesus *foretold* His Resurrection in *three days* (John ii, 19-22). His case was, in some ways, exceptional. Although killed in the prime of life, He was no doubt greatly fatigued and strained by the pre-Crucifixion events, while death on the Cross was not a sudden transition. Moreover, He may have made special arrangements in order to 'preach' to the 'spirits in prison' [='earthbound' in 'Hades'], as described in I Pet. iii. 19, 20, iv. 6 (see Appendix IV).

(*c*) *Inherent probability, support from physical science, etc.*

These statements are corroborated by two distinct groups of observed facts, namely, with the prevalence of apparitions (doubles or phantoms) of the dead within the first few days of natural death, and the rarity of communications within a few days from those who died naturally. This would be expected if, in fact, the average person who dies in a natural manner 'sleeps' for three or four days. (Such 'communications' as are received within the latter period are often of the nature of 'overheard dreams' rather than purposeful messages.)

The statements are corroborated by clairvoyants. Mrs. Garrett[1] observed and described the 'sleep' state of G. R. S. Mead: he was unaware of his transition (No. 10), and his 'sleep' was broken by dreams or 'delirium' in which he kept calling for 'Babs'.

It should be noted that the after-death 'sleep' of *three to four days* is said to apply to average people who die naturally

---

[1] Eileen J. Garrett, *Awareness*, Creative Press Inc., 1943.

in old age. That period is lengthened or shortened by several factors (see (a) above). In addition, the spiritual status of the person concerned is important: one communication[1] said that a person of very high spiritual development does not experience the "torpor" that affects "ordinary people". This agrees with St. Paul's statement: "We shall not all sleep. . . ." (I Cor. xv. 51).

As already said, in the process of physical birth, certain factors (e.g. heredity and diet) may modify, even nullify, each other, producing contradictions that are apparent and not real. The same would be true if, as communicators say, death is a form of birth.

A study of communications *en masse* regarding the important experience of an after-death sleep is unhelpful. This is illustrated by Sir Arthur Conan Doyle's[2] statement regarding the 'sleep'. Doyle merely said that the 'sleep' varies in length, sometimes hardly existing at all, and quoted Hubert Wales as saying that the period is "usually shorter than the average life-time here". Our method is to eliminate the statements of extreme people (great saints, as mentioned by Cornillier's communicator, who may have no sleep, while men of low spiritual development may have a protracted sleep). We concentrate on men of *average* type, and when we further contrast the statements of communicators who claimed to have died naturally (in old age) with those who claimed to be killed in the prime of life, thus eliminating contradictions that are apparent and not real, the whole of the accounts carry conviction and point to the statements having emanated from surviving souls.

The sleep is affected by a complex of factors. In natural death in old age the enveiling effect of the vehicle of vitality on the Soul Body is at its maximum, because the vehicle of vitality is completely exhausted of vital forces, a condition which contributes to unconsciousness. An alert, vigorous man (whose vehicle of vitality is replete with vital energies), forcibly ejected from the body, tends to remain awake, but with an 'enveiled', i.e. a 'sub-normal', or dream, consciousness. He is awake, but with a vitalised vehicle of vitality still impeding the activities of the Soul Body and he may therefore find it difficult

[1] P. E. Cornillier, *op. cit.*, 1921, p. 185.
[2] Sir Arthur Conan Doyle, *The New Révélation*, Hodder and Stoughton, 1918 p. 88.

to distinguish between 'realities' (i.e. the common environment, consisting of the 'doubles' of physical objects) and 'illusions', (i.e. mental images, created by himself or others): he is 'half awake', in 'Hades' conditions.

Other factors tending to cause (or to prolong) the after-death sleep are of more or less abnormal nature. One consists of fixed ideas of non-survival (No. 4); these act after the manner of post-hypnotic suggestions. The newly-dead man's attention may be earthwards (e.g. seeking revenge, preoccupied with the welfare of those 'left behind' or craving physical sensation) or he may be affected by undue grief of mortal friends.

(d) Possible impact on cremation

We have noted that there is evidence that, for some time after their deaths, certain people were aware of their Physical Bodies and of what happened to them and that, according to communications, this may have a bearing on cremation, etc. 'Raymond'[1] was among the 'communicators' who gave a warning on this matter. He said: "We have terrible trouble sometimes over people who are cremated too soon." Asked, "What if the body goes bad?" he replied, "When it goes bad the spirit is already out. . . ." He further said that in cases where the 'silver cord' was still attached, it had to be severed by 'spirit-doctors' [=deliverers', see Statement No. 3] and if the operation was performed "rather quickly" it caused "a little shock". (This communication is interesting, since there are several cases of people who were present at death-beds and who claimed to have seen 'deliverers' assist in the 'loosing' of the 'silver cord', etc.) In *Light*, vol. XLVIII, 1928, p. 557, Miss E. Gibbes told of a relative whose body was cremated three days after her death. Twelve days later she communicated, saying: "I have had only one glimpse of you since I fell asleep. You were with A (i.e. at the funeral) . . . I saw a long box near you and soon after that I got my last feeling of all. . . . After that everything was dark. . . . That extraordinary feeling was not pain, but it was something worse; just as if everything was breaking away, slipping from me, and I was trying to hold on and couldn't."

Light, vol. LII, 1932, p. 245, carried a letter from Kate Sedon referring to "the theory that cremation, if carried out

[1] Sir Oliver Lodge, *Raymond*, Methuen & Co. Ltd., 1916, p. 196.

within four of five days of death is liable to cause shock".
She said: "Reading H. Dennis Bradley's book, *Towards the
Stars*, I find the control 'Johannes' affirms the same thing."
The Editor then cited a message received through 'Feda' at
a sitting with Mrs. Leonard: "Listen to this very seriously.
The body should not be buried or burned for some time after
death. No funeral should be arranged until mortification has
set in." An automatic script obtained by Geraldine Cummins
from 'Bernard Shaw' soon after his death was published in
Prediction for May, 1951. It says that he was reluctant to return
to physical life and was angered by "that damned doctor
who will come and stab me with more drugs, bringing me back
—stop the fellow! . . . tired—G.B." (This would appear to be
part of the 'review' of the past life.) But, "for the benefit of
future pilgrims who seek cremation", 'Shaw' also said that when
his body was cremated, he was "sensible of a tearing, a
wrenching, a breaking, a snapping", a "temporarily annoying
experience" as if he were "hot, red hot". After this he "rose",
and "floated" and "knew what was meant by 'the beatitudes
of the saints' ".

'A.B.'s communicator (*One Step Higher*, The C. W. Daniel
Co. Ltd., 1937, p. 140) maintained: "The soul does suffer
if the body is cremated too soon. . . . If four days pass, it is
probably safe. That gives the soul time to sever itself. . . ." He
added: "Burial creates no shock."

Professor C. Flammarion (*Death and Its Mystery*, vol. iii,
After Death, T. Fisher Unwin Ltd., 1923, p. 166) cited a communication from the supposed discarnate Mme. Blavatsky
soon after her 'passing'. She said: "I am dead. I left a will . . .
in which I asked to be cremated. Cremation as it is practised
in India, in the open air, is in conformity with religious precepts,
but it is done in an oven here and means a loss of one's psychic
personality [=the 'etheric double', 'vital body', 'Odic body',
'vital soul', 'Bardo Body', etc.]. I implore you to write to
Colonel Olcott not to have me cremated." (The communicator
went on to say that Mme. Adam should be warned against
cremation—that she also had made a will that included
instructions for cremation—this was a fact, though no one
present knew of it.)

It should be noted that all these accounts of the severance
of the 'silver cord' refer to cases of natural transition. The

communicator of Mabel Beatty (*The New Gospel of God's Love*, Wright and Brown, p. 49) said that "in many cases" the 'cord' remained intact for three days after death, and that severance "often" does not take place until after three days. He continued: "Violent death may cause the cord to be separated too hastily, and the Soul Body is precipitated into the next plane of consciousness in a disconcerting manner—but help is usually forthcoming [by 'deliverers' =our Statement No. 3] from our side, and prayer from your own side enables the vibrations to be steadied." [=our Statement No. 29]. This communicator evidently regarded the retention of the 'cord' for a period of up to about three days as fairly normal—and as one of the several mechanisms that minimises the shock of natural transition.

Olivia M. Trueman (*The ABC of Occultism*, Kegan Paul, Trench, Trubner & Co. Ltd., 1920, p. 50) stated that "hasty cremation" is undesirable, since it may interrupt the "panoramic review" of the past earth-life.

The communicator of John Scott (*As One Ghost to Another*, Psychic Book Club, p. 97) said: "Sometimes it may be rather long before the spiritual body is able to separate from the material form, and it is advisable to leave the corpse undisposed of for a short period."

According to the communicator of Paulette Austen (*The Philosophy of White Ray*, Psychic Press Ltd., p. 137) some fifty to sixty hours should elapse between death and cremation.

The deceased daughter of the Rev. John Lamond, D.D. (*Kathleen*, Hutchinson & Co. Ltd., 1934, p. 131) said that, after death, "a certain sympathy between the departed Spirit and the lifeless body may exist for several days". She continued: "Where cremation is adopted, an interval of several days should be allowed to elapse before the body is consumed."

A communicator of A. W. Austen (*Spirit Guidance*, Psychic Press Ltd., 1941, p. 34) told him: "Four days, usually, is sufficient to allow the Spirit to get quite clear of the body." He added: "And cremation always means that the Spirit loses certain chains that might otherwise tie him to earth." (On this account, he recommended eventual cremation, whereas another communicator, 'Vettellini'—mentioned below—on the same grounds, was against cremation: It should always be

borne in mind that communicators commonly disclaim infallibility: when their opinions are both (*a*) practically unani-
mous and (*b*) supported by extraneous evidence, we suggest
that they are worth considering by mortals.)

According to the communications that are published in
"The White Eagle" Books (*Spiritual Unfoldment*, vol. ii, 1943,
p. 72), "Fire, in a sense, both destroys and liberates life.
Fire means a very rapid disintegration of the body. . . . There
can be suffering if the body . . . be brought into contact with
fire too soon."

'J.V.H.' (*Death's Door Ajar*, Rider & Co. Ltd., 1934, p. 99)
said that his communicators "mentioned this period of three
days during which the liberated Spirit has a gradually lessen-
ing association with its former body and, on this account, we
have been told that no body should be cremated till this
period is over". He added: "Burial does not seem to affect it
in the same way as cremation does."

'Peter', the communicator of Harry Edwards (*The Mediumship of Arnold Clare*, Psychic Book Club, p. 219), stated that
"the etheric body" [here =vehicle of vitality] remains associated
with the dense physical body "until decay is complete." He
therefore consented to cremation, "provided always that three
days have elapsed."

'Percy' communicated to his mother: "It takes a little time
for the Spirit and the emanations [=vehicle of vitality] to
withdraw completely from association with the physical body,
and when cremation takes place it sometimes causes suffering
and shock to the Spirit of the body which is being destroyed"
(Ethel Welsford, *Key of Gold*. The Society of Communion,
1929, p. 115).

Clairvoyants make the same statements concerning cremation as do discarnate communicators. Max Heindel (*The
Rosicrucian Cosmo-Conception*, 1911, p. 66) said that neither
cremation nor embalming should be undertaken until at least
three days after death, since the cord may not be severed and
the injury to the dense [physical] body will be felt, in a measure,
by the man". He gave another reason against too early cremation: "It tends to disintegrate the vital body [=vehicle of
vitality] which should be kept intact until the panorama of
the past life has been etched into the Desire [=Soul] Body."
The supposed Italian 'Vettellini', communicating to the

French P. E. Cornillier (*op. cit.*, 1921, pp. 78-9, 153, 160), mentioned an interesting corollary to this, i.e. that people whose bodies are cremated find difficulty in communicating with mortals, a statement that might explain certain observations. This statement was also made in *Light*, vol. lii, 1932, p. 136: 'D.G.' said that a communicator was "glad he was not cremated". He gave the same reason as Max Heindel gave in America: "This would have caused a quick disintegration which would have reduced his power to communicate with earth. . . ." 'D.G.' further said: "I once received communication in direct voice from a friend . . . a few months after his death. He referred to the fact that (as I knew) his mortal remains had been cremated, and he observed it as a curious fact that this had made it more than usually difficult for him to communicate." 'Vettellini' claimed that cremation had other (what may be called long-term) effects, and (p. 160) concluded: "It is better not to be cremated." The American clairvoyant, A. J. Davis (in *The Physician*), said that a corpse should not be interred "until after decomposition has positively commenced."

The statements of these communicators and clairvoyants concerning decomposition as the real indicator of death, agrees with medical opinion. Dr. Wm. O'Neill (*Lancet*, 1884, p. 1,058) said that a body should not be interred "until after decomposition has set in". Dr. G. Fagge (*The Principles and Practice of Medicine*, vol. i, p. 19, 2nd ed.) said that "putrefaction" is "the only conclusive and infallible sign" of death. The *Medical Examiner* of Philadelphia (vol. vi, p. 610) and the French doctor, Gannal (*Signs de la Mort*, Paris, 1868, p. 31), made identical statements. Our communicators are in good company in this, as in other matters.

Cremation was the custom in ancient Rome because in their *experience* it eliminated haunting by the 'larva' (vehicle of vitality). Suetonius says that the body of the murdered Caligula was only half-burnt and then buried: the 'ghost' (vehicle of vitality) of Caligula haunted the burial-place. When, however, the half-burned corpse was exhumed and destroyed by fire, the hauntings ceased. Embalming was undertaken by the ancient Egyptians partly for the same reason (also the result of *experience*) and partly with a view to supposed eventual rebirth. The ancient desire for 'proper burial' of a corpse was not necessarily based on superstition. Nor was it entirely connected with the avoidance of marauding animals. On the contrary we suggest that, in some instances at least, it was based on *experience*.

It may be said that the Roman Catholic Church forbids cremation. Among the well-authenticated cases of what we call temporary *post mortem* 'dual consciousness', i.e. of awareness of the Physical Body and physical world for some short period after death (though it was not a case of cremation) may be mentioned that of the nephew of M. Biberi which was published in *Journ. S.P.R.*, XXVI, p. 96. In 1912, Biberi took his nephew, who was very ill, to a hospital, which was situated some thirteen miles from his home. Two months later he was told, by telephone, that his nephew had died, but Biberi was unwell and unable to attend the funeral. Two months later, he had a manifestation of the dead nephew which included the words (twice repeated): "Put me in properly; the coffin is narrow, the coffin is short". In the following year, Biberi, when on a visit to the town in which the hospital was situated, was approached by a woman who said that she was the ward-servant in the hospital and that she had been present when Biberi took his nephew there. She gave him details of the 'passing' of his nephew. They included the following statement: "One thing was bad. . . . The coffin proved to be so narrow and short that, when he was being laid in it, the bones cracked." This case, and many others, strongly suggest that, in very rare instances (i.e. when transition is not quite complete, since a slight connection—the 'silver cord'—still persists between the exteriorised double and the vacated Physical Body), there may be some physical consciousness. They support the statements of supposed communicators, and of clairvoyants, concerning the advisability of postponing cremation, etc., until decomposition has commenced.

(e) *Internal consistency or coherence of communications*

Many communicators, including 'Lancelot' and 'Myers', mentioned above, independently liken the after-death 'sleep' phase to the chrysalis stage in insect development: they suggest that earth-life corresponds to the caterpillar stage (the 'nutriment' absorbed being represented by experience), the

'sleep'-and-dream phase to the chrysalis stage and the 'awake-ening' to the 'butterfly' stage in 'Paradise' conditions.
Statements Nos. 25 and 26

(a) Causes of the experiences

An occasional 'partial awakening' is understandable in view of the manner in which we sometimes awaken from natural sleep, with a vague 'Where-am-I' feeling. The cause assigned by communicators—namely, the fact that the 'sense organs' of the Soul Body have not yet begun to function—is reasonable. What causes the full 'awakening'? Life and consciousness in the Physical Body are said to be 'cribbed, cabined and con-fined': the body retards mental operations, bedims con-sciousness and restricts it mainly to physical objects and earthly activities. If this is so, it is obvious that the removal of this limitation will cause an 'expansion' and an 'awakening'.

(b) Internal consistency or coherence of communications

The coherence of Statements Nos. 25 and 26 with No. 1*b* has just been noted in considering the cause of the full 'awaken-ing'. Whereas those who die naturally, on fully awakening, typically say they feel 'secure', 'peaceful', 'serene', 'free', 'light', 'strong', 'young', 'fully alive', 'alert', 'vital', 'vigorous', etc., those whose transition was enforced typically describe definite (though temporary) 'confusion' and 'bewilderment'. These two contrasting statements, which are obviously highly signi-ficant, occur not only in numerous 'popular' books but also in communications that are received through accredited mediums.

(c) Inherent probability, support from psychical science, etc.

As already observed, the statement is often made by com-municators that things were by no means entirely new and strange, but even *'familiar'*. In this connection R. H. Ward[1] has an interesting observation concerning the (? out-of-the-body) experiences induced in him by lysergic acid: "And into the unknown the drug precipitated me. . . . And always the unknown, once I was, so to say, *there*, was paradoxically the known and familiar, it was always in some strange way recog-nisable, just as I dare say those sounds which are beyond our ordinary range of hearing would seem recognisable, could we,

[1] R. H. Ward, *A Drug-taker's Notes*, Victor Gollancz, 1957, p. 37.

by some means, become receptive to them. *The knowing of the unknown is dependent upon the widening of the range of consciousness.* . . . The unknown is that which we gradually lost when, in our earliest years, "the shades of the prison-house" began to fall, and the gaoler who was to become that 'personality' which we identify with our five-witted bodies closed the cupboard-door. . . . *Perhaps the unknown was known before we were born, and perhaps it will be known again when we die."*

Aldous Huxley[1] obtained, from a study of perception, ideas similar to those given us by communicators. Insisting that "perception . . . can be the same as Revelation", Huxley said that if consciousness survives death, "it survives, presumably, on every mental level—on the level of mystical experience, on the level of blissful visionary experience, and on the level of everyday individual existence. . . . From this world it is doubtless possible to pass, when the necessary conditions have been fulfilled, to worlds of visionary bliss or the final enlightenment." He ended with the following significant passage: "My own guess is that modern Spiritualism and ancient tradition are both correct. There *is* a posthumous state of the kind described in Sir Oliver Lodge's book, Raymond [='Hades']; but there is also a heaven of blissful visionary experience [='Paradise']; there is also a hell of the same kind of appalling visionary experience as is suffered here by schizophrenics . . .; and there is also an experience, beyond time, of union with the divine Ground [="mystical" consciousness, corresponding to the true 'Heaven']."

The conclusions reached by Huxley are of the first importance. But it should be noted that the teachings, explicit and implicit, of ordinary folk who communicate from 'beyond' go further than the learned and highly analytical Mr. Huxley in two respects: first, they insist (at least by implication) that, in general, the various states, or 'levels', of consciousness are determined by the bodily constitution at the time (the vehicle of vitality determining the 'sub'-normal state, the Soul Body determining the 'super-'normal state and the Spiritual Body determining the 'mystical' state); secondly, they describe objective environments that correspond to each body (and therefore to each 'level' of consciousness). However, our present study is not concerned with anything beyond the Soul Body,

[1] *The Doors of Perception,* 1954; *Heaven and Hell,* Chatto and Windus, 1956.

'super'-normal consciousness and the 'Paradise' environment.

Edward Carpenter[1] made the following observations: "It seems indeed probable—and a long tradition confirms the idea—*that the soul at death at first passes, with its cloud-vesture of memories and qualities* [=*the vehicle of vitality*] *into some intermediate region, astral rather than celestial, Hades rather than Paradise, and for a period remains there surveying its past, trying to understand the pattern.*"

(d) 'Paradise' is not a purely mental state

With regard to the nature of the environment in which the 'awakening' takes place—that which is called 'Paradise' 'The Garden of Eden', 'Summerland', the 'Third Sphere', 'Elysium', etc.—many communicators maintain that it is not the super-physical, spiritual 'Heaven' of orthodox Christian theology but an earth-like, 'semi-physical', condition. *'Paradise' is commonly described as intermediate between earth and the true 'Heaven' of the Bible.* In transmitting this view communicators agree with Tennyson ("No sudden heaven nor sudden hell for man . . ."), Stephen Hobhouse, Dr. W. R. Matthews, etc.

In discussing Statements 2-4 we referred to the phrase 'Abraham's bosom' as denoting 'Paradise' conditions. Hobhouse (*op. cit.*) said: "The word 'Paradise' has sometimes been used, as by Dante, for the final Heaven of light and vision, instead of being reserved for *the intermediate state of rest and purification.* Christ himself clearly meant to use it thus when He promised it, on the Cross, to the dying thief" (Luke xiii. 43). Dr. W. R. Matthews similarly observed: "When Jesus said to the dying thief, 'This day shalt thou be with me in Paradise,' He did not mean, 'in the full vision of God', in heaven, but in the place of departed spirits. . . ." Dr. L. P. Jacks[2] insisted that the world in which a man survives death "is not another world, but this". He continued: "By placing him in 'another' world, you would make another man of him and that would be tantamount to saying that *he* does not survive at all. . . . The conditions under which the departed continue after death are essentially the same conditions as those under which they lived here. . . ." The view which is transmitted by communicators that the 'next' world is 'not

---

[1] *The Drama of Love and Death*, George Allen & Co. Ltd.
[2] *Near the Brink*, George Allen & Co. Ltd., 1952.

M

immaterial' (and consequently that it is more or less earth-like) is adopted, according to Canon Marcus Knight[1] by no less an authority than Dr. Moffatt in his *Commentary on Corinthians*. Moffatt maintained: "*The spiritual, in other words, is not immaterial*." This conclusion of the learned Churchman may be compared with a typical statement of an ordinary unlettered communicator. The latter said, "Many people think that we must be living in a kind of dream-state, or in a world which is mental only. *Even in a world where one can create mentally there must be some material to work upon. On whatever sphere you may be living you have material on which to work.*"[2]

This statement applied to the 'Paradise' conditions, but others say much the same concerning the 'Hades' state—even this 'Shadow-land' or 'Plane of Illusion' is not 'purely sub-jective'. Thus: 'The intermediate plane' [='Hades'] was said to have 'material side', though it is difficult to describe because it is "insubstantial and shifting".[3] Later, speaking of 'Paradise' conditions, the communicator said: "Beyond here, *matter* becomes more etheral and *bodies* thin out into a visible presence of light and flame." Still later he insisted that matter is never transcended—that it goes through "an infinity of refinement". If, as is said, there are *bodies*, then presumably there are *realms* (worlds, spheres, planes, conditions, or 'mansions') to correspond. A communicator of Geraldine Cummins[4] stated: "Our bodies are created out of what I can only describe as an air of matter, or ether, which is, I believe, the ancestor of matter. Anyhow, to us, this air is substance." 'Vettellini' also insisted that 'matter' exists for all discarnate, as well as for incarnate, people.[5] 'Raymond' said: "People who think everything is created by thought are wrong . . . there is more than that."[6] The communicator of N. O. Davies[7] made almost the same statement as that of Drayton Thomas: "Because . . . the astral plane is a world of thought, you must not run away with the impression that it has no physical [=objective]

---

[1] *Spiritualism, Reincarnation and Immortality*, Duckworth, 1950, p. 112.

[2] The Rev. C. Drayton Thomas, *The Life Beyond Death, with Evidence*, Collins, 1923.

[3] Jane Sherwood, *The Psychic Bridge*, Rider & Co. Ltd., p. 47.

[4] *Mind in Life and Death*, Aquarian Press Ltd., 1956.

[5] P. E. Cornillier, *op. cit.*, 1921, p. 275.

[6] Sir Oliver Lodge, *op. cit.*, 1916, p. 184.

[7] *The Children of Evolution*, Psychic Book Club.

existence. . . ." 'Conan Doyle' maintained: "The 'astral' worlds or planes are composed of 'matter', but matter of so etheric a texture as to be largely malleable by thought . . . even as a man shapes his physical surroundings by action."[1] A communicator told Mrs. R. de Koven (*A Cloud of Witnesses*, E. P. Dutton, 1920, p. 255): "It is a world of spirit, but not of spirit alone, *spirit . . . has some material to act on.* The material has been called ether and out of it all objects known to the ethereal world are composed. It can be manipulated with infinite ease. . . ." H. Dennis Bradley was informed: "This is not a state of spirit, any more than the one I have left [=the earth]. . . . *I am still in a state of matter*, with a more beautiful . . . body."[2] Another communicator said: "Ours is a solid planet. . . . We walk on material ground; *we do not live on mental conditions only.*"[3] Bradley's two communicators, just mentioned, referred to both the 'world' which they inhabited and the 'body' with which they contacted it.

The communicator of Marjorie Livingston (*The New Nuctemeron*, Rider & Co. Ltd., 1930, p. 48) after saying that "the spirit-world exists in ever-widening spheres beyond the confines of the aura of the earth", stated: "This fact is a matter of *condition* [=state of consciousness, i.e. subjective] as much as of geography [=locality, i.e. objective]." On p. 75 the communicator said that Heaven and Hell are "*conditions*" which, "by means of these magnetic emanations", become "*places*" He added, "But such a place is not absolute geographically. An Ego may carry *its own* environment *or* it may move through *sympathetic environments.* When it desires to move into *an anti-pathetic environment* . . . it is obliged to subdue its own bright emanations . . . and gather grosser material from lower planes". On p. 77 he said that the idea that 'heaven' is *a place* applies to the 'astral' spheres that envelope the earth (corresponding to the 'astral' body which envelops our physical body), i.e. to 'Hades' and 'Paradise', while the Spiritual Spheres (the True Heavens of the Bible, corresponding to the Spiritual Body) are *subjective*.

The communicator of *Letters From the Other Side* (Watkins, 1919, p. 27) said "All these glories are *real, actual* as on earth, only more so, infinitely more so".

[1] Ivan Cooke, *Thy Kingdom Come*, Wright and Brown, p. 82.
[2] *And After*, p. 48.   [3] *Ibid.*, p. 34.

A communicator of Wilfred Brandon mentioned the 'material' nature of his body: he asserted, "There is more than pure thought in this 'vehicle' of ours. It is a finely attenuated form of matter. . . ."[1]

Jane Sherwood's communicator[2] after describing the 'Judgment'-experience (Statement No. 34) insisted that "The ordinary objective life goes on side by side with the Judgment". 'Hatch'[3] noticed the difference between "those things which have existed on earth unquestionably" (i.e. the objective environment) and "thought-creations" (i.e. the subjective element in some people's environments).

Mrs. Heslop's discarnate husband (*Speaking Across the Borderline*, Charles Taylor, 1912, p. 41) insisted: "Heaven is a condition of spirit [=subjective], as well as a place [=objective], a place of radiant beauty." Similarly, 'Judge Hatch' told Elsa Barker (*op. cit.*, 1914, p. 33): "This element in which we live ['Paradise' conditions] undoubtedly has a place, for it is all round the earth." This point was also made, on the basis of many communications received, by the Editor of *Light* (vol. XLVI, 1926, p. 265). He said: "The conditions of the life beyond—and, to a smaller extent, of the life here—involve considerations both of place and state. There must always be a substantial basis for every variety of experience, always an outer and an inner condition of life in every grade of being; the outer represents *the place*, the inner *the state*."

Drayton Thomas's deceased father insisted: "I must refer to this sphere as a place, for it is no mere condition."[4] Edward Randall, in America, cited several communicators to the same effect: for example: "The spirit world is part of your planet. . . . Around and about your globe . . . are separate, *material*, concentric zones or belts. . . ."[5] The communicator of Kate Wingfield, in England, said the same: "The disembodied spirit . . . enters another world, and yet the same, for it is all round your world: neither above nor below, but round it. It is far more real than the earth, for that is but a reflection of the real world."[6] The communicator of F. H. Fitzsimmons, in

---

[1] *Open the Door!*, Alfred A. Knopf, 1935, p. 106.
[2] *The Country Beyond*, Rider & Co. Ltd., p. 74.   [3] Elsa Barker, *op. cit.*, 1914.
[4] *In the Dawn Beyond Death*, Lectures Universal Ltd., p. 128.
[5] *Frontiers of the After Life*, Alfred A. Knopf, 1922, pp. 54, 63, 147, 209.
[6] *Guidance from Beyond*, Philip Alan, 1923, p. 89.

South Africa, made an identical statement: "Hades is a place and a condition of mind. . . . The abodes of those who once lived on earth are all around the earth at various distances from it."[1] 'Stewart' told Dr. J. M. Peebles, in U.S.A., that 'the next world' "has actual location, as well as conditions".[2] The communicator of F. T. Robertson said: "It is incorrect to say there are no such *places* as heaven or hell—there *are* 'many mansions'."[3] Dion Fortune insisted, "Purgatory has a definite astral location",[4] etc.

Even some of those communicators who insist that the 'spheres' are states of consciousness and not places or localities often use material terms in their descriptions. This is the case, for example, with 'Asa', communicating to J. G. Carew-Gibson (*Communication with the Dead*, Rider & Co. Ltd. p. 70). Having said that the world 'state' is better than the world 'sphere' for the succession of after-death conditions. "because a sphere is a state of consciousness", she continued: "Each sphere is a state of consciousness [=subjective] less material [=objective!] than those preceding it."

On earth, the subjective (or thought) aspect is subordinate to the objective (or environmental) aspect: as the 'spheres' are ascended, the importance of the subjective increases and that of the objective decreases (and the result of this is discussed under No. 34a). Only the 'Father', the Infinite Absolute, Transcendent and Unmanifested is *purely* 'subjective', *pure* 'Spirit', unconditioned by even the finest 'matter'.

Writing in *Light* (vol. xxxiv, 1914, p. 262), Miss H. A. Dallas pointed out: "Nowhere in the Universe have we any examples of *disembodied* existences." She defined a 'body' as "an instrument whereby intelligent beings are able to manifest themselves and to relate themselves with their environment" and pointed out that "St. Cyril taught that God's nature alone requires, neither for its own sake nor that of others, the assistance of a bodily instrument. St. Ambrose of Milan spoke in a similar manner: 'We must not suppose that any being is wholly immaterial in its composition, with One only exception'."

The importance of the physical body, and the corresponding physical environment in the development and evolution of the

---

[1] *Op. cit.*, 1933, p. 215.   [2] *Immortality*, Colby and Rich, 1883, p. 115.
[3] *Celestial Voices*, H. H. Greaves Ltd., p. 220.
[4] *Through the Gates of Death*, The Inner Light Publishing Society, p. 22.

human 'soul' was indicated by Phoebe and Dr. L. J. Bendit (*Man Incarnate*, Theosophical Publishing House Ltd., 1957, p. 5). They said: "Without a body, man, as naked Spirit, would be left in a subjective state, with no consciousness and hence no possibility of gaining objective experience or realising himself for what he is."

Clairvoyants make the same statement as communicators: the 'next world' has objective, as well as subjective, elements, Phoebe Bendit (Payne), a clairvoyant of extraordinary power and undoubted integrity, in *Man Incarnate*, written in conjunction with her husband, Dr. L. J. Bendit (Theosophical Publishing House, 1957, p. 114), pointed out that at psychic 'levels' there are objective things, as well as subjective mental images (or 'thought-forms'). and that non-psychic mortals who are in the half-asleep, half-awake condition may confuse the two [just as people who are in the 'Hades' after-death state and untrained psychics may confuse them]. After stating the fact that undue passivity 'loosens' the vehicle of vitality (which she called the 'etheric screen', the 'vital etheric field' or the 'etheric bridge'), she insisted that, on account of "the fluidity and lack of sharp barriers in the psychic realm, an untrained sensitive may confuse the images produced by his own mind [=subjective elements] with those of psychic objects and situations not so produced, but *existing in their own right outside himself* "[=objective elements].

An example of this confusion was given by H. Bland (*Psychometry*, Rider & Co. Ltd., p. 144). A sensitive described a number of discarnate souls (i.e. presumably their objective Soul Bodies), and went on to describe "an extraordinary figure with a wooden leg and a patch over one eye". The latter was a mental image (subjective) produced by someone present who had recently read *Treasure Island*—it was a mental image of Long John Silver.

Professor H. H. Price has pointed out that even if the 'next world' were not (as both discarnate communicators and incarnate clairvoyants declare) objective but were composed of mental images, it would not (as might be thought) be purely private and restricted to each surviving personality. He said: "Suppose we bring telepathy into the picture. It may well be that in this present life the physical brain [='blinkers' of communicators] *inhibits* the operation of our telepathic powers, or, at any rate, *prevents the results from reaching consciousness*. In the after-life, if there is one, telepathy might well be much more extensive and continuous that it is now. If so, one might expect that 'A's' images would manifest not only his own desires and memories, but also the desires and memories of other personalities, 'B', 'C', 'D', etc. if these were sufficiently similar to his own. [Note the correspondence of this idea with discarnates' communications concerning the 'Judgment', p. 163.] In this way there might be *a common image-world* for each group of sufficiently like-minded personalities, common to all members of the group though private to the group as a whole. There would still be many next worlds and not one (a suggestion which most religious traditions would, I think, support) but none of them would be wholly private and subjective." Thus, Professor Price showed that, *in ultimate effect, the psychological conception* of the 'next world', that held by some philosophers is less distinct from the *'higher body' conception* which is held by communicators, clairvoyants, etc. than appears on superficial view In both cases the 'next world' would be common to a number of surviving souls, they would exist in space (though not in physical space), and they would be subject to laws (though not to the laws of physics). He concluded: "It may well be that the two lines of thought, if pushed far enough, would meet in the middle. . . . There may be realities in the universe which are intermediate between the physical and psychological realms as these are ordinarily conceived. The contents of the [?immediate] other world, if there is one, may be in *this intermediate position, more material than ordinary dream images, more image-like or dream-like than ordinary material objects. . . .*" (*Does Man Survive Death?, A Symposium*, ed. by Eileen J. Garrett, Helix Press, 1957, p. 43). It is quite remarkable how the closely reasoned, factually-based conclusions of this eminent philosopher accord with the innumerable independent statements of ordinary discarnate communicators, made through ordinary 'uneducated' mediums.

Although Dr. Cyril Garbett,[1] late Archbishop of York and one of the great thinkers of the Church of England, realised that human confidence will be restored only "by a living faith in God as revealed in Christ *and the hope of life beyond the present*

[1] *In the Age of Revolt*, Pelican Books, 1956, pp. 105, 263.

world order", he was quite vague concerning the latter, observing, "There must be great reserve in describing its nature". He said: "It is Eternal Life rather than an endless cessation [?procession] of years that should interest the Christian. . . ." These statements seem to show a confusion of thought which is common in the Church: there is no necessary antagonism between the phenomenal life of this physical world (or that of 'Paradise' conditions) and Eternal Life. Moreover, until the Church can provide men with doctrine concerning the after-life that they can understand there will be no "restoration of confidence". Dr. Garbett admitted that "Christian doctrine of the future life . . . teaches both duration and quality", but failed to realise that most mortals demand more specific accounts than this. Mrs. G. Vivian[1] made our point admirably: "The life we usually want to know about when we lose a dear one is *the environmental life* they lead in the next world. This is not to be confused with Eternal life which comes from within and is the *quality* of life in which God rules, here and now, so that death brings no break in *its* continuity, but simply makes us aware of the things which cannot be destroyed."

Leslie Weatherhead (*After Death*, Epworth Press, 1923, pp. 179-80) failed to realise that the 'next world' does in fact consist of 'many mansions'. He complained that 'Raymond' (Lodge) described dead friends as smoking cigars, etc. and said that these conditions cannot be descriptive of 'the final home of our spirits'. Such a claim was not made by 'Raymond' or any other communicator: on the contrary! 'Raymond' himself was (1) "newly-dead" and (2) killed suddenly in the prime of life and he was, therefore, living among discarnate souls who were temporarily 'earthbound', i.e. in 'Hades' conditions, living among earth-memories which persisted in the (still-unshed) vehicle of vitality, imagin-ing, or dreaming, that there were smoking cigars, etc. They had not, as yet passed through the 'second death' (the dis-carding of the vehicle of vitality) and so entered 'Paradise' conditions (in the Soul Body). The subsequent shedding of the Soul Body and entrance into true 'Heaven' conditions which *are* "the final home of our spirits" was necessarily far in the future.

The usually vague, sometimes unacceptable, teachings of

[1] *Love Conquers Death*, L. S. Publications, p. 9.

the Church in general concerning the nature of transition and of the after-life has been one of the main causes of decline in religion. Canon Bezzant, Dean of St. John's College, Cambridge, speaking in 1955, said that the imagery in which the after-life had been preached "far too long" was either repellent or no longer suggested anything desirable. "If hell offends," he pointed out, "Heaven bores," and he concluded: "The only hope for the Church in this matter is to re-think the whole subject."

Dr. A. W. F. Blunt, Bishop of Bradford, at the Bradford Diocesan Conference, 1952, observed: "We have renounced the idea of hell, and we have lost belief in Heaven, except as a desirable, but probably fictitious, residential neighbourhood. . . . We have by-passed God, and in consequence, lost all feeling of crisis in this life. . . ." He concluded: "We are becoming a humanity without God or devil."

The Report of the Archbishop's Commission on Healing, 1958, admitted that the Church needs to teach a doctrine of the hereafter "more convincingly and simply". It failed, however, to indicate how this might be done. We suggest that the Church should cease to regard the Scriptures as a comprehensive and an unfailing guide-book to the after-life, since it is manifestly neither. Three hundred years ago Galileo, charged by the Inquisition with contradicting the Scriptures in saying that the earth goes round the sun, and not *vice versa*, insisted that "the Bible is intended to teach men how to go to Heaven and not how the heavens go!" (See Appendix v.)

(e) The locality of 'Paradise'

Where is the 'next world'? The following conclusion, arrived at by G. N. M. Tyrrell, a former President of the S.P.R., agreed with the statements of many communicators (and many 'astral projectors'). He considered: "At the end of our life in this world, it is very unlikely that we shall be shot off into another, the location of which we cannot imagine. *We are there already*: for a change of world is not brought about by spatial travel but by a change in what we are aware of."[1]

[1] G. N. M. Tyrrell, *The Nature of Human Personality*, George Allen, and Unwin 1954.

(f) Scriptural support

The conclusions, noted above, concerning the various states of after-death consciousness and the environments that correspond to them, i.e. (a) 'sub-normal' (or dream) consciousness, in 'Hades' conditions; (b) 'super-normal' consciousness in the 'Paradise' environment and (c) 'mystical', 'cosmic' or 'Spiritual' consciousness in the true 'Heaven' State, obtained by the present writer from the analyses of communications from 'beyond', correspond in general with Scriptural Revelation.

The argument against a state that is intermediate between earth and the true 'Heavens' of the Bible because "there is no Scriptural authority for it" is unsound. America, Australia, New Zealand and Great Britain existed in Biblical times— yet there is "no Scriptural authority" for them. When a new American cathedral was being built in the U.S.A. several clergymen objected to the representation of female angels on the ground that no female angels are mentioned in the Bible! (The architect compromised by providing the female figures with beards.) The then Bishop of London was reported[1] as making these wise observations in the course of an address: "There is no subject on which Christians are so mistaken as that of death. Death is mistaken for the pain which sometimes precedes it. Being born into another world is probably like being born into this. Death is an incident in a continuous life. There are six things *revealed* to us about the life after death: that the man was the same man five minutes after death as five minutes before it, that his character would grow, that he had memory, that he would be with Christ in *Paradise*, that there would be mutual recognition and that he would still have a great interest in the world he had left." All these things are said by communicators.

Statement No. 27.—The newly-dead, and especially those who have not yet shed the vehicle of vitality from the total after-death double (and who are consequently temporarily in 'Hades' conditions), are adversely affected, their minds being disturbed, depressed, 'befogged' and 'darkened', and their progress consequently retarded, by undue grief on the part of still-embodied friends.

[1] *Daily Telegraph*, January 30, 1911.

(a) Internal consistency or coherence of communications

'Philip'[1] urged his mother: "Shake off your dumps; . . . it hinders me in visualising you clearly." He also told her the converse—namely, that her wish to help him (when newly-dead) had had "a great effect" on his post-death experiences. One of Randall's girl communicators[2] pleaded, "Oh, Mummie, don't cry so. It makes me so unhappy. If only you would smile and be glad I'd be quite happy because I see ever so many lovely people who seem to be waiting to take me to some place . . . but I just can't leave *you*." Later this girl complained, "Why do you grieve so? I am well and could be happy, only your sad face keeps me wanting to be near you and comfort you." A boy-communicator of Randall's made identical statements: "When earth conditions do not bind me, I can attend lectures, etc. But I am bound to earth by the sorrow of my parents. . . . That holds me like bands of steel so I can only at times do what other boys do. They don't understand that I am more alive than ever before, but until they give me happier thoughts. . . . I am as unhappy as they are. I could be so happy, and accomplish so much, if they would let me go!" Katherine, a child communicator (whose identity was also well established) said, "Do not cry for me—it makes me sad."[3] Freddie Grisewood, of B.B.C. fame (and, incidentally, an honours graduate of Oxford), having described 'seeing', at various times, friends and relatives who had 'passed on', noted that they looked "well and happy" (see Statement No. 26). But he observed: "All made the same request—that those whom they had left behind should not grieve for them unduly." He continued: "In Mark's case this request was reiterated time after time. He would say, 'Freddie, do tell mother (Lady Mackenzie) not to grieve so much—*she's holding me back.*'[4]

A communication received from Nova Scotia and published in *Light*, vol. XLVII, 1927, p. 230, contained a reference to the effect of grief on the newly-dead. It was as follows: "I was still conscious of all that went on in my own home. . . . I saw my daughter weeping . . . and it seemed to put a cloud between us and give a numb sort of pain. . . . Grief . . . makes a barrier

---

[1] Alice Gilbert, *op. cit.*, 1948, p. 103.   [2] *Op. cit.*, 1922, pp. 36, 43, 131-3.
[3] *Proc. S.P.R.*, xiii, 484.   [4] *The World Goes By*, Secker and Warburg, 1952.

through which we cannot come, and it also hinders our progress upwards, for we are affected by *thoughts* and not by *physical conditions*, as we were on earth. . . . Happiness in the hearts and faces in our dear ones on earth radiates waves of light that attract us . . . grief radiates dark clouds and gives the appearance of a heavy black cloud enveloping our friends. Our new bodies are tuned to a higher key than were our earth-bodies. We are extremely sensitive to impressions."

A similar statement was made in England: "Do not grieve. Grief is so short-sighted. It blocks the outlets" (L. M. Bazett, *After-Death Communications*, Kegan Paul, Trench, Trubner & Co. Ltd., p. 108). A discarnate soldier's communication, cited in *Light*, vol. XLII, 1922, p. 706, included the following: "I could tell when Mother was fretting about me. I couldn't understand, I couldn't tell when Carrie was fretting. . . . But it was because *she was beginning to forget me* [compare 'Myers' under Statements 2-4*f*]. I was glad when you got a bit better: it made me miserable. . . ."

Clare Sheridan, the famous sculptor and cousin of Sir Winston Churchill, was described by the great philosopher Keyserling as "perhaps the most independent female spirit living". In her autobiography, entitled *To The Four Winds* (André Deutsch, 1957, p. 317) she described how she received communications from her (dead) son, first by "automatic writing" and later by telepathy. She found that "It was only when *a cloud of depression* descended on me that he could *not* contact me, and '*the fog*', as he called it, made him miserable".

Like practically all the statements reviewed in this study, No. 27 is not confined to 'popular' works. For example, a month after 'Raymond' (Lodge) died, his mother was told through the mediumship of Mrs. Leonard: "You used to sigh; it had an awful effect on him, but he is getting lighter with you." Later, although 'Raymond' promised to attend the family party at Christmas, he made this appeal: "No sadness . . . keep jolly, or it hurts me horribly."

The statement that undue grief 'holds back' newly-dead friends agrees with another made, independently, to the effect that emotions of a 'negative' type (grief, depression, self-pity, etc.) represent 'low', or 'slow' 'vibratory' rates—such as would, presumably, have that effect. The 'positive' emotions (cheerfulness, hope, faith, courage and especially love), on the other hand, represent 'high' or 'rapid' 'vibrations' and are helpful (as described by 'Philip' and quoted above). Again, the declaration that grief depresses the dead is the converse of the statement that love provides the best conditions in which they can communicate (Statements Nos. 2-4g).

'Lancelot'[1] communicated these two complementary statements. On the one hand, he said, to his mother, "When you cry I can't get near you because clouds come up round you". On the other hand, he said: "I am so glad of father's thoughts of me, because I get such big help from them: they give me a lift up and make me strong. I am helping other boys and they make me able to do it" [the father was, quite unconsciously, 'co-operating' with Lancelot—Statement No. 30].

As already said, Statement No. 27 (regarding grief) agrees with No. 29 (regarding prayer), No. 2 (concerning the 'Call') and No. 30 (regarding 'co-operation'): all illustrate the fact that mortals (though seldom aware of it) exercise a powerful influence on the 'dead', and especially on those newly-dead whose double includes the vehicle of vitality. As already said Nos. 2-4d), the physical body (with its vehicle of vitality) acts after the manner of a gun emplacement, or resistant base, to our thoughts, feelings and volitions. They are strengthened and reinforced by it. An airman communicator of Lord Dowding, for example, stated that hate, between the 'living' and the 'dead' hurts the 'dead' much more than the 'living': he gave this analogy: "It's like pitting a man in a bathing-dress against one in full flying kit."[2]

The communicator of F. W. Fitzsimmons[3] simply stated, "Intruders [=earthbound, would-be obsessors or 'gate-crashers' at séances] cannot stand up against the determined will of an earnest person in the flesh." A well-known medium, Mme. Hyver[4] stated: "The psychic forces emanating from the incarnate are more powerful than those emanating from the discarnate, as the former have in them more earthly elements." Again: "The vital fluid of a medium contains elements, borrowed from his physical body, which do not exist in the etheric bodies

---

[1] *Op. cit.*, 1931, p. 86.   [2] Lord Dowding, *Lychgate*, Rider & Co. Ltd., p. 77.
[3] *Opening the Psychic Door*, Hutchinson & Co. Ltd., 1933, p. 95.
[4] *Communication with the Next World*, The Cricket Press, 1937, pp. 36, 52.

of spirits." The communicator of Mrs. C. A. Dawson-Scott[1] said: "We get your thoughts *quite easily*, but we cannot slow ours down for the same to be true of them."

(b) Inherent probability, support from psychic science, etc.

Professor E. Bozzano (*op. cit.*, 1938, p. 86) suggested that the unusual 'strength' of Gordon Davis—a mortal who communicated through Blanche Cooper (*Proc. S.P.R.*, xxxv, 560-89)—was due to the fact that the psychic elements were impregnated with "earthly fluids" (which is exactly what Mme. Hyver said in another connection).

There is much evidence in connection with supernormally-produced 'raps' which supports the idea that the physical body acts as a gun emplacement to certain psychical manifestations. Again, the frequent injunction, in communications that when mortals try to address their dead friends (and especially their newly-dead friends) they should *speak aloud* (and not merely 'telepath' their thoughts) points in the same direction.

Another statement with which No. 27 accords is No. 1*b*— namely, that the thoughts and feelings of mortals are retarded by the immersion of the Soul Body in the sluggish Physical Body, which, it is said, gives mortals a chance to control their thoughts and emotions (see Appendix IV). The latter statement has support in the records of psychical research. For example, Professor Hyslop[2] observed that when the discarnate Dr. Hodgson communicated he often exhibited emotion that the incarnate Hodgson would have been able to control. Similarly, communicators who are of an impulsive and impatient temperament often 'speak' (telepathically) too rapidly for the medium or the recorder or both. 'Myers', who was impulsive and most eager to tell us about the conditions and methods of communication, had often to be asked to retard his speed, but found it almost impossible. 'Gurney', another communicator, commented that 'Myers' "lets the whole blaze come out in his impatience". At one sitting, in his great eagerness, 'Myers' "brushed 'Gurney' aside". At another, 'Myers' was said to be in such a state of "passionate eagerness" that he aroused a similar condition in the sensitive

---

[1] *From Four Who are Dead*, 1926, p. 100.

[2] *Psychical Research and Its Resurrection*, T. Fisher Unwin Ltd., 1908, p. 163.

and prevented communication. (*Proc. S.P.R.*, XLIII, 1935, pp. 130, 131). At a later sitting (*op. cit.*, p. 254) 'Gurney' observed: "Myers is here and, once he is 'in', so to speak, I may not be able to break in."

It is highly significant that statements that the body acts as a governor to the thoughts and emotions of mortals (and that its absence, after death, may cause discomfort, even trouble with people who fail to take the opportunity of achieving an adequate measure of control during the favourable period of incarnation—see p. 236) are also made by people who are only temporarily and partially out of the body. Thus, the engraver mentioned by Dr. P. Gibier (*Analyses des Choses*, p. 142) felt great lassitude and then found himself out of his body said, "being no longer master of my own thoughts, I found myself carried here and there as my thoughts directed. I could no longer rely on it; it seemed to scatter me before I could realise it."

Kate Wingfield's communicator (*More Guidance From Beyond*, Philip Alan, 1925, p. 26) also made this point with regard to mortals: she said that if a man does his best "in his waking hours" i.e. when the Soul Body is immersed in the physical body), then, when the soul (in the Soul Body) is temporarily released in deep sleep, etc. it will continue "learning or working or in some way rising to a higher level". The mental habit imposed through the bodily activities will tend to continue, both when he is temporarily and, eventually, when he is permanently out of the body. (See also pp. 236-7).

Similarly, 'Sir William Barrett', communicating to his wife (*Personality Survives Death*, Longmans Green & Co. Ltd., 1937, p. 146) urged her thus: "Get into the *habit* of opening your mind to me when you go to bed, and then you will find that I shall impress you with the right solution to your difficulties in the morning."

Statement No. 28.—The newly-dead often wish to assure their 'living' friends of their survival and well-being. In most cases they fail to make themselves seen or heard, since few people are psychic. However, apparitions of the dead are chiefly seen within a few days of the passing, and these (whether telepathic or bodily apparitions) may represent successful endeavours. We may, then, believe that No. 28 describes a fact.

Statement No. 29.—The 'dead', and especially the newly-dead, are helped by the prayers of mortals. Mrs. Heslop's discarnate husband stated: "We need your prayers here, just as we needed them on earth" (*op. cit.*, 1912, p. 12). As already said, this accords with Nos. 2 and 27, all three being examples of the telepathic *rapport* which may exist between the 'living' and the 'dead'. F. W. H. Myers maintained: "To believe that prayer is heard is to believe in telepathy—in the direct influence of mind on mind."

It should be noted that prayers for the dead were in use in Jewish synagogues more than two centuries B.C. (2 *Macc.*, xii, 4445). They were undoubtedly used during the Master's lifetime and He made no adverse comment. They continued for centuries as is shown by inscriptions in the Catacombs, but were discontinued by Protestants when certain Romish ideas of Purgatory were rejected. But they still are an important element in Roman Catholicism. Although St. Cyril, St. Basil, St. Augustine, St. Chrysostom, St. Ambrose, etc., all subscribed to the practice, a pamphlet published by the Protestant Truth Society in 1920 described it as pagan and contrary to the teaching of the Scriptures.

St. James (v. 16) counselled: "Pray one for another that ye may be healed. The effectual fervent prayer of a righteous man availeth much." Since prayers for the souls of fellow-mortals "avail much", does it not follow that prayers for the souls who have shed the body will also be effectual? The Protestants make the common mistake of thinking of man as a physical body and therefore supposing that there is a vast difference (and an unbridgable 'distance') between the 'living' and the 'dead', while all the evidence points to the contrary.

(a) Inherent probability, support from psychical science, etc.

Professor Flammarion (*Death and Its Mystery*, vol. iii, *After Death*) noted the fact the numerous communicators pleaded "Pray for me" or asked for Masses to be said for the repose of their souls. He also observed that when such requests were granted, unpleasant noises, etc. (at the places where such people had died) ceased. For instance, a dying man asked for Masses to be said on his behalf. His father, an agnostic, did nothing. Some nights after the son's transition both the father and mother felt a strange pressure against them and heard three knocks on a box. (In point of fact, the son, during his earth-life, had often knocked three times on this particular box.) These phenomena continued for some nights but ceased when they complied with the son's dying request. The procedure seemed to be efficacious. Flammarion could not understand these requests, with which we deal briefly in Appendix IV.

Statement No. 30.—There is so much evidence for the statement, by discarnates, that suitable mortals, namely, those who are more or less psychic, may help (i) other mortals, (ii) the dying, (iii) the newly-dead and (iv) the 'earthbound' that it would fill a small book.

(a) Cause of 'co-operation'

Many independent communicators give the same reason why mortals may be more helpful than 'ministering angels' and it is an acceptable one. The 'earthbound' often ask for help by way of prayer (see Appendix IV). In one case the mortal concerned asked them: "Why come to *us* [mortals]? Why not ask the angels?" ['deliverers', etc.]. The answer was: "Where are the angels? We have not seen any. *You are nearer to us*"[1] (compare under Statements Nos. 9 and 10).

The question has often been asked, "Why are there so many Red Indian 'guides'? Why should we expect to learn great wisdom from such people?" Apart, however, from the possible production of 'physical' phenomena, such 'guides' should seldom be expected to instruct us: in fact in many cases (though doubtless not in all) 'the shoe is on the other foot'. Sir Arthur Conan Doyle, in an article entitled 'The First Movements of the Spirit' (*Light*, vol. LXV, 1925, p. 86) said: "The Shakers [to whom the Red Indians first came, as, indeed, had been predicted] came to the unexpected conclusion that the Indians were there not to teach but to be taught. They would proselytise them, therefore, exactly as they would have done in life." He continued, obviously putting this particular matter in its right setting as an example of 'rescue circles': "A similar appearance has occurred in very many spiritualistic circles, where humble and lowly spirits have come to be taught

[1] Doris and Hilary Severn, *In the Next Room*, Constable & Co. Ltd., 1911, p. 29.

N

that which they should have learned in this world had true teachers been available." He continued, "One may well ask why the higher spirits over there do not supply this want. The answer given to the author upon one notable occasion was, '*These people are very much nearer to you than to us. You can reach them where we fail*'."

(b) Inherent probability, support from psychical science, etc.

A number of psychical researchers have suggested something of the nature of what we call 'co-operation' in various contexts. For example, Myers[1] suggested that certain cases of apparitions involved that process. He said: "I conjecture that a current of influence may be started by a *deceased person*, which, however, only becomes strong enough to be perceptible to its object when reinforced by some vivid current of emotion arising in *living minds*". (Compare our gun emplacement analogy, mentioned above). Again: "I myself hold . . . that the thought and emotion of *living persons* does largely intervene, as aiding or conditioning the independent action of *the departed*."

Statement No. 31.—We here assemble the various factors that are said to help a newly-dead man to realise that he has shed his body: (*a*) the sight of his own discarded Physical Body (No. 17); (*b*) the sight of 'dead' friends (No. 18); (*c*) the inability to make 'living' friends see or hear him (No. 28) and (*d*) the ability to pass through walls, to defy gravity, etc. In such cases the newly-dead are noting incongruities between the new and old environments. The claim that realisation of transition followed one or more of these experiences, which is a reasonable one, is not confined to 'popular' books. For example, 'F. A. Morton', communicating through Mrs. Piper, said that soon after his death (by shooting) he did not, for a moment, know where he was but his thoughts began to clear when he saw his vacated 'material body.'[2]

Statements Nos. 32 and 33.—These were considered under No. 26. Innumerable independent communicators insist that the 'next' world is 'semi-physical' in nature, earth-like, and not the 'super-physical' 'Heaven' of the Bible—that it is intermediate between earth and 'Heaven'! This has not prevented

---

Op. cit., 1907, pp. 238, 245.   [2] *Proc. S.P.R.*, xiv, p. 12.

certain clerical critics from complaining that communicators described a 'materialistic Heaven'!

Statement No. 34

(a) Causes of the judgment—experience

Whereas, our learned theologians seldom envisage the cause of the 'Judgment', and can produce no evidence for its existence (outside Biblical texts that are, nevertheless, mutually contradictory), psychic communications include both these desiderata.

Rudolf Steiner considered that the second review, or judgment-experience, was due to the loosening of the 'Astral' (here =Soul) Body from the Spiritual Body and its gradual dissolution. This may be true since the first review was regarded as caused by the loosening of the vehicle of vitality. But there is a mental, as well as a bodily, factor involved in the second review.

During earth-life consciousness, though 'normal' to us, is actually limited, 'blinkers'-like, by the Physical Body (Statement No. 1*b*). When, at death, this valuable, though restricting, instrument is shed, 'normal' consciousness gives place to the 'super-normal' type: there is an 'expansion', and a 'deepening' of awareness (No. 26), and not only do remarkable faculties (of which we may have had occasional evanescent activities during earth-life) become normal to us, but we find that we are 'nearer' than before to loved ones who are still in the flesh (No. 30). The true causes and the necessary consequences of our words and deeds, our underlying motives and true characters (which were more or less hidden from the lesser self) become clear to us in the un-enshrouded Soul Body.

Solomon said (Prov. xx. 24): "Man's goings are of the Lord (operating through the Greater Self); how can a man [the personality or lesser self] then understand his own way?" It is the Inner, Real, Greater, Higher, Transcendent and Eternal Self, the Over-Soul or Individuality, which 'judges' the works of the outer, shadowy, lesser, lower, immanent and temporary self, the soul or personality. Since all Over-Souls, or Greater Selves, as St. Paul (Eph. iv. 25) said, are "members one of another", and since, as Jesus pointed out (John xv. 5), all are "branches" of the Christ-spirit or "True Vine" (of which 'the Father' is "the Life"—John v. 26), the 'Judgment' of the Greater Self is necessarily also the Judgment of God. This conception, which differs so markedly from the current orthodox idea, was indicated by the Master (John xii. 48) when he said, "I judge no man. . . . I came not to judge, but to save", and He added: "The Word [i.e. true Conscience, the Voice of the Greater Self] shall judge you. . . ."

The fact that we are essentially "members one of another" means that, in the 'Judgment', we ourselves experience the emotions that were experienced by others as a result of our thoughts, words and deeds. Even while we were on earth our separate existence was apparent and not real: whether we were aware of it or not, we were "our brother's keeper". The fact is now realised.

Another cause of the 'Judgment'-experience is that there has been a change from the predominantly *objective* existence in the Physical Body to a predominantly *subjective* existence in the Soul Body—a change of emphasis (see remarks under Nos. 25 and 26*d*): that which was 'hidden' during physical embodiment necessarily now becomes 'manifest'. (Matt. x. 26; Mark. iv. 22; Luke viii. 17).

(b) *Internal consistency or coherence of communications*

Communicators' statements regarding the 'Judgment' accord with their statements about the total constitution of man (No. 1*b*) and the processes involved in transition (Nos. 2, 6, 8, 9, 13-33).

There is also coherence concerning the incidence of the 'Judgment'. 'Earthbound' men are said to owe their condition to the fact that they have not yet shed the vehicle of vitality (and they remain in 'Hades' conditions until they do so). Among these people, suicides, etc. often say that their after-death experiences include mechanically reviewing, over and over again, certain acts that they performed during earth-life, i.e. their abnormal 'passing' involves an abnormal first (non-emotional) review (Statement No. 5). The second (emotional) review, i.e. the 'Judgment', is said to come *after* the vehicle of vitality has been shed. In point of fact, I have not seen a single case in which an obviously 'earthbound' person (who had not passed through the 'second death') said that he had experienced his 'Judgment'. On the other hand, some communicators say that certain unrepentantly evil among the 'earthbound' are deliberately postponing the 'second death' and prolonging their stay in 'Hades' conditions in order to avoid their 'Judgment'—in the religious idom they are refusing to 'repent'; in the psychological sense they are refusing to 'ab-react'; in financial terms they are refusing to discharge their liabilities. As one communicator said: "Only those who have shed that dense body [=the vehicle of vitality] which was theirs on quitting the still denser Physical Body, experience the 'Judgment.'"[1] The examination of numerous independent individual accounts reveals harmony with this generalisation.

Communications contain concordances concerning the idea of the 'Judgment' as regards its cause, its occurrence, its nature and its incidence. Its effects are also concordant and understandable. Communicators claim that it cleanses and purifies the surviving soul from any remaining selfish tendencies. In this connection we note that Ivan Cooke (*Light*, vol. 1, 1930, p. 538) stated, "During a long experience, I have not met with one 'devil'," and F. W. H. Myers[2] observed: "I can find nothing worse than living men; I seem to discern not an intensification but a disintegration of selfishness, malevolence, pride." (Compare the conception of Group Souls, p. 48.)

The orthodox idea corresponds with that given in communications and that at which Ivan Cooke and F. W. H. Myers arrived from a study of communications. "Judgment", says the *Report Towards the Conversion of England* (1945, p. 35), "is the ultimate separation of the evil from the good, with the consequent destruction of all that opposes itself to God's will." It adds: "Such must be the precursor and condition of unfettered life with God. . . . Ultimately all that is found valueless in God's sight will be abolished, that that which He can use may be set free and 'God may be all in all' (I Cor. xv. 28)."

Dr. Leslie Weatherhead (*After Death*, Epworth Press, 1923, p. 58) pointed out that the popular idea of the Judgment (as a general sort of Assize), based on Matthew xxv, describes a *principle* rather than a *form*. His idea of the Judgment corresponds to that given by numerous communicators through mediums who had no theological training whatever. Weatherhead said: "When a soul passes into the next world, spiritual values shine out supreme. In this light, the soul views its own spiritual state. It passes Judgment on itself. . . . So a man is

[1] Ivan Cooke, *Thy Kingdom Come*, Wright and Brown.   [2] *Op. cit.*, 1907, p. 252.

. . . judged both by himself (I Cor. v. 10) and, in a sense, by Christ. But he is not judged as a prisoner is judged by a magistrate."

(c) Inherent probability, support from psychical science, etc.

As already said (No. 5), the claims, made by the 'dead' that at the very point of death, they experienced a panoramic, non-emotional review of the past earth-life, is supported by the fact that many men (who almost died) independently described having passed through that experience. This is also true of the 'second review', the 'Judgment'-experience: a few men (people, we suggest, of a relatively advanced type and therefore with relatively 'loose' Soul Bodies) who almost died and yet recovered, have independently described having experienced this type of review of the past earth-life. The following are examples:

(1) We first cite the case of Violet Burton (*My Larger Life*, Rider & Co. Ltd., pp. 58, 123) as a person who, on different occasions, experienced each of the 'reviews', the 'first' and the 'second'. When she was nearly drowned, she said, "The pictures of my life presented themselves to me exactly as the events had taken place", but they were unaccompanied by emotion, a realisation of motives, effects, responsibility, etc. On a later occasion, she reviewed the "same pictures" but the motives by which she had been actuated became clear to her.

(2) Dr. J. Haddock (*Somnolism and Psycheism*, London, 1851) and H. Martineau[1] mentioned the case of Admiral Sir Francis Beaufort, who was almost drowned when a "youngster". Beaufort said that *as soon as, considering it useless to try and save himself, he relinquished all effort, pain vanished* (No. 7) and his sensations were "of a rather pleasurable cast". He continued: "Though the senses were thus deadened, not so the mind; its activity seemed to be invigorated in a ratio which defies all description." The whole of his life, including "many trifling events", passed before his mind: *each act was "accompanied by a consciousness of right or wrong, or by some reflection on its cause or its consequences"*. Beaufort considered that, since he had undergone temporary death, a similar experience may well follow actual death—that he had had a fore-taste of the 'Judgment'.

[1] *Biographical Sketches*, 4th ed., pp. 219-30.

(3) The case was reported of a man who, on three successive nights, reviewed his past life, being affected by their *"moral significance"*.[1]

(4) 'John the Prophet', almost dying, on awakening from coma, said that "his sins had been read out to him."[2]

(5) An officer who was left for dead in war said that he saw "all his sinful actions pass in review through his mind".[3]

(6) 'Starr Daily', an ex-convict, sank into a coma [=shed the body]. He said: "I dreamed while I seemed to be wide awake. It was like a scroll or a motion-picture film, which began to unroll slowly before my vision. *The only pictures on it were of people I had injured.* A vast number of these people I knew or had seen. Then there were hundreds I had never seen; these were people who had been indirectly injured by me. The minute history of my long criminal career was thus re-lived by me, *plus* all the small injuries I had inflicted unconsciously by my thoughtless words and looks and omissions. *The most terrifying thing about it was that every pang of suffering I had caused others was now felt by me as the scroll unwound itself* [compare the experiences described by the newly-dead, cited in the First Part]. This dream occurred no less than a dozen times during the next few weeks. . . . One morning I woke with a sense of well-being, quite free from pain and fear. I knew I would recover."[4] This portion of the total experience was followed by a review of all the good deeds he had done and all the men he had helped. (It should be noted that Beaufort, 'John the Prophet' and 'Starr Daily', like the 'deliverers' mentioned in No. 4*j*, did not wait until "the end of the Age" for the 'Judgment'. Also that still-embodied persons often have the death-experience, up to and including the first review, but few proceed as far as the second review.)

(7) Just as partial experiences of the first review are known among people who are still in the flesh (and, indeed, can be produced experimentally, by hypnosis), so partial 'Judgments' can be produced experimentally in mortals—by stimulating areas of the brain with a fine electrode. Dr. Penfold found that when a patient, under a local anaesthetic, was so treated, the procedure aroused detailed memories, each memory

[1] Dr. Carl du Prel, *The Philosophy of Mysticism*, Redway, 1889.
[2] *Ibid.*   [3] *Notes and Queries*, 12th Series, vol. 1, p. 97, 1916.
[4] 'Starr Daily' (*nom de plume*), *Release*, Simpkin, Marshall.

being accompanied by the appropriate (original) emotion.

The present point is that communications concerning 'the second review', like those concerning the first review (cited in our discussion of No. 5), cannot be dismissed as due to telepathy from the 'living' or to the potential omniscience of mediums (since they are also described by 'living' people who did not consult mediums). This phenomenon is also observed among people who claim to have left their bodies temporarily, i.e. 'astral projectors'—some, after having shed the Physical Body, described experiencing the first review and a few claimed to undergo the second; again no mediums were consulted. The evidence strongly suggested that the statement of the 'dead' concerning the two 'reviews' refer to actual experiences of surviving personalities.

The concordance that subsists between the statements of *discarnate communicators* and those of *psychics* concerning acts committed during earth-life is also remarkable: they have an obvious bearing on the nature of the 'Judgment'-experience, as outlined above. A communicator said, "I, like you, was insensitive (while in physical embodiment) to the physical effects of anger, love, etc. I had to wait for them to issue in tones, words, expressions. I thought that I responded in my behaviour only to these. I was, of course, wrong in so thinking because *the hidden interplay of emotions was always the largest part of every situation in life.* But now [that I am dis-embodied] I can make no such mistake. . . . The etheric [here = Soul] body must register them as 'physical' facts."[1]

Statements identical with these are made by the well-known psychic, Mrs. Eileen J. Garrett, on the basis not of communications received but of her own personal observations. She said: "The impacts which I saw taking place in the 'surrounds', or 'auras', of people as they met and reacted to each other's thoughts and emotions, constantly disturbed me [as a young child]. I saw how people's conflicts rocked them without their understanding why, and I became aware that people were thus the unconscious victims of each other's moods."[2]

Phoebe Payne[3] another psychic of outstanding ability and

[1] Jane Sherwood, *The Psychic Bridge*, Rider & Co. Ltd., p. 34.
[2] Mrs. Eileen J. Garrett, *My Life as a Search for the Meaning of Mediumship*, Rider & Co. Ltd., 1939, p. 15.
[3] Phoebe Payne and Dr. L. J. Bendit, *The Psychic Sense*, Faber and Faber, 1943, p. 120.

undoubted integrity, also referred to this subject. She mentioned people who are so fundamentally different that they are unable to meet without mutual irritation and said "When they clash actively, their auras strike one another with a hard edge and psychic sparks literally fly." She continued: "When the situation has not actively flared up, their concealed irritation makes their auras act like a file or sand-paper: there is *objective* friction between them, which causes psychic wear and tear. . . . To the clairvoyant they look frayed and worn." Miss Payne (Mrs. L. J. Bendit) pointed out that children are particularly sensitive to psychic impacts: "An excited and exuberant person may cause a real psychic assault on the aura of a little child. It is not necessary for the excitement to have been directed at the child, nor for it to have been unpleasant and angry; if the victim has been within the radius of the blast, he can be badly jarred."

A similar statement occurs in Jane Sherwoods' communications from 'Scott'[1] though in a different connection. When she (incarnate) became attuned to her (discarnate) communicator, she said that she felt his emotions and *vice versa*, giving this example: "I am immersed in activity and have forgotten 'Scott's' presence. He is immersed in his own thoughts and has forgotten me. *He* recalls some incident from his past which kindles anger in him, and *I* feel a searing pain which has no connection with my present thought or present experience. . . . In the same way, *my* anger or impatience harm *him*." 'Scott' went further: he said that he had 'registered', with great pain, anger that had been directed to the incarnate Jane Sherwood. Moreover, *he* had felt the *full* effects of it, whereas *she* [because shielded, insulated, screened, 'blinkered' and protected by the Physical Body] did not.

The same idea was given in *Life Beyond the Grave*: "All persons are more or less *en rapport* with the spirit-world; and their spirit-friends know more of the thoughts that are directed against them than they do themselves."

This anonymous communicator[2] said that appreciation and kindly thoughts of other mortals benefits the 'senders' (by raising their confidence in themselves) while criticism and harsh thoughts injured the 'senders' by lowering their confidence

[1] *The Psychic Bridge*, Rider & Co. Ltd., pp. 33, 34.
[2] *Life Beyond the Grave*, E. W. Allen, 1876, p. 108.

in themselves, and pointed out that, "in a world where *all* forces are spiritual [i.e. in the 'next' world] these effects are much more marked than in the physical world". He then made the following statement (which links these matters up with the 'Judgment-'experience): "You see, from this, that spirits can never be happy until they have obtained the forgiveness of those they have injured." He added: "The harbouring of evil thoughts brings its own punishment, for it prevents the thinker from rising in the spirit-world. . . . Without love, he cannot rise."

Jane Sherwood's communicator[1] made the same declaration that, in the 'next' world, "no one willingly courts the hostility of others; it is too painful". On the contrary, "He desires, above all things, to avoid the experience of another's anger and to enjoy the flooding-forth of that other's goodwill". He said: "*You* know that *fire* will burn . . . *we* avoid *anger* because we know it will burn us in just the same actual sense." He insisted that, to them, the only wealth is love and goodwill.

Statements such as the above, made both by clairvoyants and discarnate communicators, accord with others (made independently) by communicators to the effect that we mortals are by no means so distinct and separate from each other as the 'blinkers'-effect of the body makes us imagine: each has grave responsibilities as his 'brother's keeper'. The physical body, while permitting the development of individuality, facilitating the formation of mental habits and encouraging the development of initiative, tends to hide the fact that we are essentially "members one of another". When earth-life terminates and the body is shed, this fact becomes abundantly clear in the course of the 'Judgment'-experience.

(d) Support from eminent theologians

The Judgment-experience is an essential element in all religions. The ancient Egyptian dead were described as first affirming their freedom from certain evil deeds ("I have not blasphemed; I have not stolen", etc.) and then claiming their good deeds ("I have given food to the hungry . . . and clothes to the naked").[2]

---

[1] *The Psychic Bridge*, Rider & Co. Ltd., p. 61.
[2] Le Normant, *Book of Hades* in *Records of the Past*, x, pp. 79-134, and *The Funeral Ritual*, *Manual of Ancient History*, i, pp. 308, 313 (English trans., 1869).

Christian theologians are divisible into three main groups concerning this matter.

The first, and largest, group consists of those who still subscribe to the old idea of a *general* Judgment (for all mankind) which will take place at "the end of the world" (or Age).

The second group comprises those who admit their essential ignorance of this matter. In spite of the fact that they had ample opportunities for comparing views, and in spite of their great theological and philosophical learning, the authors of the authoritative volume *Doctrine in the Church of England* (1938) admitted that the question of an after-death state that is intermediate between earth and 'Heaven' (i.e. of 'Paradise'), and the idea of a general Day of Judgment (for all mankind, at 'the end of the Age') present such "great difficulties" that they could not agree on the matter. [Note the marked contrast in the teachings of communications on these questions: this is remarkable whether they are regarded as emanating from the incarnate mediums or discarnate communicators. In spite of the fact that the latter had no opportunity to compare views, and in spite of their lack of theological or philosophical training, all make the same readily-understood statement: that the 'Judgment'-experience is normally undergone relatively soon after death and that it is not a general and a universal, but an individual, experience. It should be said that "the end of the Age"—John iii. 16; Matt. xxv, 46—refers neither to the end of the *world* nor to anything '*everlasting*', but to the completion of a quite indefinite period of time, an epoch.]

At a recent Churchmen's Congress in Cambridge, the Rev. C. J. Wright pointed out: "There are a *number* of possible and permissible theories of what is called the Resurrection,[1] the Ascension and the Judgment." D. H. C. Read, B.D.,[2] considered: "The most that we have a right to believe *in the light of the Gospel* is that the life beyond the grave is richer and fuller than this one, and that it consists in a continued growth into the image of Christ—together."

The third group consists of thinkers and their teachings are in agreement with those of the unlearned communicators.

---

[1] An excellent study of the Resurrection by the Rev. J. Pearce-Higgins is published by the Churches' Fellowship of Psychical Study.

[2] *The Christian Faith*, English Universities Press Ltd., 1956, p. 163.

Dr. Cyril Alington (*The Fool Hath Said*, Longmans, Green & Co. Ltd., 1933) said: "You all know what you have chosen to be, and what you choose must ultimately be your destiny. There is no need to look forward to that spectacular Day of Judgment which the Jews conceived and the Romans elaborated. The Judgment has already begun and it is you who pronounce your own inevitable sentence."

The learned Dane, Dr. H. Martensen, Bishop of Seeland, said: "The Kingdom of the dead, unlike that of the physical world, is not one of *words and deeds*, for they no longer possess the conditions upon which words and deeds are possible. . . . Theirs is a Kingdom of *subjectivity, of thought, remembrance and self-fathoming*. . . . The soul now enters into its own recesses. . . . Hence rises the purgatorial nature of this state." Martensen continued with a passage very reminiscent of the communicator of the English Jane Sherwood: "As long as man is in this present world, he is in a Kingdom of *externals*, wherein he can escape from self-contemplation and self-knowledge by distractions . . . but at death . . . his soul finds itself in a Kingdom of pure realities. The voices of this world grow dumb . . . ; hence the realm of the dead becomes a realm of judgment."[1]

Statements Nos. 35-42.

(a) *Internal consistency of coherence of communications*

These affirmations have all been discussed incidentally above. They are coherent with each other and accord with the general philosophical basis of communications.

(b) *Inherent probability, support from psychical science, etc.*

There is clairvoyant support for the statements of communicators concerning the 'earthbound' (people who are in a protracted 'chrysalis' condition, since the vehicle of vitality has remained enshrouding the Soul Body for a period markedly beyond the average three or four days.) Mrs. Garrett[2] described such a case. She said: "He loved himself and he loved his life and clung to it decade after decade of our time. . . ." Then followed a typical description of the 'chrysalis' state in general: "Those who return [to communicate] in such fashion would appear to be in a half-world of confusion—a world

---

[1] *Christian Dogmatics*, Clark's Foreign Theological Library, p. 460.
[2] Mrs. Eileen J. Garrett, *Awareness*, Creative Press Inc., 1943, p. 213.

caught between waking and sleeping, where the dream-experience becomes a reality and too often a nightmare." The latter is a good description of the environment which is variously called the 'astral plane', 'Hades', 'Shadow-land' or the 'Plane of Illusion' (the 'hypnagogic' state of psychologists). In this state, mental images (or 'thought-forms'), may be mistaken for, and confused with, objective persons (Soul Bodies) and things (the 'doubles' of physical objects): the environment is therefore, shifting, uncertain and bewildering. In Appendix III we point out that those in the 'Hades' state relatively easily communicate with mortals—but, like 'Raymond' (Lodge), they are liable to communicate their *'dreams'*, either in place of, or as well as, genuine observations.

A communicator told Lord Balfour (*Proc. S.P.R.*, xliii, 1935, p. 188) that there are three kinds of telepathy, i.e. (1) "something like two big clouds coming together and then the lightening"; (2) "the coma-business, dream-business", and (3) "a leak".

CORRELATION SCRUTINISED AND TESTED

(a) inherent probability, support from psychical science, etc.

The basic idea implied in communications, that earth-life and the successive after-death states ('Hades', 'Paradise' and the true 'Heavens') exhibit corresponding 'levels' of consciousness ('normal', 'sub-normal', 'super-normal' and 'Spiritual' respectively) both of which are determined by the bodily constitution at the time (Physical Body, vehicle of vitality, Soul Body and Spiritual Body respectively—see Fig. 2) is supported by independently-made statements, and these by actual observations.

(1) In the process of transition the Soul Body leaves the Physical Body first and most easily, then the vehicle of vitality is exteriorised, though relatively slowly and sometimes with more or less difficulty. Correlated with this succession of events there is a succession of states of consciousness. While the vehicle of vitality is in process of disengaging from the Physical Body, neither the latter nor the Soul Body is available as an instrument of consciousness: hence there is a period of coma which varies in duration according to circumstances.

(2) The correlation is supported by the statements of numerous people who did not obtain communications from discarnate friends through mediums (and some of whom were even markedly averse from doing so), that when *temporarily* out of the body, they also experienced the various 'levels' of consciousness that are described by the 'dead'. The present writer (*The Theory and Practice of Astral Projection*) show sthat in these cases also the 'level' of consciousness was determined by the bodily constitution at the time. An actual instance may here be briefly cited. A man who had a weak heart and who left his body temporarily, described his experience in *Borderland*, vol. iii, 1896: when his double was free from the physical body his consciousness included "a magnificent sense of freedom, knowledge and power" and his environment was the 'glorified earth' which is designated 'Paradise' or 'the Garden of Eden'.

He continued: "Then I felt a slight pull upon me and saw that *a shadowy thread . . . extended from me through the air . . .* [=*the 'silver cord' by which his liberated double was still attached to his vacated physical body.*] *It was as if this pull had altered all my vibrations and changed my state of consciousness, for now I ceased to see the wonders about me* [='*Paradise*'] *and saw instead the buildings on the snow far beneath* [*the physical world*]. *Yes, I had returned to a lower order of matter. . . .*"

(3) It is stated by discarnate communicators, and confirmed by the observations of 'astral projectors', that the latter, while visiting 'Paradise' conditions and with some 'super-normal' consciousness, never attain the full state that will be theirs after transition has completely detached them from the Physical Body. The reason given in a number of independent communications is such as one would expect if the 'level' of awareness were, in fact, determined by the bodily constitution—it is that in 'astral projection' the complete Soul Body of the earthly 'visitor' is not available as an instrument of consciousness, since part of it forms the 'cord'-connection between the (exteriorised) Soul Body, and the (vacated) Physical Body. The 'level' of consciousness is thus affected by a bodily factor, in this case the 'silver cord', which, as it were, the Soul Body, 'lends'! (In addition, it is probable that the exteriorised Soul Bodies of many 'astral projectors' are slightly enveiled by portions of the vehicle of vitality, constituting another bodily factor.)

(4) Communications include the statement that the 'vibrational gulf' between mortals and relatively 'advanced' discarnate souls (in 'Paradise' conditions) may be so great that, in order to achieve the attunement necessary for communicating, the difference has, as it were, to be halved—the discarnate communicator is obliged to 'borrow' a bodily factor, in this case extoplasm, from the medium. The process involves a partial re-embodiment by the would-be communicator and therefore affects his 'level' of consciousness. In this case, the '*borrowed*' bodily factor 'lowers' his 'level' of consciousness (see Diagram 5). Meanwhile, as would be expected, the process has the reverse effect on the medium concerned: her '*loan*' of this bodily factor was a partial disembodiment, 'raising' her 'level' of consciousness. With this double effect, communication became possible.

(5) When the bodily-factor (ectoplasm) is *'borrowed'* in very large amounts by a discarnate soul from a 'physical' medium (if such a process does indeed—as we believe—occur), there is a correspondingly great effect on the 'level' of consciousness of both the discarnate and incarnate souls concerned. The medium who *'lends'* the ectoplasm is typically unconscious (in deep trance) and her Physical Body is death-like, while the discarnate 'borrower' exhibits relatively poor intelligence. A. Campbell Holms[1] made this point. He said: "The so-called 'materialised spirit' is but a dim reflection of the spirit's own personality. Even the most perfect materialised form usually displays mental capabilities of a very feeble order." The explanation which he proffered for his observation agrees, in part, with that which we advance: "Probably the continuous materialising effort and *the close association with flesh-and-blood conditions* is sufficient to inhibit the display of the higher mental faculties."

A communicator of Oswald Murray (*The Spiritual Universe*, Duckworth, 1924, p. 166) said the same as Holms. He insisted that "materialisations" usually represent discarnate souls who are in "the first after-death state", i.e. 'Hades', and continued: "In such cases the spirits themselves are not the operators—they are subjects acted upon by higher operators who have the requisite knowledge and power. . . . The original spirits thus represented are then subjects acted upon, so *they are temporarily in a second state. This explains why so little information with regard to their normal environment, etc., can be got from such forms.*"

(6) The correlation between the bodily constitution and the 'level' of consciousness attainable, was obtained by the present writer from analyses of statements by supposed *discarnate communicators*. The well-known *clairvoyant*, Mrs. Eileen J. Garrett (*My Life as a Search for the Meaning of Mediumship*, Rider & Co. Ltd., 1939, p. 214) arrived at an essentially similar conclusion from personal observations of her own supernormal faculties—namely, clairvoyance, telepathy, 'astral' projection', prediction of the future, etc. She said: "Each phase of consciousness is wrapped within some form of vehicle, subtle and invisible though it may be, which is appropriate to the state of evolution of its being" (see also p. 224).

---

[1] *The Facts of Psychic Science and Philosophy*, Kegan Paul, Trench, Trubner & Co. Ltd., 1925, p. 381.

(7) This idea was also held by the ancient Polynesians (who, it should be noted, could neither read nor write and who had been cut off from the rest of the world until the discoveries of Captain Cook in 1778: see Max Freedom Long's book *The Secret Science at Work*, Kosmon Press Ltd., 1953, p. 10).

(8) We have frequently pointed out that ideas which are unanimously given to us by 'communicators' from beyond (who had no means of comparing each other's statements) were eventually arrived at by psychical researchers (as the result of decades of investigation and co-operation). The present one that the bodily constitution determines the 'level' of consciousness—is another example of this noteworthy fact. Dr. Raynor C. Johnson (*Psychical Research*, English Universities Press Ltd., 1955, p. 165) said: "It may well be that the psychical faculty is the normal and characteristic faculty of mind when not geared closely to a physical body. The physical brain may normally be an organ of limitation. It canalises the sensory aspects of the psychical faculty through the special senses, and it canalises the motor aspects of the psychical faculty through the cerebrospinal nervous system and the muscles." He suggested: "There is a fringe or slight residue of unchannelled psychical faculty which can be detected statistically by the experimental methods of psychical research. *The marked and dramatic phenomena become evidence, however, only when the mind and brain are uncoupled to a substantial extent, as in trance. . . .*" Using the terms employed in this book, it is when the Soul Body is almost entirely released from the 'blinkers'-like physical body that telepathy, clairvoyance, etc., are seen at their best: the Soul is then almost in its normal state—on earth it is 'in exile', 'in prison', etc.

(*b*) *Internal consistency or coherence of communications*

(1) Many individual communications accord with the basic idea under consideration. For example, 'Philip'[1] observed: "It is difficult for me to visualise the ['Hades'] condition of those described in Lychgate." He gave the reason for this in another communication later in his book (without reference to this one): it was that after death, he had been "only a couple of hours" with the vehicle of vitality enveiling the Soul Body. This was doubtless because he was of high spiritual

---

[1] Alice Gilbert, *op. cit.*, 1948, pp. 139, 206.

development. He had had practically no experience of 'Hades' conditions. Later (p. 219) 'Philip' said: "Once you enter the flesh, nothing can save you from its laws and conditions. You just have to adapt as well as you can." (This statement about the 'blinker'-like effect of the body (No. 1*b*) offers an explanation of many puzzling things, including our forgetfulness of out-of-the-body experiences.)

(2) Another 'pointer' to the fact that the 'level' of consciousness is determined by the prevailing bodily constitution is represented by the 'dual' or 'alternate' consciousness (which obtains when two almost separate bodies are employed (either simultaneously or successively) as instruments of consciousness—No. 21). When, during earth-life, a single body (the physical) is the effective instrument (since the Soul Body is 'in gear' with it), there is a single 'level'—namely, 'normal' consciousness; when (after the 'second death'), there is again a single instrument of consciousness (the Soul Body), there is also a single 'level', i.e. 'super-normal' consciousness. But during the earliest stages of death, in those (relatively rare) cases in which the 'silver cord' remains intact for an appreciable time, consciousness may operate simultaneously, or alternately, in *two* bodies (the Physical Body and the Soul Body), producing 'dual' or 'alternate' consciousness.

It is significant that this phenomenon, the existence of which is supported by communications from women who stated that wedding-rings had been removed soon after transition, that a lock of hair had been cut off, that the face had received a slight accidental scratch, etc., though (as might be expected) rare in *permanent* separations of the double from the physical body, is quite common in *temporary* separations (i.e. in accounts of 'astral projectors'). This accords with the claim that the 'silver cord' transmits impressions both from and to the double. Only rarely, we are told, does it remain intact for an appreciable time after death: in temporary separations, however, it invariably remains intact throughout. The severance of the 'cord' means death.

(3) A circumstance that is even more significant is commonly observed in temporary separations of the double from the body: 'dual' consciousness obtains so long as the exteriorised double remain within *a certain 'distance'* of the vacated body ("the range of cord activity" or "critical distance"—commonly up

to about twelve or fifteen feet), but if and when the exteriorised double moves beyond that 'distance', the 'cord' is too 'thin' to transmit ordinary physical stimuli to the double and consciousness ceases to be 'dual'. It then operates through the double alone, giving impressions of the environment corresponding to it and not that corresponding to the Physical Body.

But an unusually violent physical stimulus, such as the banging of a door, is transmitted to the double, in spite of the tenuity of the 'cord', causing a return to the body, often with a 'jump', 'jolt', 'jerk', technically called a 'repercussion.' There is evidence of repercussion' in the closely-related phenomena of 'materialisation' (in which almost all of the densest portion of the double, i.e. the vehicle of vitality, is exteriorised from the Physical Body): here 'repercussion' undoubtedly occurs and may cause physical injury (including bleeding). These matters are discussed in detail in two books to be published by the present writer, *The Theory and Practice of Astral Projection* and *Events on the Threshold of the After-life.* They are mentioned here to show that the phenomenon of 'dual' consciousness supports the idea that the 'level' of consciousness is determined by the prevailing bodily constitution, whether during earth-life, during the process of transition or in the successive states of the after-life.

We suggest that certain mortals who exhibit dissociation of the mind will eventually be found to have a corresponding dissociation in the total bodily constitution (and especially a 'break' between the physical body and the vehicle of vitality). It is probable that in some cases the mental dissociation is caused by bodily defect: if so, it will prove intractable until the latter has been remedied.

(c) Converse communications

Conversely, discarnate souls are said to be unable to see our physical bodies, or physical surroundings, unless and until they enter the 'auras' of mediums, i.e. *re-embody* themselves in substance from the vehicle of vitality. Thus, when the mother of 'Raymond' (Lodge) asked the 'control', "When does Raymond see me?" she received the reply: "When a medium is present."[1] Curtiss[2] was similarly told that the newly-dead do

---

[1] *Op. cit.*, 1916, p. 159.   [2] *Op. cit.*, p. 46.

not see the Physical Bodies of mortals except in the presence
of "certain types of physical medium". 'A.B.'s'[1] communicator
also said: "We do not see your Physical Bodies unless a very
strong medium is present."

In these cases, that portion of the 'physical' medium's
vehicle of vitality which is exteriorised enables discarnate
souls in the neighbourhood to become *partially re-embodied*, a
process which 'lowers' their 'level' of consciousness so that
physical matter can be cognised. Here also the '*borrowed*' bodily
factor (ectoplasm) has 'lowered' the 'level' of consciousness.

This ectoplasmic bodily factor may not be 'borrowed' from
others but may be *one's own* and merely reassumed by an incarnate person who is out of the body—yet the effect described
is essentially similar. The well-known and non-professional
medium, Mme. d'Espérance (*Shadow Land*, Redway, 1897),
when out of the physical body, and in the unenshrouded Soul
Body, wished to help certain of the 'earthbound' (=men whose
Soul Bodies were enshrouded by the vehicle of vitality), she
said: "*I must clothe myself with mist*" [=re-embody herself in
her own vehicle of vitality in order to attune to the 'earthbound'
conditions]. It was a repugnant thought, yet I would do it."
(*See also* 'Stead', etc., cited on p. 224, Appendix III.)

[1] *Op. cit.*, 1937, p. 169.

CONCLUSIONS

(a) The internal consistency and inherent probability of communications

The statements from 'beyond' concerning man's experiences at, and soon after, death, have been neglected by psychical researchers, yet they exhibit significant coherence and, in addition, many are inherently probable, since they accord with certain observations and established facts. Although a number of these statements, when envisaged in isolation, are incredible, when they are considered in the light of the whole philosophy that is advanced, they are at least eminently reasonable. Internal coherence, by itself, it not a satisfactory criterion of truth, but when to this is added concordance with extraneous facts, the case is extremely strong.

It may be asked, "Why do not communicators provide a simple, systematic and logical account of the process of death and the conditions of the after-life, with all the complicated inter-relationships rendered explicit from the start?" Many people have feebly suggested, "We are not meant to know!" The answer is twofold. In the first place, psychics, artists, poets, musicians and geniuses produce their distinctive works from a 'deep', non-systematic, non-logical, normally inaccessible 'level' of the total self, i.e. from the intermediate, or psychic, self and the Greater Self: they (the lesser selves) can seldom analyse and systematise them. Other men (who may lack the psychic sensitivity or genius) must undertake that work. Psychic productions, we suggest, come from consciousness working through the Soul Body (which gives 'super-normal' consciousness), while the work of genius involve the use of the Spiritual Body (which gives 'Spiritual', 'mystical' or 'cosmic' experiences). Intellectual, logical and systematic thought is produced when consciousness works through *the physical brain*. We should not expect psychic communications to be systematically and logically expressed or to have a noteworthy content of physical science. Analysis and synthesis is essentially the work of ordinary mortals. "I have noticed", said Leonardo de Vinci, "that when one paints one should *think of nothing*." On the other hand, a perusal of Sir

Joshua Reynold's *Discourses on Art,* representing an analysis of
the artist's methods, though interesting, is quite barren without
an essential touch of genius.

In the second place, those who communicate with mortals
most easily and most often are not highly advanced and
knowledgeable souls (see Appendix III); in general, their
opinions are as diverse as they were during earth-life. (This
does not prevent their descriptions of what they *experienced,*
at and soon after, death bearing a definite relationship to
fact.)

(b) A basic conception in communications

A basic conception implicit in communications from
'Beyond'—the idea that the 'level' of awareness is determined
by the bodily constitution that prevails at any given period of
our existence (whether here or hereafter)—is clearly of great
importance.

First, it suggests that there is Consciousness that immeasurably transcends anything that mortals can imagine or con-
ceive. (The various names which men have given to this
transcendent Consciousness are unimportant.)

Secondly, it provides us with a reasonable explanation of
the fact that, while all the greatest men, namely, the true
mystics, true poets, etc., are convinced of a Supreme Being and
of an after-life, the majority of ordinary people are either
indifferent to, or vaguely doubtful about, such important
matters. Coleridge insisted that "Poetry has a logic of its own,
as severe as that of science and more difficult, because more
subtle, more complex and dependent on more fugitive causes".
"'Tis we musicians know", declared Browning. Dean Inge
said: "New outpourings of the Spirit come rather to poets
than to theologians. . . . Our clearest visions of the invisible
are enshrined in our poetry." Average people have little, if
any, knowledge of the physically invisible realms that are
glimpsed by true poets, artists, musicians and mystics (each of
whom expresses his vision in his own way). Most average people
are entirely *unconscious* of any details of any out-of-the-body
experiences (which they nevertheless very probably enjoy
during deep sleep) and most are *unconscious* of the receipt of
either psychic impressions or Spiritual impulses (which they
doubtless nevertheless receive at all times and in all places,

whether 'asleep' or 'awake'). We all live, as it were, at the bottom of a well—the Physical Body—which not merely limits but tends entirely to suppress, our knowledge of these high matters. "Surely," declared Jacob (Gen. xxviii. 16) awakening, i.e. re-entering the body, from an inspired 'dream', "the Lord is in this place—and *I knew it not.*" Like all true mystics (and poets) he had had a convincing glimpse of the Spiritual world. Most people reject such reports not because they are untrue but because their own 'wells' are so deep, their own bodies so dense, their own activities so predominantly worldly, that they are *unaware* of their own 'higher' contacts, on both psychic and Spiritual 'levels'. "In the Kingdom of the Blind the one-eyed man is King."

Nevertheless, *intellectual* studies, such as those given in this book, show that the psychics and the true mystic and poet, by and large, have been reporting truly. Such being the case, would it not be wise if those who, at present, are among the 'blind' provisionally accepted our main thesis and ordered their lives on that basis? They would at least then provide the conditions under which they could obtain certainty, i.e. by way of first-hand, conscious experience (see Appendix V).

"If any man will do the will", declared the Master, "He will know of the doctrine, whether it be of God" (John vii. 17). While it is true that *intellectual* studies, by themselves, may be barren and even deceptive (I Cor. xiii. 8), they should not be despised. They may provide the beginnings of a successful search for "the pearl of great price" (Matt. xiv. 45)—for only when the modern man sees that there is good reason to believe in its existence will he begin to seek it and, having found it, pay "the price"—which is "all that he has".

(c) *The harmony of the several lines of approach*

We have mentioned five lines of approach to the problem of transition and the immediate hereafter. Although, as might be expected, there are differences in detail, all lead to substantially the same conclusions. The first consists of *Scriptural revelation*. The second is represented by those results of clairvoyant investigation that are grouped under the general term '*Occultism*'[1] (a modern statement of which is Theosophy). The

---

[1] See, for example, C. M. Waterlow, 'Psycho-analysis and Occultism', *Light*, LXXIV, 1954, p. 16.

third is *Aldous Huxley's study of perception*.[1] The fourth consists
of *mediumistic communications concerning earth-memories that constitute direct evidence for surviving personalities*. This evidence,
however, as already said, suffers from the possibility that some
(though not all) of it may be explained as due to the telepathic
powers of mediums, to their potential omniscience, etc. The
fifth line of approach—that considered in this book, *analyses
of psychic communications concerning experiences*—provides evidence
of an indirect nature only, but it is unaffected by the telepathy-
or-omniscience hypothesis. *These "travellers' tales" clearly bear
the stamp of truth.*

(d) The nature of communicators

There are undoubtedly *pseudo*-communications, as well as
possible *genuine* ones that emanate from surviving souls (see
the introductory sentences to Appendix III). The present
question is whether the communications that have been cited
and analysed in these pages came from the living dead (and
are therefore examples of genuine communications) or from
the 'sub-conscious minds', 'splits' or 'partial personalities' of
the mediums concerned (and are therefore merely *pseudo*-
communications).

There are several significant considerations. If these 'messages' are from 'splits', what these *'partial' and 'sub-conscious'*
minds say was experienced at, and soon after, death, is identical
with what certain *complete and conscious* minds say—the latter
people (those who 'returned' from the 'dead', 'astral projectors', observers of transitions, etc.) did not transmit their
statements through mediums.

Secondly, these supposed *'partial and sub-conscious'* minds
(usually of unlettered people) stated many of the chief facts
that have been established as the result of the investigations of
many *complete and conscious* psychical researchers. They also
forestalled practically all the fruitful theories that have been
advanced of researchers to explain these facts! For instance,
the fact that there is a constant difference between natural and
enforced death, obtained by the writer as a result of laborious
analysis (as already said) was stated by several independent
communicators. Again, the 'psychic factor' of Professor
C. D. Broad clearly corresponded to the 'astral shell' of

[1] *The Doors of Perception*, Chatto and Windus, 1954; *Heaven and Hell, ibid.*, 1956.

communicators. The present writer indicated many such facts and theories in an article in *Psychic News* (January 19, 1957): others are mentioned in these pages. There is no sign of 'fragments' of minds here!

Thirdly, while (in their attempts to avoid the acceptance of the Theory of Survival), some psychical researchers assumed that all such communications come from *'partial' and sub-conscious'* minds, others (e.g. Professor Richet) assumed that all come from *super-conscious, virtually omniscient minds!* (Yet, as already said, these minds are usually of relatively uneducated people.)

Both of these attitudes are partly right and partly wrong: 'partial' and 'sub-conscious' minds undoubtedly exist in the total minds of mediums (and of us all): they often 'communicate' dream-stuff, and, apparently, occasionally facts that must have been obtained by super-normal means (i.e. other than by the physical senses). The error, in both cases, was to argue from the particular to the general and to say that *all* communications are of these types—mere dreams of mediums in one case, supernormal mentation of mediums in the other. As communicators themselves say (incidentally correcting these psychical researchers) when we mortals are *partially and temporarily* disembodied (as occasionally occurs with non-mediums and more commonly with mediums) the 'level' of awareness is 'higher' than 'normal', since it includes *partial and occasional* flashes of super-normal consciousness (clairvoyance, telepathy, foreknowledge, etc.) and *partial and occasional* glimpses of the 'next world' ('Paradise'), and, when, eventually, we are *completely and permanently* released from the 'blinkers'-like effect of the Physical Body on the Soul Body, our consciousness is *fully and continuously* of the super-normal type and our environment is the full 'Paradise' condition.

The fact that some genuine communications (with some supernormal content) can and do emanate from mediums who are only partially and temporarily exteriorised, does not exclude the possibility that others come from the totally and permanently exteriorised living dead; on the contrary, when seen in proper perspective, the first forms a valuable link in a very strong chain of evidence that ends in the second; it points unmistakably to the fact that we do receive genuine communications from surviving souls.

The writer has advanced no new evidence, cited no new or startling cases: on the contrary, most of our evidence has been extant for approximately half a century. We have merely subjected it to systematic analysis, bringing into relief truths that are otherwise obscure.

Psychic communications are like a jig-saw puzzle. Once solved, jig-saw puzzles are not 'proved' by experiment or statistics—they are *seen* to be correctly assembled. This, we venture to assert, is true also of communications from 'the other side'. The majority of these communications occurred in 'popular' books, such as have been rejected by most psychical researchers as valueless. "The stone which the builders rejected, the same has become the head of the corner." (Matt. XXI, 42).

The whole of the available evidence is explicable only on the hypothesis of the survival of the human soul in a Soul Body. There is no longer a 'deadlock' or a 'stalemate' on the question of survival. On the contrary, survival is as well established as the Theory of Evolution.

"The souls of the righteous are in the hand of God. In the eyes of the unwise they seem to have died. But they are at peace. Their hope is full of immortality" (The Wisdom of Solomon).

APPENDIX I

THE ADMISSIBILITY OF THE EVIDENCE

(A) THE QUESTION OF COLLUSION

THE Statements by supposed discarnate souls as to what they *experienced* at, and soon after, death (itemised in the Second Part) came mainly through British and American mediums. A number of the Statements had already been noted, though not in any systematic way, by Sir Arthur Conan Doyle.[1] These were cited in Part II. But similar statements come from France, Germany, South America, Tibet, India, China and, indeed, most countries, and some of the authors specifically declare that they had no previous knowledge of such matters.

The statements concerning permanent exteriorisations from the body that occur in 'popular' books are identical with those obtained through accredited mediums and published by the S.P.R., etc. A similar situation obtains with regard to case histories of 'astral projection', i.e. to temporary exteriorisations from the body. Professor Hornell Hart,[2] who has made scientific investigation of these phenomena (using strictly evidential and statistical methods) found that the content of narratives which had little evidential backing was identical with that of his most evidential cases. Camille Flammarion,[3] writing after sixty years of psychical research, in reference to accounts of psychical phenomena in general, said: "Cases in which there was a possibility of there being concerned farceurs, liars and minds that were given to illusions . . . constitute a minimum." He added: "In almost every instance in which I have been able to make a personal investigation, I have encountered perfectly trustworthy people."

[1] *The New Revelation,* Hodder and Stoughton, 1918.
[2] *Proc. S.P.R.,* 50, 1956, 241.
[3] *Death and Its Mystery,* T. Fisher Unwin, vol. iii, 1923, p. 113.

(1) A German Priest

Johannes Greber,[1] a German Roman Catholic priest, after twenty-five years of ministry, was asked by one of his parishioners about communication with the dead. He knew nothing about it and admitted the fact. But he accepted an invitation to attend a meeting. He said: "I was inwardly convinced that I would be able to expose the whole affair with ease as a fraud." Again: "I had no knowledge of the possibility of any such intercourse, having read neither books nor periodicals dealing with the subject." Nevertheless, the statements which the priest published (at the cost of his livelihood) are identical with those which we obtained by an analysis of the communications received chiefly through English-speaking mediums. Thus: *"Very numerous indeed were the Spirits who did not realise at all that they had been divorced from the flesh by death* [=our Statement No. 10]." *He mentioned the first review of the past earth-life* [No. 5], which is necessarily prolonged for criminals who are delayed in 'Hades' conditions, as "like a film which repeats itself over and over again". He also claimed that those in 'Hades' hear the prayers of mortals on their behalf [No. 29] and said that their thoughts were thereby "turned towards God". This German priest also described 'the silver cord' and its functions [Nos. 19-21]: he said that it is "a luminous band of od" which (a) transmits vitality and (b) along which the odic [=Soul] body of the medium, exteriorised from the Physical Body in trance, "finds its way back". (This is exactly what the American medium, Mrs. Piper, who had been out of the body in trance, said, "I came in on a cord, a silver cord,"[2] and exactly what the Englishman, G. B. Crabbe, said on returning from being temporarily shocked out of the body: "I came down that silver cord and returned to the old body."[3] This concordance is most significant. Moreover it is coherent with what other communicators tell us concerning the nature of the 'cord'—they say that it is, in fact, an *extension* of the two separated bodies (consisting of some of the densest part of the Soul Body and some of the most tenuous part of the Physical Body): in other words, they claim that the Soul Body never

[1] *Communication with the Spirit World*, John Felsburg, New York, 1932.
[2] Sir Oliver Lodge, *The Survival of Man*, Methuen, 1909, p. 276.
[3] J. Arthur Hill, *Man is a Spirit*, Cassell & Co. Ltd., 1918, p. 69.

completely leaves the Physical Body until it *finally* does so. This independent statement is in agreement with the three phrases cited, one from Germany, one from U.S.A., and one from England, about the exteriorised Soul Body returning to the Physical Body 'via' the 'silver cord'. The latter, therefore, is not a separate and distinct feature, but merely an extension of the two partially-separated bodies: reunion would, presumably, be 'along' it.

Greber also said that, in deep trance, "the entire od [=double], except an odic cord, is separated from the spirit [-body]" and added that the latter "is thereby set free, being enabled to leave the body and to travel for great distances from it, thanks to the great elasticity of that cord". He noted that death is essentially due to "the breaking of the cord" [No. 20]. *Greber mentioned 'meeting cases' and 'deliverers'* [Nos. 2-3] thus: "Spirits from the Beyond surround every dying person. Generally they are those of deceased friends and relatives. . . . Many dying persons themselves can see these Spirits by clairvoyance [and his continued account should be compared with our Statement No. 6], for *at the time of death the soul is already partially released from the body, and hence is endowed with the power of spirit-vision.* . . . It is the duty of these Spirits not only to escort the dying into the Beyond, but to assist in freeing their souls [soul-bodies] from their [physical] bodies."

The priest's communicator insisted that the odic [Soul] body is primary, and the physical body a 'condensation' of it, thus: "All bodies of terrestial beings are condensed od. . . . *Your material body is only the material shell of your Spirit* [-body]. . . . " *He also explained why the 'next' world is earth-like* [Statement No. 25]. It is because all physical objects, not the physical body only, have 'doubles' or 'duplicates' (which, according to many communicators, are primary).

(2) *A German investigator*

Dr. Rudolph Schwartz[1] said: "No one, so far as I know, has yet attempted a thorough comparison of mediumistic reports from the Beyond. So I decided to do this. First I had to find a medium who was unaware of all existing reports. In German literature . . . there are almost no reports of life after death obtained through a medium. Consequently, when I met Landmann (pseudonym) in 1950 I felt he was the ideal type. An 85-year old German, honest and respectable, he had no knowledge whatever of English literature."

Dr. Schwartz compared the statements obtained through this medium with those published in fifteen English books and summarised his conclusions in a book (which the present writer has not seen) entitled *Wie die "Toten" leben* (How the "Dead" Live). He stated: "I can assure you that the conformity of the Landmann scripts with the English books was striking even in minor details."

(3) An English lawyer

'King's Counsel'[1] insisted: "Neither my wife nor I, nor any of my children (two of whom were the psychics used in the course of his investigations) had read any psychic book or studied occultism in any way, until some time after many of the messages set out below had been received." Yet these communications also are identical with those from other sources. The communicators said that they saw the medium as 'a light' (as with Mrs. Piper in U.S.A. and many others in Europe) and that *death is followed by a sleep* [No. 22]. The latter, it was said, "may be brief or may be prolonged for several weeks" [No. 24]. It was stated that, "*There is often difficulty in making the person who has died realise the fact*" [No. 10], that '*deliverers*' often assist at 'passings' [No. 3] and that relatively advanced discarnate souls undertake '*rescue work*' for those delayed in 'Hades' conditions.

(4) An Indian investigator

V. D. Rishi, was reported[2] as saying in his book,[3] "*Death is painless* [No. 7]; it is like going to sleep. A man who 'passes over' is just the same person five minutes after death as he was five minutes before" [No. 10]. . . . One communicator described the change as "similar to that which a serpent might feel when it has sloughed its skin."

Rishi continued: "*A discarnate individual can see his friends and*

---

[1] *I Heard a Voice*, Kegan Paul, Trench, Trubner & Co. Ltd., 1928, p. 2.
[2] *Psychic News*, April, 28 1956.   [3] *Spiritualism in India*, Bombay, 1956.

relatives in the flesh [No. 17] *and he is greatly pained to see them mourning for him* [No. 27]. *He tries to prove his existence in various ways to them . . . but within a short time realises the futility of his attempts* [No. 28]."

Rishi further quoted from an unpublished MS. by an Indian named Emil as follows: "*Normal death is preceded by unconsciousness* [No. 9], *during which state all the incidents of earth-life pass before the dying man* [No. 5]. . . . *Simultaneously, the etheric body starts emerging from the head* [No. 13] *in the form of a cloud of vapour* [No. 14]. *This condenses and gradually forms into a replica of the dying person* [No. 15]. *When the* [new] *body is completely formed, a process which usually takes from one to two hours, it stands erect over the prostrate physical body, yet connected by a cord* [No. 19] *about two feet long* [No. 16] *similar to the umbilical cord of earthly birth* [No. 20]. *The dying mortal's last gasp indicates the snapping of the cord* [No. 21] *and the completion of the death process.* Thus is the chicken hatched from the egg. The Spirit, the Real Man, hitherto enveloped in two shells, the physical and the etheric bodies, starts functioning in only one—the etheric body."

(5) *The natives of Hawaiian Islands*

Perhaps the most convincing data in favour of the admissibility of our evidence comes from the Hawaiian Islands. These were cut off from civilisation for centuries before being discovered in 1778 by Captain Cook. In spite of this fact, and of the inability of the natives to read or write, they held ideas as to the nature of man and the succession of events that takes place at, and soon after, the 'passing' that are practically identical with those received in communications in England, Germany, U.S.A., etc., from the dead. For instance, they held that the total man consists of a hierarchy of three selves (an animal self, a human self and a High Self) and that each of these possesses its own 'body'. They held that the (physically invisible) body of the animal self [=our 'vehicle of vitality'] (*a*) contains memory traces and (*b*) stores vitality, etc. These facts were brought to light by Max Freedom Long as the result of a study of the 'magic' of the natives and of the language used by the kahunas or priests. (*See The Secret Science Behind Miracles*, 1950, *The Secret Science at Work*, 1953, Kosmon Press.)

(6) A Chinaman

The letter of a Russian correspondent in China was published in *Light*, vol. xlii, 1922, p. 13. It included the following passage: "An old monk who was living there (i.e. in 'a mountain district between the Korean border and Ninguta') sometimes was entranced and had communications with the spirit world. I know from the Colonel only a little; but *nearly everything he told me . . . I see now in the Rev. Vale Owen's books*."

(7) The Maoris

Dr. Horace Leaf, Ph.D., F.R.G.S. (*Light*, vol. xlvii, 1927, p. 449), after a visit to New Zealand, reported that the phenomena which are known to us as 'spirit control' (i.e. 'possession') were well known to the Maori priests. Their name for 'spirit control' was *tohunga-kehua*, while a person who was capable of producing the phenomena was called a *waka*.

(8) The Tibetans

The 'oracles' of Tibet are ordinary mediums who are given to the 'possession' form of mediumship (as was Mrs. Leonard and Mrs. Piper, two of the chief mediums investigated by the S.P.R.), but they are despised by the mystics, who regard psychical phenomena in general as genuine but as distracting one from "the true path" (which is union with God). The 'Bardo Body' of Tibetans corresponds to the vehicle of vitality.

Sufficient has been said to show that the similarities in the evidence we have adduced cannot be dismissed as due to collusion between those who provided it. While it is highly desirable that the *bona fides* of those who submit evidence should be established wherever possible, that is not always possible.

A policy of dismissing such evidence is unwise and unproductive. If the Secret Service, drawing up accounts of the disposition of the forces of a potential enemy did nothing until the absolute trustworthiness of all informants had been established, their work would fail dismally. The wise procedure is provisionally to accept all available evidence and plot it on the maps: any complete fabrication will then stand revealed since it will be in clear disagreement with the whole of the other evidence.

(B) THE MEDIUMISTIC 'CLIMATE OF THOUGHT'

(1) *The status of the conception*

Although the similarities that abound in numerous independent communications from 'Beyond' cannot be attributed to collusion or fraudulent manipulation, they are considered by some to be due to a prevalent mediumistic "climate of thought".

Categorically to refuse even provisional consideration to any evidence on such grounds is to adopt an illogical standpoint: the all-embracing "climate of thought", thus treated as an established fact, is no more than a hypothesis, one which is envisaged expressly to explain the similarities observed. There is, of course, another hypothesis which even more adequately performs that function, namely, the Theory of Survival. Moreover, since the Theory of Survival must be accorded a very high degree of probability on grounds other than the similarities in mediumistic communications, the presumption is surely that these similarities are (at least in part) due to their having come from surviving personalities (and not entirely from the mediums themselves).

There may well be a 'climate' of mediumistic thought which 'colours' many communications, but it does not affect the communications with which we are primarily concerned, namely, those descriptive of *experiences* at, and soon after, death. The *experiences* are obviously simple events the description of which are 'uncoloured', though they may be described in symbols. Even the symbolic 'robes', 'lecture halls', 'hospitals', etc., probably describe realities of some sort. One communicator,[1] mentioning these, insisted: "This language is symbolic. A thread of actual events runs through the symbolism. . . . I fear to be misunderstood." The symbolic interpretation of references, in mediumistic communications, to the 'robes' and 'garments' worn by the 'dead' is obvious from the Scriptural references to those features (Matt. xiii. 43, xxviii. 3; Mark xv. 5; John iv. 14; vii. 38; Rev. iii, 5; iv, 44; vii, 9, 13; xix, 8; xii, 3; Acts x, 30; 1 Cor. xiii, 12; Eph. 4. 14; II Thess. ii. 8).

[1] W. T. Pole, *Private Dowding*, Watkins, 1917, p. 76.

P

(2) *Against the hypothesis*

Critics must explain on what grounds they invoke the hypothesis of a common 'climate' to explain similarities in the statements (concerning the experiences of the dead) that are *transmitted by mediums,* when identical statements are made *without mediumistic intervention,* i.e. by people who are in process of transition ('death-bed visions'), by watchers at death-beds, by 'astral projectors', and by people who claimed to 'return' from the dead, etc. Is it not obvious that the similarities which are brought to light in *all* these circumstances (and not alone in mediumistic communications) are due to the fact that they bear a direct relationship to the simple truth?

Again, some of the statements, derived from mediumistic communications, are supported by facts: *these* statements, at least, presumably describe the actual experiences of surviving personalities and there is no justification for a supposition that they are mere products of 'sub-conscious', 'partial' minds or a general 'climate' of thought. The others dove-tail into them and thus qualify to escape the same fate.

For instance, the statement, obtained through mediums, by those who claimed to have actually died, that there is an early 'review' of the past earth-life, is supported by the statements of many people who did not consult mediums but who nearly died (by drowning, etc.): the latter also described experiencing a review of the past life.

The statements that in natural transition there is an after-death sleep (which averages three or four days) whereas in enforced transitions the person concerned tends to be awake at once are supported by the observed facts that those who communicate after natural transition often do so after three or four days, while those who were forcibly ejected from the body often do communicate quite soon after their 'passing'.

Still again, communicators tell us that during earth-life our total (available) consciousness is limited ('blinkers'-like) by the Physical Body through which it must operate and that in many cases when they communicate, in order to achieve attunement, they must partially re-embody themselves by borrowing ectoplasm from the medium: this partial re-embodiment, like our complete embodiment, necessarily lowers their 'level' of consciousness and may affect their

THE ADMISSIBILITY OF THE EVIDENCE 195

memories and the clarity of their communications. These
statements by communicators are in agreement with the subsequent findings of many eminent psychical researchers (see
Appendix III).

(3) Converse and complementary statements

Converse and complementary statements are difficult, if
possible, of explanation on the theories of 'sub-conscious' or
'partial' minds or the 'climate of thought'.

Among the converse statements that are particularly significant may be mentioned those concerning the shedding, on
the one hand, and re-entering, on the other, of the Physical
Body: these statements are made by different people. Moreover,
the analogy of 'passing through a tunnel' is used (at a later
stage in disembodiment) to describe shedding the vehicle of
vitality, and (at a still later stage), the Soul Body. Thus, this
symbol is independently used to describe not only what *we*
call death but also the '*second*' and '*third*' deaths and the
re-entering of a body (when possible)—as would be expected if
the narratives are descriptive of fact and not mere 'sub-
conscious' productions. (These matters were considered in
detail in Part III under Statement No. 9.)

Again, the differences between natural and enforced death,
the exceptional conditions that obtain in regard to death by
explosion, etc. are all beyond adequate explanation on the
basis of 'sub-conscious' or 'partial' minds or a 'climate of
thought'. These differences also were given by several independent communicators: the present writer obtained them by
laborious analysis.

We maintain that those who dismiss *everything* that occurs in
mediumistic communications as merely products of the 'climate
of thought' are guilty of 'begging the question'. What has to
be determined is whether *anything* avoids that taint, and we
maintain that this applies to *personal experiences*. Those who
sweep all aside, without systematic investigation, unconsciously
use the *a priori* argument. Dr. Alfred Russell Wallace, the
co-discoverer, with Charles Darwin, of Evolution, observed:
"The whole history of science shows that whenever scientific
men have denied the facts of other scientific investigators on
a priori grounds of absurdity or impossibility, *the deniers have
always been wrong.*"

(c) DIFFERENT FORMS OF MEDIUMSHIP YIELD SIMILAR COMMUNICATIONS

Professors Bergson and Lodge suggested a study of unverifiable communications in general. In the Foreword to *One Step Higher* (The C. W. Daniel Co. Ltd., 1937), Hester Dowden, the automatist, suggested a somewhat different procedure, i.e. a specific comparison of communications that are received through different forms of mediumship. If, she considered, they are essentially the same (though naturally differing from each other in the forms of expression), this might provide "the best" evidence for survival. There can be no doubt that different forms of mediumship yield essentially similar communications concerning death and the after-life. For example, the contents of *On the Edge of the Etheric*, by J. Arthur Findlay (Rider & Co. Ltd., 1931), obtained by 'direct voice', are identical with those published in *One Step Higher*, obtained by 'automatic writing'.

'POINTERS' TO SURVIVAL

WE concluded the Introduction to the First Part of the book by saying that the 'travellers' tales' that are represented by communications concerning experiences, when examined in the light of observed facts, yield many 'pointers' to survival. A number of these have been indicated in the foregoing pages. Here are some more.

(A) DIFFERENCES IN 'PHYSICAL' PHENOMENA

Natural Death

Significant differences are to be observed between those 'physical' phenomena that are typically associated with natural death and those produced by enforced death: they differ in frequency, incidence and continuity. In either case, their origin is doubtless to be found in the relative amount of vital energy in the vehicle of vitality that is newly-released from its life-long association with the Physical Body. This amount is small in natural death, great in enforced death. It must be dissipated.

'Raps' and other noises, the stopping of clocks, the falling of pictures, the breakage of crockery, etc. (i.e. telekinetic effects), which are beyond chance coincidence, typically occur in natural death. These phenomena differ from hauntings in that they occur very near the moment of death and are rarely repeated; hauntings generally begin later and may continue over a considerable time.

An example of a telekinetic effect that was produced just before natural death is given in *Ann. des Sciences Psychiques*, 1899, p. 106. Alfred de Musset, lying in his armchair at the point of death, was too weak to rise. Two people present saw him look intently at the bell near the mantelpiece, as though wishing to ring it. Both saw the bell-pull (which the dying man could not reach) move, as though pulled by an invisible hand. Not only did both hear the bell actually ring, but a servant came in response to the summons. This narrative is particularly interesting, since de Mussett had 'astral projections' during his life-time.

Enforced death

In enforced death the vehicle of vitality is often *super-charged* with vitality. Professor E. Bozzano[1] investigated over three hundred cases of haunting that involved a death and found that two out of every three were correlated with death of a tragic (i.e. enforced) nature. He concluded that the great majority were due to personalities who had survived death. Although in some instances the activities were of an unconscious automatic or habitual nature, in others they were conscious, deliberate and intelligent. (Bozzano considered that the rest might be due to some sort of 'trace' left either at the places at which the hauntings occurred or in the neighbouring 'ether'.)

Although they made no numerical evaluations, many nations including savage tribes, *observed* the connection between enforced death and hauntings. Professor Raymond Firth,[2] for example, mentioned the Tikopia tribe, a primitive people of Polynesia, who made this observation, suggested that, when a man dies naturally, friendly spirits were aware of his transition, met him and ushered him into the 'next' world [Statement No. 3], while in death by accident, etc., the soul was expelled from the body so suddenly that deceased friends were unaware of the 'passing' and consequently failed to meet him [Statements Nos. 2 and 36].

(B) DIFFERENCE IN THE TIME-INTERVAL BETWEEN DEATH AND COMMUNICATION

Natural death

As already said, in natural death it is common for communications to begin some three or four days after death (Statement No. 22). The following are among many observations to this effect.

S. Stromberg communicated through Mme. d'Espérance's hand *three days* after his death. He asked her (in Europe) to tell his parents (in Sweden) of his death (in Canada). The facts

[1] *Phenomenes des Hantise*, Alcan, Paris.   [2] Talk on B.B.C., November, 1955.

were verified by Mr. Fidler.[1] According to Harry Edwards, the deceased Jack Webber transmitted a message *three days* after his passing.[2] Bozzano cited the case in which Sirchia jokingly made a death-compact with his doctor: he said that if he predeceased him he would notify the fact by breaking a hanging lamp in the doctor's room. Raps, announcing his de\th, began *three or four days* after his 'passing'.[3] Usborne Moore said that he had been told two or three times by the departed that a dead man "generally recognises his new environment on the *third day* after physical death". He added: "Once a discarnate lady came to me and told me that she had been able to impress her sister in earth-life with the conviction that she was alive *"on the third day."* He added: "I made enquiries two months later and found that this was true."[4] Hodgson, in his 1898 Report on Mrs. Piper's psychism, said: "That persons just deceased should be extremely confused and unable to communicate directly, or even at all, seems perfectly natural after the shock and wrench of death." One man was unable to write the second day after his death; another wrote, "I am all right, adieu" within *two or three days* of his death; a third was unable to write on the morning after his death. A few days later he wrote: "I am too weak to articulate clearly." Not many days later he wrote fairly well and quite accurately.

Enforced death

In enforced death communication typically begins at once if at all (though in some cases there is delay). This occurred in many cases of airmen, etc., cited by Lord Dowding[5] and in the case of Mrs. Kelway Bamber's son, Claude, killed in an accident.[6] 'Blanche Abercrombie' communicated through the Rev. Stainton Moses the same evening as she died (suddenly) though she was confused. It was only after several days that she could write coherently. A girl of seventeen who committed suicide communicated *the day after* death.[7]

These observations were made by the writer from a study of many accounts. But, as in most, if not all, other matters it was

[1] Mme. d'Espérance, *Shadow Land*, George Redway, 1897.
[2] *The Mediumship of Arnold Clare*, Psychic Book Club.
[3] *Discarnate Influence in Human Life*, Watkins, 1938.
[4] *Glimpses of the Next State*, Watts.   [5] *Lychgate*, Rider & Co. Ltd.
[6] *Claude's Book*, Psychic Book Club.   [7] Myers, *op. cit.*

already stated, quite explicitly, by communicators. A man killed by a steamroller communicated through Stainton Moses *a few hours* later. Moses asked his 'Guides' why this stranger could communicate so early when a personal friend (who had died naturally) had not done so? They said that the friend who had died naturally was 'asleep' [No. 22], while the former had 'not rested' [No. 39]. It was explained that the man whose death was enforced would be 'earthbound' (in 'Hades') because the "rude shock" of his transition "stirred him to action rather than lulled him into repose".[1]

(c) THE RELATIVE FREQUENCY OF AFTER-DEATH APPARITIONS AND COMMUNICATIONS

As the result of an investigation of apparitions (doubles or phantasms) by the Society for Psychical Research[2] the conclusion was reached that *"Between deaths and apparitions of the dying a connection exists which is not due to chance alone"*.

Again, Professor Richet[3] observed: *"If a time-curve of post mortem apparitions were drawn, it would show a very rapid fall within the first few days after death, becoming almost nil for longer periods."*

Other investigations, both in America and in France, pointed to the same conclusion and it is now established fact that a man's 'double' (whatever its nature) is most often seen either shortly before, at the time of, or soon after his death. Sir Ernest Bennett[4] considered that the hypothesis of telepathy from the dead is the only one that covers all the facts established concerning such apparitions. Later, Bennett[5] criticised the authors of *Phantasms of the Living*: they had invented far-fetched explanations in an attempt to avoid envisaging that of survival. By their first hypothesis (that a corpse remains vitalised for twelve hours after death) they hoped to dispose of apparitions of the dead that occur within that period as due to the still-vitalised body and not to the surviving personality. They then tried to account for still later apparitions by the suggestion that they were due to telepathy, but the

[1] *Spirit Teachings*, L.S.A. Publications Ltd., 1933 (11th ed.).
[2] E. Gurney, F. W. H. Myers and F. Podmore, *Phantasms of the Living*, Kegan Paul, Trench, Trubner & Co. Ltd., 2 vols. 1886; abridged ed., 1918.
[3] *Thirty Years of Psychical Research* (trans. Stanley de Brath), Collins, 1923.
[4] Sir Ernest Bennett, *Apparitions and Haunted Houses*, Faber and Faber, 1939.
[5] In Th. Besterman, *An Enquiry into the Unknown*, Methuen, 1954.

telepathic image, or impression, had been sent out by the dying man *before* death, and had been 'latent' in the mind of the recipient until after the transition took place. Bennett described these two theories as "pure hypothesis, unverified and unverifiable". If some apparitions of the 'living' are due to telepathy from the 'living', then some apparitions of the 'dead' are presumably due to telepathy from the 'dead'.

Myers (*op. cit.*) discussed the theory of 'latent' telepathy. He pointed out that "*Apparitions . . . increase very rapidly for the first few hours that precede death, and decrease gradually during the hours and days which follow, until, after about a year's time they become merely sporadic*". He referred to Gurney's statistics[1] representing cases in which death and the appearance of the double were known to be in 'close proximity'. (Of these, few, if any, deaths can have been of the enforced type.) They may be summarised as follows.

Apparitions, phantasms or doubles of the dead:

	No. of cases	Percentage of total
Seen more than twenty-four hours before death	19	9
Seen within twenty-four hours of death .	19	9
Seen at (or within one hour of) death .	134	63
Seen within twenty-four hours after death	40	19

Moreover, Myers pointed out that in almost all cases of a veridical phantasm *preceding* the agent's death, that death was the result of illness and not of accident: he could not explain this. He also remarked that phantasms that exhibit purpose and intelligence (most, though not all, of which are probably telepathic images) are rarely seen collectively (or successively), while those that are mere purposeless automata are often seen collectively (or successively). He said: "I do not know how to explain this apparent tendency."

The available facts are adequately explained by the statements of supposed discarnates. The purposeless automata would, presumably, be isolated vehicle of vitality, or 'astral shells'. These are 'semi-physical'; they are 'objective' in a

[1] *Proc. S.P.R.*, v, 408, pp. 888-9.

sense that telepathic images are not and they may, consequently, be visible, audible, etc. to non-psychic mortals. They
would tend to be seen collectively (or successively).

The observation that death tends to produce an apparition
of the dying (or nearly dead) man fell short of what it was
possible to conclude. The latter, we venture to suggest, was
nothing less than survival.

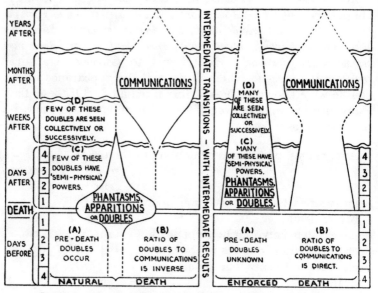

DIAGRAM No. I — ILLUSTRATING OBSERVED FACTS REGARDING
APPARITIONS & COMMUNICATIONS.

In our Diagram No. 1 the number of (usually purposeless
and unintelligent) apparitions is set off against the number of
purposeful and intelligent communications (by automatic
writing, etc.), the two extreme conditions of transition (natural
and enforced death) being given separately.

We make three sets of notes on this diagram. First, as regards
apparitions: (1) 'Doubles' that are seen before the death of the
man they represent are (as Myers pointed out but did not
explain) almost always associated with illness—that is, with
natural and gradual death—in many cases the man is 'half-
dead', 'half' out of the body; his vehicle of vitality is 'projected'. (2) The 'doubles' produced by those who die naturally

tend to be typically purposeless, 'pale', 'haggard', 'cadaverous', etc.—that is, they are mere 'wraiths', 'spectres', 'shells', or 'shades', partial corpses, remnants of the total Physical Body. (3) Such phantoms relatively seldom perform 'semiphysical' acts. (4) They are seen, and they act, over a period of only a few days. All these features are correlated with the fact that, since these men died gradually (of debilitating illness or in old age), the separated vehicle of vitality contained little vital force.

Turning to the apparitions produced by those whose death is suddenly enforced: (2) These are traditional 'ghosts', purposeless automata; they are characteristically not 'pale', etc. but so life-like as often to be mistaken for 'living' people. (3) They often perform definite 'semi-physical' acts and that over relatively long periods of time. These features are correlated with the fact that there has been no depletion (by sickness or old age) of the vital energies—on the contrary, the vehicle of vitality is often 'super-charged' with energy that was intended to be used in physical activities—it must now be dissipated in 'semi-physical' phenomena.

Secondly, as regards the approximate numerical relationship that exists between 'doubles' (when seen just before, or just after, death often representing vehicles of vitality) and telepathic communications from the 'dead': (4) *In natural death there is an inverse ratio between the number of 'doubles' seen and the number of communications received.* This ratio (*a*) accords with Statement No. 23 (that the unshed vehicle of vitality, especially if in a depleted state), tends to enveil the Soul Body and therefore to enshroud consciousness and cause a 'sleep'; (*b*) it strongly suggests that doubles that are seen within a few days of death are more often isolated vehicles of vitality than telepathic images. Turning to enforced death: (5) *In enforced death there is a direct ratio between the number of 'doubles' seen and the number of communications received.* (This accords with Statement No. 39, that those whose death is enforced tend to be 'awake' at once.) Again, since many of these doubles perform 'semiphysical' acts, presumably they are not merely telepathic images.

Thirdly, regarding telepathic communications: (6) The communications from those who die naturally are coherent from the first (though they may be dream-like at first as would presumably occur in a 'partial awakening'—No. 25): those from men whose death is enforced are very incoherent at first. This agrees with Statement No. 42) that natural transition involves less shock than enforced transition) and No. 23 (that the aged have a brief post-mortem period of 'sleep' (and dream).

Two facts show that it is *surviving souls or personalities* and not,

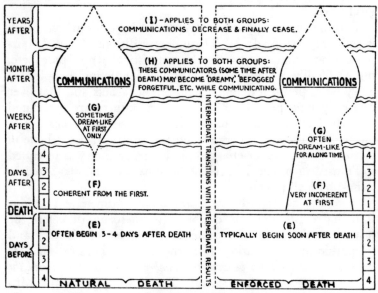

DIAGRAM No. 2 – ILLUSTRATING <u>OBSERVED FACTS</u> REGARDING <u>COMMUNICATIONS</u>

as some have suggested, mere 'memory-traces' ('psychic factors', 'mindlets' or 'astral shells'), that provide *purposeful and intelligent* communications: the first is that, as already said, differences in the nature of transitions cause differences in the nature of early communications: the second and more significant fact is that these differences are of brief duration—those whose death was enforced soon communicate just as clearly as those who 'passed' naturally (see Diagram No. 2).

Again, The S.P.R. Census of Hallucinations of 1889-90 (in which 17,000 replies were received, indicating that about 10 per cent had seen apparitions) produced results that are inexplicable on the hypothesis held by most psychical researchers that all apparitions are of a purely telepathic nature or on that held by many medical men that all are 'purely subjective' (imaginary).

Of those doubles that were identified (66·8 per cent of the total), and that could be assigned to a period either before or after the death of the person represented, about 70 per cent.

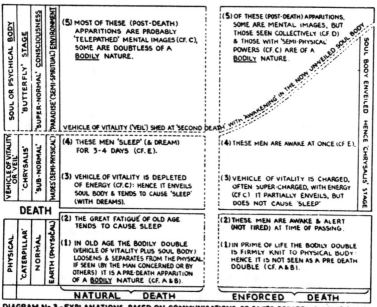

DIAGRAM No.3 – EXPLANATIONS, BASED ON COMMUNICATIONS, OF FACTS REGARDING APPARITIONS: BODILY DOUBLES SURVIVE DEATH; THEY MAY BE THE INSTRUMENTS OF CONSCIOUSNESS – OF SURVIVING SOULS

were doubles of the '*living*' and about 30 per cent were doubles of the '*dead*'. This noteworthy ratio is readily explicable if (as communicators say) the Physical Body is vivified by a 'vehicle of vitality': the double of a 'living' person would presumably often include elements from this 'semi-physical' feature: it would be denser and more visible than that of a person who had been dead for some time (and who had shed the vehicle of vitality). Similarly any telepathic image created by a 'living' person would probably also be more 'dense' and more visible than that of a 'dead' person because it was re-inforced by both the vehicle of vitality and the Physical Body which acted after the manner of a gun-emplacement. This suggestion that the vehicle of vitality and the Physical Body of the 'living' act like a gun-emplacement to thoughts, etc., is supported by cases in which impressions from the 'dead' seem to be too subtle to affect mortals until they have been reinforced by other mortals (who being more or less psychic, 'co-operate',

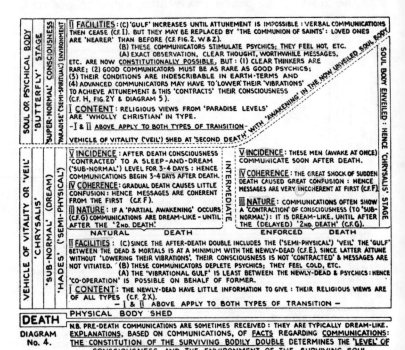

DIAGRAM No. 4.

N.B. PRE-DEATH COMMUNICATIONS ARE SOMETIMES RECEIVED : THEY ARE TYPICALLY DREAM-LIKE. EXPLANATIONS, BASED ON COMMUNICATIONS, OF FACTS REGARDING COMMUNICATIONS: THE CONSTITUTION OF THE SURVIVING BODILY DOUBLE DETERMINES THE 'LEVEL' OF CONSCIOUSNESS AND THE ENVIRONMENT OF THE SURVIVING SOUL.

though all unconsciously, with discarnate souls in such operations (No. 30). Another instance in which there is a strong suggestion that the vehicle of vitality and the Physical Body of a 'living' man acted like a gun-emplacement is the famous Gordon Davis case. Davis, still 'alive' (but evidently exteriorised from his body), manifested through a medium by 'direct voice'. The 'control' twice interrupted his communications, stating that he was 'too strong' for the medium. At the close of the seance, the medium complained of exhaustion and headache (symptoms which she had not experienced with *discarnate* communicators). Hence, at the second séance, the 'control' would not allow Davis to communicate directly: she questioned him herself (the whispered conversation between her and Davis being audible) and then passed the answers on to the sitter.[1]

The essential ideas that are indicated in the foregoing pages are summarised in Diagrams 3-5.

[1] *Proc. S.P.R.*, xxv, p. 560.

THE TWO SOURCES OF GENUINE COMMUNICATIONS

In addition to 'sub-conscious' productions by mediums, there are *pseudo*-communications that include (*a*) 'messages' that are due to telepathy from the 'living', (*b*) those due to a medium (unconsciously) vivifying and 'reading' an 'astral shell' (a partial corpse—the discarded vehicle of vitality) which bears memory-traces and (*c*) those due to a medium (also unconsciously) 'reading' the memory-traces in the vehicle of vitality of a 'living' person. In these three cases, no surviving soul is directly involved.

Other *pseudo*-communications may emanate from surviving souls, but may not be transmitted intentionally—the medium may, as it were, 'overhear' the dreams or thoughts or share the emotions of a surviving personality.

Intentional, i.e. genuine, 'messages' from actual survivors of death tell us many things including their mental condition while engaged in communicating and their conditions or environments.

(*a*) *The many communications from 'Hades'*
(*corresponding to the vehicle of vitality*)

In considering the numerous 'messages' that reach us from the 'lowest' of the 'next world' environments, namely, 'Hades' conditions, it should be remembered that they may emanate from people who belong to two different groups, and chiefly from (*a*) men of average spiritual development who, having died suddenly in the prime of life, are in a half-awake, half-dream state and (*b*) men who (whether their transition was enforced or natural) were so markedly below average spirituality that they are delayed in these conditions—'earthbound' men. These latter are often jokers, impostors and liars though not 'devils' or 'demons'. We have already (Third Part, Statement No. 34*b*) pointed out that there is very little, if any, evidence of (non-human) 'devils' and that the Statement

[No. 30] that 'Spirits in prison', i.e. in 'Hades' conditions, can be assisted through the 'co-operation' of incarnate psychics and discarnate helpers is supported by a considerable body of evidence.

Fitzsimon's *South African* communicator[1] pointed out: "When you sit at a séance, a glow goes out from you all and

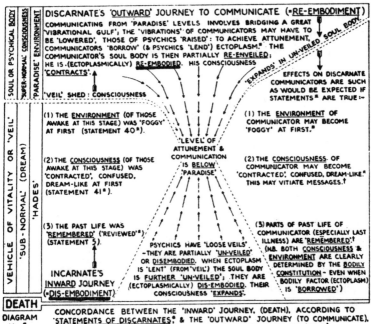

DIAGRAM No. 5. CONCORDANCE BETWEEN THE 'INWARD' JOURNEY, (DEATH), ACCORDING TO 'STATEMENTS OF DISCARNATES,' & THE 'OUTWARD' JOURNEY (TO COMMUNICATE), INCLUDING ESTABLISHED FACTS OF PSYCHIC SCIENCE.

strange spirits—*mostly earthbound*—are attracted. . . . Casual spirits are always watching for the opportunity to speak. . . ." The German Roman Catholic priest, Johannes Greber,[2] was told that 'controls' supervise the work of mediums of high spirituality, adding that most séances become the playgrounds of the *lower* spirit-world. . . ."

Another *German* had discovered this more than a century before Father Greber, though the latter was unaware of the fact. Dr. Kerner, an eminent physician at Weinsburg, in 1829, published *Die Seherin von Prevorst* (which was translated into

---

[1] *Op. cit.*, pp. 73, 172.   [2] *Communications with the Spirit World*, 1932, p. 53.

English by Catherine Crowe under the title *The Seeress of Prevorst* (J. C. Moore, 1845). Frau Hauffe, the Seeress, insisted that "the spirits in the mid-region" [='Hades'] of the 'next world' are "more ignorant than when alive". Dr. Kerner understood this situation: he said: "Wrenched from those worldly connections and dependencies which constituted *their* wisdom, there remains only *their former desires*, without the means of gratification, together with the recollection of their sins." He cited Plato: "He who has lived a vicious life is more a brute after death than he was in life." Kerner further observed: "These relations will appear to many incredible and absurd —especially to those who are of opinion that a spirit must know more than a human being: but I answer that this is not the case with these *earthbound spirits* [*in 'Hades'*]; they are in a very inferior state, are mostly entangled in error, and can more easily approach man, with whom they are in a sort of nervous relationship [because they have still to shed the vehicle of vitality from the total after-death double], than heavenly [here ="Paradise"] spirits [whose effective body consists of the Soul Body un-enshrouded by the vehicle of vitality]. A spirit who has lived in darkness here on earth remains dark after death. And thus *a weak spirit becomes weaker after death*, when . . . the amount of his weakness is exposed by his standing alone and unsustained. A sinful and worldly-minded man may shine on earth by the strength of his *intellect* but his *spirit* is only the weaker and darker. . . ." Dr. Kerner maintained that the ability to see true 'ghosts' [i.e. 'earth-bound' spirits, whose double still includes the vehicle of vitality, a remnant of the discarded physical body] belongs to all mortals and not only to such rare people as the Seeress of Prevorst. "But", he said, "it is seldom active, and only momen-tary, since it must be excited by something that calls forth the inner man, and *this is generally dispersed and suppressed by reason*." Kerner's observation is doubtless true—extremely few highly logical and scientific men are aware of receiving psychical impressions of any kind—since they cannot 'still' their own mental activities, they fail to observe the delicate impressions that impinge on their Soul Bodies from without. Illiterate natives who have some psychical faculties may 'know' what is hidden from our greatest scientists and philosophers!

The *Italian* 'Vettellini', communicating to P. E. Cornillier

(*The Survival of the Soul*, Kegan Paul, Trench, Trubner & Co. Ltd., 1921, pp. 378, 380, 456), said: "The *lower ones* [discarnate souls] communicate easily enough—they have not to plunge into dense and suffocating atmosphere which, for high Spirits, is exactly what sinking in a mud-bath would be for you. They can speak abundantly, and abundantly they can blunder and lie. . . ." Later he stated: "Very evolved Spirits communicate rarely. *The immense majority of those who communicate are mediocre entities*: as a rule, they retain in the Astral ['Hades' plus the lower 'Paradise'] the opinions which they held on earth." 'Vettellini' insisted: "No great confidence should be accorded to the majority of communications."

The *English* Charles Moore was similarly told *The Unseen World*, Moore's Publications, London, p. 55) that "practically all" communications come from "*the lower bound* [*=bound-to-earth*] *zone*" of the Beyond, and not from the truly Spiritual realms. According to the communicator of J. J. Morse (*Light*, vol. XLVI, 1926, p. 230), "The great majority" of 'messages' are due to discarnate souls whose passing was "more or less recent". They have had neither time nor opportunity to study the "many mansions" in after-death conditions. The communicator of M. Hoey (*Truths from the Spirit World*, 1907, pp. 104-5) stated that when materialists die they become 'earthbound', i.e. they live in the 'planes' that are essentially portions of the earth. He continued: "*These are the souls who need the prayers of those on earth*, even as they need the aid of those behind the veil. They are not bad, but rather materialistic." 'A.C.D.', whose communications were published by Ivan Cooke (*Thy Kingdom Come*, Wright and Brown, 1931, p. 149) said: "The representations of life in the Astral Planes . . . are often only the experiences of souls who are still closely linked with earth. . . ."

The *English* medium, the Rev. Wm. Stainton Moses[1] wrote (of the equally famous *Scottish* medium): "Mr. D. D. Home . . . believes with me that *most* of the manifestations proceed from *a low order* of spirits who hover near the earth sphere." 'A.B.'[2] was told: "Those spirits who are *nearest to your earth* plane, and have not evolved very highly, come through easier and more

[1] *Notebook*, December 22, 1872.
[2] *One Step Higher*, The C. W. Daniel Co. Ltd., 1937.

quickly than those in a higher sphere. . . ." Brandon's communicator[1] also made a typical statement: "Eagerness to communicate is common to all here. But few have any organised ideas or information to impart. These *average* 'departed' desire only to assure their friends in earth-life that they still live [Statement No. 28]. *Communications mostly come from earthbound souls.*" 'Philip' also stated: "The people who crowd round controls . . . are *mostly* people still in the *earth-place*. . . ."[2]

The *American*, Elsa Barker (*Letters from a Living Dead Man*, Rider & Co. Ltd., 1914, p. 39), was told by her communicator, 'Judge Hatch': "This is not a place where everyone knows everything—far from it. Most souls are nearly as blind as they were in life." The communicator of Emma Hardinge (*Addresses*, J. Burns, 1865, p. 27) said that those who describe houses, landscapes, etc., as part of their 'next-world' environment are "still earth-centred"—they are still 'earth-bound', and 'Myers' said much the same through Geraldine Cummins (*The Road to Immortality*).

'W. T. Stead', communicating through Mme. Hyver (*Communication with the Next World*, The Cricket Press, 1937, p. 18) states: "All except a small number of the 'dead' are as ignorant as are men on earth. That is why so many seances are disappointing. . . . There is, in the atmosphere of the earth, an innumerable crowd of wandering, desolate souls who watch for any 'light' on earth, the light of a spiritual psychic, and who rush in whirling throngs to the spot where a possibility of manifesting themselves occurs."

As already said, the communicator of M. Hoey (*Truths from the Spirit World*, 1907, pp. 29, 104-5) said that people who live "purely material lives, pleasure-seeking, money-seeking, etc., become 'earthbound' after their deaths. Like many other communicators, he advised people to avoid "public seances", since, he said, owing to the mixed motives of those present, they tend to draw "earthbound spirits only".

It was no doubt such communicators that made Ecclesiastes (ix. 5) say, "The dead know not anything", and Plato, "It is not the pious, but the ungodly souls who return to earth".

---

[1] *Open the Door*, Alfred A. Knopf, 1935.
[2] Alice Gilbert, *Philip in the Spheres*, Aquarian Press Ltd., 1952, p. 120.

Dr. Joad, the English philosopher, similarly observed, "The dead may have souls but they have no brains", while Cesare Lombroso, the Italian psychiatrist and criminal anthropologist, concluded: "There is a great probability . . . that there is a continued existence of the soul after death, preserving a weak identity. . . ." 'Private Dowding',[1] killed in his prime and communicating at once (i.e. while the Soul Body was enshrouded by the vehicle of vitality and he was in illusory 'Hades' conditions) made certain communications. Then, a 'Messenger' appeared to him and 'Dowding' said: "He impressed on me the importance of reminding you [the recipient of the messages] that the conditions around me are impermanent . . . that I am still living in a fog, a fog of my own creation." Similarly, soon after 'passing', 'Stead' transmitted the contents of *The Blue Island*.[2] In a later communication,[3] however, he confessed: "The Blue Island was a *dream*. . . ."

'Wilberforce'[4] mentioned Lodge's book, '*Raymond*' (in which 'cigars' etc. are mentioned in the early after-life) and said: "I know of the men who slept here [=in 'Hades' conditions] and in their *dreams* enjoyed banquets: and remember, those *dreams* are often transmitted by mediums, as well as the waking experiences of those who are here". Similarly, 'A.B.'s' communicator (*op. cit.*) admitted that when he had previously written through his medium had been communicated in a "*sleep state*": he commented, "I must have expressed myself strangely".

'Myers'[5] stated: "These souls . . . enter into *a dream* that, in its main particulars, resembles the earth. . . . Such *infant souls* frequently communicate with earth when they are in a state almost analogous to the earth sleep. . . ."

Light, vol. XLIV, 1924, p. 274, carried the following statement by a communicator. "After the sleep [i.e. after the enveiling vehicle of vitality is shed] there is a difference. Before, there is always a certain amount of illusion that you are still just the same person that you were in earth-life. That illusion does not get dispelled before sleep. . . . *Earthbound* spirits [in 'Hades' conditions] have not yet passed

[1] W. T. Pole, *Private Dowding*, Watkins, 1919.   [2] Hutchinson, 1922.
[3] Hester Travers Smith, *Life Eternal*, Wright and Brown, Ltd., 1933.
[4] *Letters from the Other Side*, Watkins, 1919.
[5] Geraldine Cummins, *The Road to Immortality*, p. 37.

through their sleep-stage; being earthbound means still that you really belong to the earth life and that you are in *some curious dream.*"

'Conan Doyle', communicating, said: "There have been a variety of communications as from myself, not always projected consciously from me." He held that communications *in general* are 'often' from "souls still *closely linked with earth*", and added: "The majority of communications received by the Spiritualist come from the denizens of the higher astral spheres, from souls both good in intention and pure in motive, although of limited knowledge and outlook. Remember, they pass on, more or less, but personal opinion and personal experience."[1] A communicator told Mrs. de Morgan (*From Matter to Spirit*, Longmans, Green & Co. Ltd., 1863, p. 205) that discarnate souls who were of an 'advanced' type were "shy" of communicating, but that those who lived *'near' the earth* were "ready to communicate under any name they could take to ensure them attention. . . ."

'Julia' (*After Death*, Stead's Publishing House Ltd., 1897), gave an early communication (p. 10) to the effect that many of the newly-dead desire to communicate with mortals (but mostly fail to do so). Later (p. 135) "After more experience and with better opportunities for observation," she remarked that this applies to "comparatively few"—that when they first arrive in the 'next world' "their hearts are in the old world", but "after a little time new interests arise".

The American lawyer-investigator, Randall (*Frontiers of the After Life*, Knopf, 1922) was told: "Some . . . spirits *who have not progressed far enough* to see and realise the beauty about them, when communicating with their friends on earth, give them quite wrong and dissimilar impressions of conditions over here."

Among the communicators from relatively 'low' levels must be mentioned those who also produce 'physical' phenomena ('direct voice', apports, levitations, 'materialisations', etc.). 'C.E.B.' (Colonel), writing in *Light*, vol. XLII, 1922, p. 646, pointed out: "The value of messages received through the 'direct voice' . . . are, on the average, below the standard of the communications received through a good clairvoyant or trance medium, apart from [as might be expected if these

[1] Ivan Cooke, *Thy Kingdom Come*, Wright and Brown, pp. 77, 149, 156

things are true] a curious and rather special faculty of *speaking in foreign languages*. The great majority of messages consist in merely of gasping ejaculations of pleasure at having been able to speak, of attempts to give names and to establish identity, etc." Much the same applies to the utterances of those discarnate souls who are so 'near' to earth conditions that they can produce levitations, materialisations, etc. These are inhabitants of 'Hades' conditions, knowledgeable beyond mortals as to the production of 'physical' phenomena, and able to 'read' our thoughts, but usually ignorant concerning scientific, philosophical or religious matters.

The observations of investigators, and those of intelligent mediums, agrees with these communications.

According to the *German* physician, Dr. J. Kerner,[1] Frau Hauffe, the 'Seeress of Prevorst', often saw and conversed with the 'departed' and they were almost all of the *'earthbound'* type. They desired her prayers (see Appendix IV). Although the *French* Curé d'Ars (Jean Baptiste Vianney, 1786-1859) did much good, he was similarly troubled over a period of thirty-five years by *'earthbound'* men. These poor people needed his prayers, but his religious 'education' made him avoid them as 'demons'.

The *American* Judge Edmonds (*Letters*, p. 96) found that 'earthbound' spirits "spoke so many *falsehoods*" that he was "disgusted". As the result of many years experience, Sir Arthur Conan Doyle[2] observed: "Communications usually come from those who have *not long passed over*, and tend to grow fainter, as one would expect."

Oswald Murray, (*Light*, vol. XL, 1920, p. 50), like many others, considered that discarnates who communicate with us directly are merely in the "inner-earth plane", or "psychic earth-plane", and not in "spiritual spheres", about which they know "very little" [and which they will not enter until the Soul Body has been shed at the 'third death']. He said: "They think that the state they occupy is the real Spiritual World, which is not the case. . . . So their communications may unintentionally mislead."

Psychical researchers, such as Dr. Hereward Carrington and Professor Hyslop, note that communicators who only recently

---

1 *Die Seherin von Prevorst* (1829), trans. Catherine Crowe, 1845.
2 *The New Revelation*, Hodder and Stoughton, 1918, p. 95.

died, or who are of the 'earthbound' type, often mention that
their mental state is temporarily 'confused', 'depressed',
'drowsy', 'dreamy', 'half-alive', semi-delirious, etc., and that
their environment is temporarily 'misty', 'foggy', 'like crossing
a dark river', etc. These states of consciousness we have termed
'sub-normal' and these environments are of the 'Hades' type.
They are more or less abnormal (due either to enforced death
or to exceptional grossness). They are left behind when the
vehicle of vitality is shed. But we shall see that some of those
who communicate from 'Paradise' conditions may be obliged
temporarily to accept these dream-like mental states and to
enter these 'foggy' environments—as would indeed be expected
if the accounts are true.

(b) The rarer communications from 'Paradise'
(corresponding to the Soul Body)

Discarnates whose instrument of consciousness in the Soul
Body, and whose environment is represented by 'Paradise'
conditions, enjoy consciousness at the 'super-normal' level.
These, in their normal state, so far from being 'confused', etc.
are particularly clear, serene and intense. But there may now be
a greater ('vibrational') gulf to be bridged for the purpose of
communication. 'Myers' wished he had not "been taken so
far", and gave this reason: "It makes it difficult to communicate." However, he said he had made a "voluntary choice"
and "the missionary spirit," i.e. the desire to demonstrate
survival, kept him "from felicity awhile".[1]

In order to communicate, those in 'Paradise' conditions may
be obliged to "lower their vibrations" (to achieve attunement
with the physically-embodied medium). When necessary, this
is done by borrowing ectoplasm from the medium; their
minds are then more or less dulled and their descriptions may,
in some respects, resemble those of the temporary inhabitants
of 'Hades' conditions: they may complain of being "befogged",
"semi-conscious", "drowsy", "dreamy", "suffocated", "not all
there", etc., and their mental condition may affect their
memories and therefore their 'messages'. Jane Sherwood[2]
transmitted a typical statement on this subject. "Coming back

[1] Sir Oliver Lodge, op. cit., 1909, pp. 292, 302.
[2] The Psychic Bridge, Rider & Co. Ltd., p. 40.

is difficult. . . . One has to lower one's vibration—something like going into a trance or being *drugged* and finding oneself again in the misty, half-alive [=‘Hades’] state." Another communicator said: "Realise that between us and you a great psychic gulf is fixed."[1] Nevertheless, he gave this assurance: "There is an underlying truth in every wrongly-transmitted message." (Examples of the latter may be cited. ‘Pelham’ promised to prove his identity after ‘passing’ if at all possible. In so doing Hyslop found that he mentioned an incident "that is wholly false in relation to me, though possibly true in relation to someone else."[2] Lodge, commenting on a communication from ‘Myers’ said that "a good many of these phenomena are not precisely what their surface-aspect implies, yet neither are they fraud".[3]

‘George Pelham’, a communicator whose identity has been exceptionally well established, said (to Dr. Hodgson): "See here, H. Don't view me with a critic's eye. . . . You have brain enough to understand my explanation of being shut up in this body [that of the medium, Mrs. Piper], *dreaming, as it were,* and trying to help on science."

Hodgson (*Proc. S.P.R.*, xiii, p. 28) compared the condition under which a discarnate communicator contacted a mortal friend with that of two mortals who were obliged to communicate with each other by employing a messenger who was *dead drunk!* Mrs. E. B. Browning made a very similar comparison. On one occasion, ‘Myers’, communicating, said it was "like entrusting a message on which infinite importance depends to a *sleeping person*";[4] on another it was like "dictating feebly to a reluctant and *somewhat obtuse* secretary".[5]

Mrs. Gladys Osborn Leonard was told by a communicator that "sometimes the spirits who are not ordinarily in touch with the earth conditions would find themselves overcome by a *sleepy, dreamy condition* when actually entering physical vibrations. This only lasted a short while with most people, but if is lasted longer . . . they would not be able to communicate or manifest satisfactorily. . . ."[6]

The communicator of ‘A.L.E.H.’[7] said: "When we come to

---

[1] Mrs. A. L. Fernie, *Not Silent if Dead!*, Fernie.   [2] *Op. cit.*, 1908, p. 171.
[3] *Op. cit.*, 1909, p. 305.   [4] *Proc. S.P.R.*, xxxi, p. 188.   [5] *Ibid.*, xxi, p. 230.
[6] *My Life in Two Worlds*, Cassell & Co. Ltd. 1931, p. 148.
[7] *Fragments from my Messages*, Women's Printing Society, Ltd., 1929, pp. 34, 52, 60.

you *a portion of ourselves rests*. We are in a *drowsy* state . . . it makes it easier for us to pick up earth-vibrations and talk to you." He maintained: "There are many layers of mind within our being." He also insisted that "not all would-be communicators are efficient". Certain of the dead become confused when communicating, and sometimes fail to send the desired message, because "they do not understand how to communicate". He pointed out: "It requires a skilled operator, one ripe in mind and quick in understanding, to speak fluently and correctly."

'Joyce', communicating to her mother, Mrs. G. Vivian, B.A. (*The Curtain Drawn*, Psychic Press Ltd., 1949, pp. 33, 37, 55), after communicating, said: "I found the earth-atmosphere *stifling* and I was glad to get back." Later she stated that being in the "earth-atmosphere" "for a fairly long time" caused "*a faint, stuffy feeling*". Still later she said: "When we plunge down into your atmosphere *we feel stifled at first and can't think*—but improve with practice."

The communicator of *Letters from the Other Side* (Watkins, 1919, p. 6) also noted a "befogging" effect. He said: "I am, as it were, but *semi-conscious* while communicating thus." He added: "It is one of the reasons for fragmentary communications."

A Doctor of Divinity, known during his earth-life to the Rev. C. Drayton Thomas, communicated after his death (*In the Dawn Beyond Death*, Lectures Universal Ltd., p. 143) and gave certain details of his 'passing'. However, he stated that some were but vaguely remembered. He said: "In my own sphere and place it would all be clear, but I now find a difficulty with my memory which is curious. . . ."

'E.K.' communicating to Jane Sherwood (*The Country Beyond*, Rider & Co. Ltd., p. 125), describing first his transition and then the process of communicating, said: "I felt as if I had gone through a door into a world where the time-consciousness did not exist, and having lived effortlessly in that world for a long time, had come back through the door to find myself exactly where, in point of time, I had started."

The communicator of Marjorie Livingston (*An Outline of Existence*, Wright and Brown, 1933, p. 19) said: "As I speak to you, I am not manifesting with complete consciousness.

Much of which I am normally aware is indistinct to my vision. *I am troubled by the miasmas of earth.*"

'Sir William Barrett' (*Personality Survives Death*, Longmans, Green & Co. Ltd., 1937, p. 198) told his wife that "*Only a part of the consciousness* [of the communicator] is getting through to earth conditions".

Admiral Moore's 'guide' explained her difficulty in remembering earthly people, places, etc., while in control of the medium's body as follows: "In all these matters my memory is perfectly clear when I stand free and unhampered in the spiritual atmosphere, but somehow when I return into earth's atmosphere, so many things became hazy and incomplete."[1] Still another said: "In certain circumstances we are only able to communicate with *a fraction of our mentality here*, which means that the messages get through to you in a *hazy state*".[2]

The reason adduced is the same as was given to 'A.L.E.H.': it is because "There are degrees and layers of consciousness" and "*the whole personality*" *is not engaged in communicating—that which communicates is* "*ourselves as we were on earth*", the 'greater' and 'higher' levels being 'asleep' [as it should be noted, they are in the 'normal' consciousness of earth-life, when the Physical Body acts like 'blinkers']. Statements such as these are not confined to 'popular' books: 'Pelham' made similar remarks to Dr. Hodgson through Mrs. Piper: "I am more awake than asleep, yet *I cannot come just as I am in reality.*"

Hyslop (*Psychical Research and the Resurrection*, T. Fisher Unwin, 1908, p. 349) received this communication: "You [mortals] to us are more as we understand sleep and, in order for us to get into communication with you, *we have to enter into your sphere, as one like yourself, asleep. This is why we make mistakes. . . .*"

Those discarnate souls whose instrument of consciousness consists of the un-enshrouded Soul Body may have something worthwhile to tell us but have difficulty in transmitting it. 'Myers', communicating through Geraldine Cummins, said: "When we . . . desire to communicate through some sensitive, we enter *a dream (or subjective) state.* . . . If we are but slightly entranced we are detached from the memory of concrete facts in our past life . . . we are frequently unable to

---

[1] *Glimpses of the Next State*, Watts.
[2] Roy Dixon Smith, *New Light on Survival*, Rider & Co. Ltd., 1952.

communicate through the medium's hand or voice many exact facts about our past career on earth, sometimes not even our own names."[1] He also described the 'lowering' of his 'vibrations' thus: "My perceptions, when adjusted to earth, are not rapid in their working."[2]

In a later series of communications, 'Myers' stated: "When we seek to communicate, we . . . slow down our processes of thought. . . . I may compare the experience with a passing from active life into *a still, sleepy world* [='Hades']. . . ."[3]

Still further, 'Myers' pointed out that one result of the 'Control's' mental condition, so produced, may be apparent fraud by the medium. He said that, since the discarnate 'Control' is often (temporarily) in "a partially hypnotic state", he is very open to suggestion. He continued: "Many instances of fraud, committed by mediums who practise physical phenomena may be traced to this condition. If any of those persons present at the seance suspect or anticipate, even sub-consciously, deception and trickery on the part of the medium, their thoughts . . . will be as powerful in their effect as the commands of a hypnotist to his patient. Acting on the auto-suggestions made by those present, an honest medium will commit fraudulent acts, and yet will be completely innocent."[4] (Fitzsimmons, the South African researcher (*op. cit.*) independently came to this conclusion.)

When communicating through Mrs. Thompson, 'Myers'[5] described it as "like looking at *a misty picture*" [='Hades' conditions] and admitted that he was more "*stupid*" than those from whom he had received communications during his earthly investigations. He said: "I thought I should do better, but I cannot. . . . How easy to promise and how difficult to fulfil."

Further, 'Myers' offered the same reason as was given by the communicators of the Rev. C. Drayton Thomas, 'A.L.E.H.' and others: "It is not my whole self [the Greater Self] talking." Professor Hyslop gave many examples of the effect of 'lowering the vibrations' in befogging the minds of would-be communicators (*Science and a Future Life*, Herbert B. Turner & Co.,

[1] *The Road to Immortality*, Ivor Nicholson and Watson, 1932, p. 124.
[2] *Ibid.*, p. 24.
[3] *Beyond Human Personality*, Ivor Nicholson and Watson, Ltd., 1935, p. 32.
[4] *Op. cit.*, 1935, p. 193.   [5] *Proc. S.P.R.*, xxiii, p. 200.

Boston, 1905, p. 326). Thus, his (deceased) father said: "If you will wait for me, I will remember all. . . ." "I seem to lose part of my recollection. . . . I intended to refer to Uncle John, but I *was somewhat dazed*." "Strange, I cannot think of the word I want." Again: "I am working to keep my thoughts clear." Still again: "It will help to keep my thoughts from rambling," etc. Hyslop stated: "Illustrations of this sort could be multiplied into the hundreds."

The communicator of Frieda Hohenner-Parker described his difficulties thus: "Our first reaction is that of being encased, *feeling very limited.* . . . In the process of entering the medium's body, we lose much of our thoughts, ideas and knowledge, all so clear to us a moment or two previous to our contact with the body, and so, on many occasions, the controlling spirit cannot answer some seemingly simple questions from the sitter concerned." He added: "The feeling of being limited and encased fades away after a few times of trance."[1]

'Feda', the child-control of Mrs. Leonard, explained the limitation of Mr. Drayton Thomas's deceased father, while communicating, thus: "*He* brings only a part of his intelligence into the medium's [i.e. Mrs. Leonard's] mind. All *your* [i.e. Mr. Thomas's mind] is not in your brain at one and the same time: *you* have your conscious and your sub-conscious mind. *He* also develops a conscious and a sub-conscious section when he comes here. . . . The part left outside the medium's mind forms, for the moment, *his* sub-conscious mind. When *you* wish to recall what *your* conscious mind has lost, you try to obtain it from the sub-conscious. . . . It is more difficult for him than for you, because *a smaller portion of his mind is operating in the medium.* . . . You see, therefore, why he cannot, while controlling, think so clearly or remember so much as you can."[2]

Explanations of the difficulties of communication from 'Paradise' levels, similar to those given by communicators and exemplified above, were envisaged by Dr. Hodgson,[3] Professor Hyslop,[4] Dr. Hereward Carrington,[5] G. N. M. Tyrrell,[6]

---

[1] *A Crusader Here and There*, A. J. Stockwell, 1952, p. 116.
[2] The Rev. C. Drayton Thomas, *The Mental Phenomena of Spiritualism*, L.S.A. Publications, 1930, p. 102.
[3] *Proc. S.P.R.*, xii, 284.   [4] *Op. cit.*, 1908.
[5] *The Story of Psychic Science*, Rider & Co. Ltd.; *Your Psychic Powers and How to Develop Them*, Kegan Paul, Trench, Trubner & Co. Ltd., 1920.
[6] *The Nature of Human Personality*, George Allen and Unwin, Ltd., 1954.

Dr. R. C. Johnson,[1] and other psychical researchers.

Hyslop said: "The general supposition which, to the mind of Dr. Hodgson and myself, explains the persistent *triviality* of the communicating spirit at the time of communicating (not necessarily in his normal state in the spirit world) is in a sort of *abnormal mental state, perhaps resembling our dream-life. . . .*" He referred to communications received from 'Hodgson' after the latter had 'passed on', saying that 'Hodgson' alluded to the danger of "making a botch" of his messages and broke out with the statement: "It is so *suffocating* here. I can appreciate their [i.e. former communicators, during his own life-time] difficulties better than ever before." Here he was intimating ideas which he held as to the difficulty of communicating before he himself passed away, and he had often compared the influence of the condition to that of mephitic gases, and we know what effect they have on the integrity of consciousness."[2]

Hyslop (*op. cit.*, 1908, p. 175) further commented on the obvious significance of this phenomenon—it lends strong support to the survival hypothesis. Whereas those who try to avoid accepting that hypothesis make the most of apparent trivialities in communications, apparent failures of some communicators' memories, the apparently *dream—or delirium—like state* of some of them (at least during the process of communicating), all these things are not merely explicable, but are to be expected under the conditions that are described.

An interesting case was mentioned by Dr. Hereward Carrington (*The Story of Psychic Science*, Rider & Co. Ltd., 1930, p. 326). A communicator said that he had performed a certain act during his earth-life. Actually, it was known that he had not performed this act—but he had made the same statement when, in the course of 'passing' he had been in a *delirium*. The suggestion is that, in order to attune with the medium and communicate, he had had to 'lower his vibrations' to near-earth 'level': this caused him to re-enter the pre-death *delirious state* and so he mechanically repeated a statement which was, nevertheless, erroneous. In this connection it is interesting to note that 'Stead', communicating (*op. cit.*, 1933, p. 68), called the 'Hades' state "the plane of *delirium*".

[1] *The Imprisoned Splendour*, Hodder and Stoughton, 1953.
[2] *Op. cit.*, 1908, p. 195.

Carrington (*loc. cit.*), discussing communicators, observed: "They experience great difficulty in holding their thoughts together connectedly during the process of communication." He added: "This does not mean that they are ordinarily in this confused state, but (very often) *as soon as they come in contact with the medium's psychic atmosphere and magnetism, they become confused and their minds tend to wander as they would in delirium or in a state of trance.*" Carrington made a further point: "It is because of this that many of the messages we receive commence well but dwindle off into incoherence and triviality."

G. N. M. Tyrrell (*loc. cit.*), after indicating that 'Gurney', 'Myers' and 'Sidgwick', while communicating through Mrs. Willett, were "*Very like what they were during earth-life*", said "But when we reflect, the answer occurs to us that perhaps they are not. Having entered into a larger and a different world [='Paradise' conditions] they may also have entered into a larger and different phase of selfhood [=the intermediate, or psychic, self] which match that world. *Perhaps, therefore, they have to pass through the same narrowing and specialised channels that the messages themselves have to traverse, they may become temporarily narrower and 'crystalised' too.* Like the messages, they may be reduced to this worldly forms of themselves—in fact, to what they were when they lived in this world." This conclusion of an eminent psychical researcher is identical with the statements communicated to 'A.L.E.H.' and cited above. Similarly, Geraldine Cummins (*Unseen Adventures*, Rider & Co. Ltd., 1951, p. 75) summed up a communication concerning this matter as follows: "In other words, the 'Messengers' are said to *resume their incarnate human personalities in order to approach the earth.*" On p. 156 of the same work, when discussing a (supposed) surviving Egyptian who communicated and who did not seem to have 'progressed' since being on earth (i.e. in some thousands of years of our time), Miss Cummins similarly said: "Might not the ancient Egyptian temporarily discard the accretions of personality obtained during a discarnate existence of several thousands of years . . . and be once more the *limited* personality, the *human* soul, she once was. . . .?" 'Tien Sien Tie', the Chinese inspirer of J. J. Morse, said the same as the communicators of 'Questator Vitae' (Oswald Murray)—namely, that, while communicating, they were 'temporarily projected' into earth-conditions, "the original

Spirits they represent [=their Greater Selves] are in a state of somnolency" (*Light*, vol. XLVI, 1926, p. 15).

P. E. Cornillier (*op. cit.*, 1921, p. 149) not only made this point, but he correlated it with the conditions that obtain in hypnosis. He said: "When the spirit comes back into the body, he forgets the astral [here ='Paradise'] life and is conscious only of his incarnated state. Whatever may be the reason of this oblivion of astral life, we are forced to admit its reality since we can verify it experimentally. As a matter of fact, Reine [the sensitive] manifests it at every seance when, passing from one degree of hypnosis, into another less profound, she loses all recollection of what she has seen and heard in the more profound sleep: and finally, on waking, has no longer the least consciousness of what has passed in her astral excursion."

Our Diagram 5, based on analyses of statements by *communicators*, shows that the latter not only state the fact but also offer a highly plausible explanation of it which Hodgson, Hyslop, Carrington, Tyrrell, and the other psychical researches, failed to envisage, i.e. that the 'level' of consciousness is determined by the bodily constitution. 'W. T. Stead', communicating,[1] made the latter point quite specifically. Having said that "After you die the soul suddenly seems to expand", he continued: "*When we communicate with you, we have, in a sense, to form a body; a body that will compress the soul again to the dimensions it had before it cast off the [physical] body.*" (Compare Mme. d'Espérance, cited above.) 'Stead' then described the effect of the process: "The whole thing is a strain. When we speak to you we are in an *unnatural* condition." 'Nellie', communicating through Mrs. Piper, expressed the converse of this idea when she said that when 'Myers' was *not* engaged in the process of communication he was "much more lively" and "much more wakened up" than when so engaged. The communicator of 'A.B.' (*op. cit.*, 1937, p. 116) similarly stated that, though transition brings an expansion of consciousness to the soul, "If it is to return to earth [for purposes of communicating] it must be compressed again. . . .".

This idea—that the 'lowering of vibrations' to achieve the attunement necessary for communication, involves a kind of

[1] 'W. T. Stead' (via Mrs. Hester Dowden-Smith), *Life Eternal*, Wright and Brown, 1933, p. 170.

[2] Sir Oliver Lodge. *The Survival of Man*, Methuen, 1909, p. 298.

re-embodiment in ectoplasm—was also communicated to Montgomery Smith and E. M. Taylor: "When you think of me, I am born again into your life . . . an etheric being *and body*. Here I am all spirit, but to work on earth I must be *partly materialised*. Your mental image of me draws matter [ectoplasm] round me, *creates me as I was, and I can manifest on earth*."[1]

The communicator of Marjorie Livingston (*The New Nuctemeron*, Rider & Co. Ltd., 1930, p. 75) stated that discarnate souls who are in relatively "high spheres" cannot contact mankind unless they "gather *gross material* from lower planes" and that this "material" affects both the body and the mind of the would-be communicator—it subdues "the bright emanations" of his Soul Body and has a "*heavy, choking, exhausting*" *effect*, preventing free manifestation—"Yet only so can it reach those outside its own orbit of life". In a later book which was communicated to Marjorie Livingston (*The Harmony of the Spheres*, Rider & Co. Ltd., 1931, p. 60) the communicator said that "progressed", or "advanced" Spirits, i.e. "the angels of God", "have not affinity with man save through the highest within him". He went on: "They must needs, therefore, attune themselves *outwardly* in order that they may approach him", and he pointed out that "Unprogressed spirits, on the other hand, are beset with no such difficulties".

J. Arthur Findlay (*Looking Back*, Psychic Press Ltd., 1955, p. 472) described how certain 'physical' phenomena of psychical research are produced by discarnate souls. He said: "Under suitable conditions, the so-called dead can *lower their vibration by means of a lace-like substance called ectoplasm* which is found in mediums in greater supply than in ordinary men. Thus, these other-world men and women can regain contact with physical conditions, vibrate the atmosphere and be both seen and heard."

The Rev. G. Vale Owen (*Facts and the Future Life*, Hutchinson & Co. Ltd.), like various communicators, attributed the 'lowering of vibrations' by some communicators to ectoplasm which they obtained from the medium. It is of course, the 'vibrations', and therefore the reactivity, of the Soul Body to which Mr. Findlay and Mr. Owen refer. In the cases mentioned by the former, which are relatively rare, the reduction was

---

[1] *Light in Our Darkness*, Psychic Press Ltd., 1936, p. 127.

great enough to render them visible and audible to non-clairvoyants; in those mentioned by the latter, it was relatively small, so that 'mental' phenomena only were produced—'communication' (which has various degrees) became possible.

Our immediate point is that those of the 'dead' who communicate most often and most readily (i.e. the newly-dead and the 'earthbound', whose Soul Bodies are still 'enveiled', limiting them to 'Hades' conditions) may unintentionally 'transmit' dreams, while some of those who have emerged into clearer and more stable 'Paradise' conditions, in order deliberately to communicate, may be obliged to approach, if not actually enter, that same semi-dream or semi-trance state. This explains many apparent failures of memory, errors and trivialities in communications even from 'Paradise' conditions. Moreover, they are limited to the vocabulary of the medium. Still again, since only earth-terms mean anything to mortals, they must fail adequately to describe 'next-world' conditions. (The last-mentioned limitation necessarily applies to communications between mortals themselves: whenever Livingstone told African natives of the great possessions of Queen Victoria, they invariably asked him to express them in terms of the number of cows she possessed!) Again, since in the after-death states the physical brain no longer operates, as already stated, we should not expect predominantly logical, systematic and scientific communications, but those of the moral, religious and 'mystical' type. These do, in fact, emanate from the 'higher levels' of the 'beyond'. There are other reasons for difficulties in communication, but they need not be considered here.

The clairvoyant, Mrs. Eileen J. Garrett (*Does Man Survive Death?*, Helix Press, 1957, p. 16), speaking of her own supernormal experience said: "I am unable to find any words that could translate the experience into mortal understanding. And surely this must happen to others who are in the habit of passing to and from this state. It may be why people say that nothing of importance comes through. *I believe that much of importance is transmitted,* but I do not think that we ourselves have the capacity to translate it, and it is in this stage that we fail" [i.e. the physical body and brain acts on the Greater Self and the intermediate, or psychic, self, like the 'blinkers' on the harness of a horse, precisely as the dead say].

Mortals, not unnaturally, expect communication with departed souls to be as simple and straightforward as is conversation between mortals. But it cannot be so: conversation is simple, communication is complex. It is particularly complex in those cases in which the communicator must retard his mental activities in order to attune with the medium. This process has two results. First, what is received by us may well include trivialities, confusions, contradictions and even actual errors: the person 'speaking' is 'not himself' but is like a man who has just suffered the severe shock of a road-crash, or one who is half-anaesthetised. A man whom we knew in earth-life to be of a well-informed and clear-thinking type may communicate inacurate or vague statements: he may, never-the less, be doing his best to 'get through'. The claim that a communicator may forget details of his past life—even his own name—is paralleled by what can occur in partial anaesthesia or hypnosis. The argument often advanced, therefore, "*That* can't be 'X'—it must therefore be either the 'sub-conscious' mind of the medium or an ignorant impersonating discarnate personality" is not necessarily sound.

A second effect is that a communicator may not know what is 'getting through' to 'our side'. The communicator of Mrs. C. A. Dawson-Scott (*op. cit.*, 1926, p. 100) simply said: "We give you a message . . . but are in ignorance as to whether you have got it." The supposed discarnate Edmund Gurney, after communicating to Lord Balfour through Mrs. Willett said: "There's a longing to know, when one has struggled, how far one has succeeded in making oneself. . ."[1]

Similarly, the communicator of *Letters from the Other Side* (Watkins, 1919, p. 74) said, "As to whether the things I say do get through, I have often very little means of knowing."

Sir Oliver Lodge was told, regarding the communications of his son, 'Raymond': "He does not seem sure if he got anything through. It is so peculiar. Even here [i.e. after returning to normal 'after-life' conditions], he is not always quite certain that he has said what he wanted to say except sometimes when it is clear and you jump at it. Sometimes then he feels, 'I've got *that* home, anyway!' "[2] 'Raymond' himself stated: "I

[1] *Proc. S.P.R.*, xliii, p. 232.
[2] *Raymond*, Methuen & Co. Ltd., 1916, p. 159.

was not quite sure of what I did get through."[1] In a script of Mrs. Holland, 'Myers', communicating, asked: "Does any of this reach you, reach anyone, or am I only wailing as the wind wails?"[2] A communicator of Miss L. M. Bazett's said: "You won't be disappointed if I have failed to get this correct. I will try again if you are."[3] 'Gurney', speaking through Mrs. Willett to Lord Balfour, said: "Is he there? Does it reach him?" Again: "Does he hear? How can I know that he hears?"[4]

In the 'cross-correspondence' experiments, the communicator often asked, "Did you get that?" or "Was that all right?" and 'Myers' once said: "I saw the circle, but was not sure about the triangle."

(c) The absence of communications from 'Heaven' conditions (corresponding to the Spiritual Body)

Many communicators agree with Rudolf Steiner and others in saying that, once the Soul Body is shed (at the 'third death', or unveiling), the 'vibrational gulf' between discarnate souls and mortals is too great to permit the attunement necessary for *direct* communication. Those few 'missionary' souls who do communicate from 'Heaven' conditions must employ intermediaries or 'relays' who are in 'Paradise' conditions.

In a similar way, when 'physical' phenomena are required, these cannot be directly provided by discarnate souls in 'Paradise' conditions, or beyond: others, who are in 'Hades' conditions, and whose outermost 'body' is the semi-physical vehicle of vitality, must be used as intermediaries.

Communion—a sharing of affection, aspiration and prayer—is possible between those in 'Heaven' conditions and their mortal friends, where *verbal communications* are precluded: this is the true Communion of Saints.

Let us sum up and appraise the above. It will be seen that the accounts which communicators give us concerning the processes of communication and their effects on their memories and mentalities are in complete agreement with the conclusions reached, after years of study, by certain psychical researchers. It is true that a fairly large proportion of people who have

---

[1] *Raymond*, p. 183.   [2] *Proc. S.P.R.*, xxi, p. 233.
[3] *After-death Communications*, Kegan Paul, Trench, Trubner & Co. Ltd., p. 40.
[4] *Proc. S.P.R.*, xliii, 1953, p. 233.

contacted discarnate souls have supposed (and often pro-
claimed) that *their* communicators were of a remarkably elevated type, even divine. This is not surprising. Of all the people
who possess a piano, a fairly large proportion similarly proclaim
that *their* instrument has "an exceptionally good tone" and of
those who own a camera, most think that, in *their* case, "the
lens is a very good one"! We know that the vast majority of
pianos have a mediocre tone and that most cameras have
indifferent lenses. The same applies to communicators: both
they and researchers insist that, of discarnates who both desire
and are able to 'get through' to mortals, the *vast majority are of
mediocre type*: a few are admirable, a few are pathetically weak
and some are more or less definitely wicked.

All this is to be expected: it is what obtains on earth. The
Scriptures (I John. iv. 1) exhort us to "Try the spirits, whether
they are of God". It will be clear that a vainglorious, boastful,
flattering 'spirit' (discarnate *soul*), or one who makes specious
promises, is not "of God". With communicators, as with all
things, there is the test: "By their *fruits* ye shall know them"
(Matt. vii. 16, 20).

Communicators in general are in one of two environments
and have corresponding mentalities: probably 99 out of every
100 communicators are in the semi-awake, semi-dream, condition that is known as 'Hades'. These comprise two chief
groups of people: first, newly-dead men, of average mental and
spiritual status, many of whom 'passed' prematurely and who,
in the main, merely repeat the opinions they held during
earth-life, and, secondly, the long-dead who are delayed in this
more or less abnormal condition, i.e. the 'earthbound', who
are often essentially ignorant and sometimes anti-social.
Among these are the boasters, jokers, liars and impersonators
of the immediate 'next world'. Yet these men have abilities
which may impress unthinking mortals—they know our
thoughts and wishes (and may, therefore, prepare traps that
will disgust or confuse the most honest and clear-thinking
of investigators) and they may be able to impress us by 'reading'
our 'auras' (vehicles of vitality) and telling us (*a*) events in our
past lives, (*b*) things about our present or even future health
or (*c*), by noting the trends of our thoughts, emotions and
volitions, correctly forecast certain future events. They may
also be able to produce apparent miracles—the 'physical'

phenomenon of psychical research (levitations, 'apports', 'materialisations', etc.). Some, though not, of course, all, Red Indian 'guides' are probably of the 'earthbound' type: they are probably reluctant to abandon earth-conditions. Yet they can impress non-critical enquirers in these ways.

'Physical' mediums, i.e. mediums whose vehicles of vitality are relatively 'loose', naturally tend to contact discarnates who are in 'Hades' conditions, and even those mediums who have integrity and honesty beyond that of average men (and who will eventually also contact 'higher' levels) may have to '*pass through*' 'Hades' conditions.

With 'mental' mediums it is the Soul Body that is relatively 'loose', and therefore useable separately from the Physical Body. In a few cases both the vehicle of vitality and the Soul Body are easily separated from the Physical Body, and these mediums produce both 'physical' and 'mental' phenomena.

When a 'mental' medium contacts a discarnate soul who is in 'Paradise' conditions, they may need to 'halve' the difference in their 'vibratory rates' if communication is to take place. If this is necessary, the communicator (who in any case is usually only of average mental and spiritual development) is obliged to enter the semi-awake, semi-dream condition which characterises the inhabitants of the abnormal 'Hades' conditions: this may cause disconcerting (apparent) lapses of memory and the transmission of trivialities and even errors. Nevertheless, highly-spiritual communicators (in 'Paradise' conditions) who contact mediums of a high type are not obliged to 'lower their vibrations'; they give highly satisfactory messages. The deceased father and sister of the Rev. C. Drayton Thomas thus communicated satisfactorily through Mrs. Osborn Leonard.

Whereas Ecclesiastes complained that the majority of communicators (average folk who were in the half-awake, half-asleep, 'Hades' state) "know not anything", those who receive messages from communicators of high mental and moral type through mediums of similar status make the opposite observation: discussing the Ear of Dionysius case (*Proc. S.P.R.*, xliii, pp. 41-318), the material of which consisted of a complex literary puzzle that was apparently set by the discarnate Myers and Gurney, Sir Oliver Lodge being the 'sitter' and Mrs. Willett the sensitive, G. N. M. Tyrrell (*The Personality of Man*, Pelican Books, 1946, p. 158) commented: "If these are the dead speaking [and many have come to that conclusion] *they have all their wits about them.*"

Again, whereas the religious content of communications that emanate from 'Hades' conditions merely re-echoes the babel of earthly opinions, the communicators on high 'levels' in 'Paradise' conditions, as G. N. M. Tyrrell[1] observed, are "wholly and unequivocably Christian".

Although communication may be difficult and sometimes unsatisfactory, even the difficulties are such as would be expected. Everything points to survival. True, genuine and worth-while communications are undoubtedly received under appropriate conditions. But they are relatively rare. So are true, genuine and worth-while conversations among mortals!

'Vettellini', the communicator of P. E. Cornillier (*The Survival of the Soul*, Kegan Paul, Trench Trubner & Co. Ltd., 1921) like many others, made a useful distinction between various discarnate souls by the 'colour' of their bodies. Those whose after-death double still included the vehicle of vitality (and who were therefore in 'Hades' conditions, and often 'earthbound') were *'reddish-grey'*. Such people are usually more or less ignorant, even when well intentioned, while some are 'jokers', some are impersonators and some even malicious. Many are pretentious and boastful. It is these 'earthbound' folk who cause disquiet among mortals by either contradictory or lying communications. They are responsible for such books as *The Dangers of Spiritualism*, by A Member of the S.P.R. (Sands & Co., 1901), and *Communication with the Dead*, by J. G. Carew-Gibson (Rider & Co.).

The bodies (Soul Bodies) of communicators who are in 'Paradise' conditions vary in colour from *'grey-blue to bright blue'*. The 'grey-blue' type, though more or less well intentioned, are, in fact, more or less ignorant. The 'bright blue' ones are both more honourable and more knowledgeable. But these 'Paradise' communicators (unlike many from 'Hades') lay no claim to either infallibility or omniscience—on the contrary, they often specifically disclaim both. They do not wilfully mislead. The teachings from the 'lower' ('grey blue') levels, like those from 'Hades', reflect all earthly opinions and may be Christian or other, but those from 'higher' ('bright blue') levels, as G. N. M. Tyrrell pointed out (*Grades of Significance,*

[1] *Grades of Significance*, Rider & Co. Ltd., 1930, p. 196.

Rider & Co.), are *"wholly and unequivocally Christian"*. Examples are in "The Deeper Issues Series" of J. M. Watkins (*Christ in You, The Thinning of the Veil, The Coming Light,* etc.) and *The Silent Voice* (G. Bell & Sons Ltd., 1935).

The bodies (Spiritual or Celestial Bodies) of those who are in the true 'Heavens' vary from *'white' to 'golden white'* (since they have passed out of 'Purgatorial' conditions by "washing their robes". These can seldom, if ever, communicate directly in words, though they may do so by using 'relays' who are in 'Paradise' conditions. *They always stand ready and willing, even anxious, to inspire, encourage and sustain, by telepathic process, those who will ask for this and whose intention it is to pass on what is received to others in service and other ways.* This involves no mediums, no ouija boards, planchette, trance, etc., but "prayer and fasting". Oswald Murray (*The Process of Man's Becoming* and *The Spiritual Universe,* Duckworth, 1921, 1924), Rellimeo (*An Explanation of Psychic Phenomena,* Fowler, 1911) and many others rightly insist that our main concern should be to attune our hearts and minds to the Christ Spirit within, so that He (often through His 'ministering angels'—Heb. i. 14) will inspire us with worthy purposes and the strength to implement them (Phil. iv. 13).

On the one hand, *we have to 'still' the outer, lesser, temporary, everyday self, and personality* (Ps. xlvi. 10), since "getting and spending, we lay waste our powers", and on the other hand, we have to arouse and *'awaken' the Inner, Greater, Eternal, Hidden Self, the Individuality, Over-soul or Christ-in-you* (Ephes. v. 14) and, having deliberately, definitely and repeatedly *asked* (Matt. vii. 7), *"waited upon"* (Isa. xl. 31) the Christ within, we must "bring the Kingdom of God" to earth through service to our fellows.

This approach is to Truths of a spiritual nature, and not to scientific or philosophical truths: it is a pragmatic search and does not proceed via a series of suppositions or hypotheses (none of which is finally clinched, proven and established) but via incontrovertible and utterly convincing *experience.* Any person who provisionally accepts the spiritual nature of the Greater Self (p. 57) and acts upon that conception will find it true because it 'answers' and 'works'. "If any man will do His will, he shall know of the doctrine whether it be of God or whether I speak of myself", declared the Master (John vii. 17).

The fact that first things must be put first (Matt. vi. 33) by no means implies that any and every contact with communicators from 'beyond' is wrong or undesirable. Much depends on the person, the time, the place, the aim, object and motive, the background of the activity.

"PRAY FOR ME!"

'Ghosts' may represent (1) temporarily exteriorised 'doubles' of 'living' people; (2) ensouled 'doubles', i.e. representing the 'bodies' of surviving souls—sometimes the vehicle of vitality in addition to the Soul Body and sometimes the latter only; (3) soul-less vehicles of vitality, partial corpses, 'astral shells' shed from the total after-death 'double' at the 'second death' or (4) soul-less 'doubles' representing mental images (created by either 'living' or 'dead' people) that are usually highly charged with love, hate, fear, etc., and which may be more or less 'materialised' by ectoplasm derived from a mediumistic person in the vicinity and which, therefore, may be seen or heard by non-psychics.

When 'ghosts' do represent surviving souls, or personalities, the latter are usually delayed in 'Hades' conditions and have not attained 'Paradise', the normal 'home' of the newly-dead, as indicated by Jesus to the dying insurgent ('thief'): "This day shalt thou be with me in Paradise"; they are 'earthbound' and, when they manage to make themselves seen or heard by mortals, they often plead: *"Pray for me!"* (Statement No. 29).

As early as 1829, Frau Hauffe, 'The Seeress of Prevorst', a German woman claimed that she could see and hear 'earthbound' souls, and they her: she explained this ability—which she greatly deplored—as due to the fact that she herself was in a half-dead condition (i.e. with the vehicle of vitality partially released from the physical body). Her medical adviser, Dr. J. Kerner (*Die Seherin von Prevorst*), pp. 199, 239, 267) described several instances in point. A 'dead' criminal told the Seeress that he had wandered for a long time "without being able to address himself to prayer". Kerner said: "She instructed him as she would have done a child". The sounds which this poor soul made became less audible and he became more cheerful. Another 'dead' man in the 'earthbound' state was asked by Frau Hauffe why he was where he was, i.e. in the

'mid-region' or 'Hades', and he replied, "For my sins." He
pleaded: "Teach me to pray!" On one occasion, Frau Hauffe
was awakened by a woman-'ghost' who said, "Who sits in
darkness, as I do, endures great torment. Will you pray for
me?" Another said, "Pray for me", and asked the Seeress to
open her hymn-book at a certain hymn and read it. This she
did, and so helped the enquirer. Frau Hauffe stated:"A mortal
can show them the way, but cannot redeem them. . . . I am
not afraid of spirits generally, but it is hard to be persecuted
by them". She also found that her statements (which are
highly evidential) were disbelieved by most of her friends and
she tended to lose them.

One 'earthbound' man complained that he was "unable
at present" to leave the man he was 'haunting' (as the above-
mentioned spirits 'haunted' Frau Hauffe), and he urged two
procedures: first, that the man whom he was troubling should
"exercise his will-power" and resist him and, secondly, that
he should pray for him (A Member of the S.P.R., *The Dangers
of Spiritualism*, Sands & Co. Ltd., 1901, p. 42.)

Light, vol. XLVI, 1926, p. 255, quoted from a work entitled
From Matter to Spirit, by 'C.D.', to the effect that the statement
that requests for prayers are commonly received from 'earthbound' souls was "strongly confirmed" by his own experience.
He further referred to what we call 'co-operation' (see p. 161)
thus: a poor carpenter who was 'earthbound' asked for prayers
on his behalf. The account continues: "As similarity of state
in the spirit constitutes *nearness*, he was far removed from his
guides, who were able to approach him only through the
intervention of *one in the body* with whom he was in a kind of
rapport and whose assertions he believed."

As already said, Professor Flammarion mentioned the
frequent plea, "Pray for me", and could not understand it.
(He thought it must always come from Roman Catholics, who
believe in prayers for the dead.) I have seen no explanation of
the phenomenon, yet the matter seems clear, and the implications are of the first importance.

They suggest an adequate answer to those people who—for
various reasons, mostly unknown to themselves—refuse to
consider the question of an after-life and say, "I believe in
living one life at a time."

During earth-life the Physical Body acts like a governor or

damper—it retards our thoughts, feelings and willings, since they have to overcome the resistance represented by its sluggishness. Ernest Oaten, a psychic, realised that he received thoughts from both incarnate and discarnate souls and he could distinguish between them: those from the physically disembodied came "like the flash of a cane", whereas those from the physically embodied were "heavy, slow and ponderous" (*Light*, vol. XLVI, 1926, p. 73). The damper-like effect of the body on the mind, which was thus recognised by Oaten, is important: it provides us mortals with opportunities to control thought and emotion (see e.g., Hyslop's observation concerning the discarnate Hodgson, p. 158). But, for the same reason, the Physical Body also operates like a gun emplacement to thoughts, feelings and willings: they overcome the resistance of the sluggish Physical Body only when we exert sufficient effort. (Hence the insistence, in Holy Writ, of the importance of 'overcoming'—'He that overcometh shall inherit all things', Rev. xxi, 7; see also John ii. 13; Rom. xii. 21; Rev. ii. 7, 11, 17, 26, iii, 5, 12, 21). Similarly, 'A.B.', communicating (*The Coming Light*, Watkins, 1924, p. 85) said: "Your world is the hardest school of your round of experiences. Prizes won here are won for eternity. The very density of the material in which you work makes the overcoming of it a finer conquest. . . . Experience on your planet is a unique opportunity and a privilege. . . . Make the best use of every opportunity. A strenuous life on earth is of immense value." 'Myers' communicated the converse statement, pointing out that in 'the World of Illusion', there is "an almost entire absence of conflict or effort" and he indicated the result— "accordingly there is an absence of any true creation."[1]

Dorothy Grenside similarly insisted that what we do when out of the body (temporarily, during deep sleep) is determined by our chief desires while in the body (during our 'waking' hours), that if, on the one hand, our daily lives are empty and without worthy purpose, our 'astral life' will be empty and boring, while if, on the other hand, we have some deep interest during the everyday life of physical embodiment, "whether there be an opportunity or not to follow it here" on earth, it will eventually be realised "because" (like 'Myers') she said:

[1] Geraldine Cummins, *The Road to Immortality*, Ivor Nicholson and Watson, 1932, p. 85.

"in the astral world [='Paradise'] there is *only continuation of endeavour*—there is no creation of fresh interests." She added: "Hence, the enormous importance of earth-life. It is here we sow the seeds which elsewhere come to flower."[1] (See also p. 159.)

The highly comforting statements made by many communicators that if we mortals faithfully try to develop and express any strong interests (whether artistic, musical, scientific, social or other) that we may possess, even though circumstances may deny their fruition in this life, our efforts are not lost and wasted, since we have set in motion, through the body, forces that will work themselves out in the after-life. In other words, in the world of high endeavour, as well as in the moral and spiritual spheres, we eventually 'reap' that which we 'sowed'. (This insistence on our need to put forth a maximum of effort is by no means incompatible with the fact that the eventual victory is not won by us, i.e., by the work of our lesser selves, but is the "gift of God"—see Appendix V.)

'A.B.', communicating to Mary Bruce Wallace, stressed the importance of mortals discarding materialistic conceptions before transition, "since, although death does not change a person, it certainly seems to crystallise the thoughts and feelings which the soul has strongly impressed upon it as the result of its incarnation". (Compare the effect of 'fixed ideas' mentioned on p. 77.)

Wm. James pointed out that it is *at the moment of doing* that the brain receives a trace, or kink, to correspond. It will be evident that the body facilitates the formation of mental habits, whether 'good' or 'bad', and thereby conserves mental energy and provides continuity. Life in the body is consequently a great opportunity for the acquirement of valuable modes of thought, feeling and willing: it is during earth-life that we are best able to form not only habits of honest thinking, sincere feeling and determined willing, but also *the habit of praying*, of asking the help of the Christ-spirit in these endeavours (I Thess. v. 17), for without this help from 'within', we (lesser selves) can "do nothing" (John xv. 5) and are foredoomed to frustration and failure. "I [the lesser self] can do all things", declared St. Paul (Phil. iv. 13), "through Christ [the 'Vine' of whom our Greater Selves are 'branches'] who strengtheneth me." Although the Master Himself constantly

---

[1] *The Meaning of Dreams*, G. Bell & Sons Ltd., 1923, p. 90.

turned to 'the Father' in prayer, modern man, and especially
in the West, sadly neglects the only sure source of victory.

Professor Wm. James also likened habit to the flywheel on
an engine—it carries us over possible 'dead-centres' in life.
Our study shows that immediate after-life necessarily has a
pronounced 'dead-centre'.

Earth-life is clearly a time when we have the initiative and
those who fail to make full use of the initiative which the
physical body and physical world afford will find it hard to
initiate desirable activities in the after-life: among these is *the
habit of prayer*—not feeble, purely verbal and only occasional
petition. People in 'Hades' often need the prayers of mortal
friends (whose bodies act as gun-emplacements) in overcoming
the inertia which characterised their mortal lives and which
they have taken with them. That which was not 'sowed' in this
life was not 'reaped' in the next.

Many communications urge us to take full advantage of
earth-life and warn us that those who fail, to any considerable
degree, in doing so will "long to come back" to the protection
of the body—that their thoughts and feelings will "run riot"
and be impossible to control once the governor-like physical
body has gone.

The 'Seeress of Prevorst', described the 'ghosts', or 'earthbound spirits', as more or less unhappy. She stated (p. 248):
"I would rather be here on earth than in the mid-region
(='Hades'). *They feel their sins more acutely than they did here*,
and the evil ones trouble those that are better than them.
A mental trouble is worse than a bodily one." Frau Hauffe
(p. 159) explained that "earthly thoughts" had resulted in
these poor folk being 'earthbound' and added: "*But it
must not be thought that improvement is easier there, in the mid-
region, than here on earth*. It must originate with themselves. ...
I am unhappily so constituted (i.e. with a partially-released
vehicle of vitality) that I can see them and they me. They come
to me that I may aid them through prayer and give them a
word of consolation. . . ." This description of unprogressed
discarnate souls as being in a 'mid-' region between earth and
'Paradise' (corresponding to the vehicle of vitality which is
intermediate in certain properties between the physical body
and the Soul Body) has an exact counterpart in the trance
addresses of Emma Hardinge (*Extemporaneous Addresses*, 2nd

Series, 1886, J. Burns, p. 44). The communicator stated that when a man dies "he does not quit the earth at all—*until*, through various stages of progression, *he passes from the earthly spheres into higher ones*". He continued: "*Hades is here; the mid-region where dwell the souls of men during their second sphere of eternal existence—within this natural earth of yours.*"

So much for people who fail to take advantage of their opportunities during earth-life, who fail to use them as "stepping-stones" to "higher things". Most of us have a sufficiency of difficulties, but the wealthy are often deficient in that type of soul-making material. Hence, the Master (Matt. xix. 23) insisted: "A rich man shall hardly enter into the Kingdom, of Heaven." It is hard for easy life to be a fruitful life.

The point just mentioned as coming from many independent communicators was also made by one of our foremost psychical researchers, Dr. Hereward Carrington (in *Problems of Psychical Research*, Rider & Co. Ltd., 1914, p. 32). He said: "It is probable that the brain is as much an inhibitory organ as anything else; and when this inhibition is removed, it is natural to suppose that the *the flow of thought would be far less controllable and far more automatic than it is with us*. It would be impossible for spirits to check and go on with their stream of thoughts at will as we do on this hypothesis." (He considered that this may be one of the reasons for some of the confusions that occur in certain communications.) "Hell", observed Coleridge, "is conscious madness." On this view, life in the physical body is a valuable opportunity: it helps us to control our mental processes and to initiate desirable lines of activity.

Again, as both the learned Bishop of Seeland and many unlearned communicators say, the 'next world' environments are less objective and stable than this world of "slow vibrations". Hence, a person who is 'half-awake' in the 'Hades' state (because he 'passed' before his time) will have trouble if his thoughts and emotions were uncontrolled during earth-life—there is no steady and stable environment that would assist him in regaining the initiative against them: the forces that he himself called forth must work themselves out in pain and frustration. This is reasonable. A similar thing occurs in connection with sleep. If we work on some problem all day and far into the evening and then go to sleep, we keep waking to find that the energies which we set going during our waking

hours have continued to work themselves out in our 'sleep'—
we '*dream*' that we are working. The vicious circle can be
avoided by ceasing work some time before retiring and re-
focusing the attention on some practical activity—by using the
physical body to break the mental habit prior to retiring.

Mortals who are very worried and highly 'nervous', whose
minds are, as it were, on a treadmill, constantly going over
some difficulty (yet fully aware of the futility of that activity),
find that they can re-capture the initiative, and break the
vicious circle, by playing golf, gardening, sewing or engaging
in some other occupation that utilises the stable environment
of the physical body. People who are not abnormally 'nervous'
also do this far oftener than they realise and the fact is recognised
in stage-craft where much apparently incidental 'business' is
actually carefully provided—the setting of tea-things, pouring
out of beverages, drinking, smoking, telephoning, etc. When
many people meet each other, or engage in discussions, they
often exchange cigarettes, etc.; when many speakers address
meetings they make great 'play' with their spectacles, stroke
their hair, scratch their noses, etc., all using the stable physical
environment to retain the initiative and to prevent thoughts
and emotions "running riot", i.e. to avoid 'stage-fright'.

On the other hand, many men and women have risen above
bodily defects, have not only overcome them, but even used
them as sources of strength and victory and not causes of
weakness and defeat. Demosthenes, the Athenian statesman-
orator (b. 384 B.C.) originally had serious defects of speech:
he overcame them by increasing his handicap: he forced himself to speak clearly with pebbles in his mouth. Among those
who, in modern times, have turned bodily handicaps to positive
advantage are Helen Keller and Douglas Bader. It is considered that doctors who (usually unconsciously) possess defects
of lungs, heart, ear, eyes, etc., are drawn to specialise in that
aspect of healing. The body seems to 'war' against the spirit,
but if we adopt the positive attitude, the body is a friendly
enemy, an ally. 'Earth-life' should be lived to the full and as
long as possible.

Suicides are, of course, 'earthbound'. Although special
arrangements may be made to compensate those few suicides
who willingly sacrificed their lives for others, those who cast
off the body deliberately in an endeavour to escape the trials,

tribulation and duties (which, properly viewed, are inestimable opportunities) of earth-life are 'earthbound'. One reason for this is that the vehicle of vitality is charged with energy that has to be dissipated. Another, is the mental factor—namely, the rejection of opportunity, of life itself. The deliberate suicide has *not* "ended it all": he survives the death of the body and takes his problems with him, but into harder conditions— he has lost the steadying, and the initiative-providing, physical body. Suicides who communicate typically plead, '*Pray for me*', and there must be many who are unable to 'get through' to mortals who also need our prayers (Jas. v. 16). When seen in their proper perspective, the characteristic plea of 'earth-bound' souls, "*Pray for Me!*" is a 'pointer' to survival. All these inter-related considerations are otherwise inexplicable.

According to *The Cyclopedic Bible Concordance*, Humphrey Milford, p. 218, the 'leading lesson' of the Parable of the Talents (Matt. xxv. 4) is "the use of advantages", and this is the level on which some clergymen deal with it. But when it is considered in the light of the conceptions indicated by com-municators the matter not only becomes much more insistent but much more reasonable (I Pet. iii. 15). It is the sluggishness and unresponsiveness of the body that makes earth-life, to a large extent, a 'seed-time' and the immediate after-life, to a large extent, a 'harvest-time', as was said by the Master. This is also the teaching of the Parables of the Talents (Matt. xxv. 14), the Sower (Matt. xiii. 3), the Labourers (Matt. xx. 1), the Ten Virgins (Matt. xxv. 1), etc. "Whatsoever a man soweth, that shall he also reap. . . . Let us not be weary in well-doing: for in due season we shall reap, if we faint not" (Gal. vi. 7, 9.).

The sluggishness of the body has another noteworthy effect: during earth-life a beautiful body may be associated with an evil mind (and *vice versa*); good people necessarily mix with wicked people. This, however, ceases to obtain after death— the delicate Soul Body responds immediately to every thought and feeling, and they are 'visible' to others. In these cir-cumstances the wicked feel rebuked, inferior and uncomfortable in the presence of the good: they therefore segregate themselves (our Experience No. 7), precisely as described by the Master (Luke xvi. 19-31). "There is nothing hid that shall not be known" (Matt. x. 26).

s

THE PLACE OF PSYCHIC STUDIES IN RELIGION

THE 'Report Towards the Conversion of England' (1945) notes that the Gospel comprises eight elements: (1) that God is love; (2) that "He has intervened and done for man that which he could not do for himself"; (3) "that God was, in Christ, reconciling the world to Himself"; (4) that this involves "the restoration of all things in Christ" (Acts iii. 21); (5) that the new life is to be "enjoyed in the fellowship of Christ's Church"; (6) that the power of the Holy Spirit is available to its members; (7) that this involves "redemption to Eternal Life"; (8) that "the good" will finally triumph, with "escape from the power of sin, from the fear of judgment and from everlasting death".

Communications that come from 'high levels' agree in general with the above but the aspect which they emphasise is not that which is emphasised by many clergymen. Three main aspects demand treatment, (a) *the historical Jesus* (the subject of the first three Gospels); (b) *The Cosmic Christ*, the *Logos*, by whom "all things were made" and who, at the same time, is "the true Light which lighteth every man that cometh into the world", giving all who receive Him "power to become the sons of God" (John i. 1-15) i.e., the 'Christ-in-You' of St. Paul, "the hope of Glory" because the mediator of forgiveness, of salvation and Eternal Life (Col. i. 27); and (c) *the Christ of History*, i.e. the impact of the Cosmic Christ, through the Church, on men and their institutions.

"The Kingdom of God is *within* you" (Luke xvii. 21). Men may be 'saved' from original sin and may enter Eternal Life here and now because of the Love (which is God) that is mediated by the Cosmic Christ (John xiii. 35, xv. 12; I John iv. 8, 12). This 'mystical' aspect of the Gospel is that which is invariably emphasised by communicators from 'high levels', whereas many clergymen emphasise the historical, the ritualistic, the institutional and the social aspects of religion. The

Churches have often demanded doctrinal tests of discipleship—
that one must believe this and not that, etc.—but the Master
gave a much simpler criterion: "Thus shall all men know that
ye are my disciples—if ye have love one for another" (John
xiii. 35). Again, "This is my commandment, that ye love one
another as I have loved you" (John xv. 12). Still again, "If
we love one another, God dwelleth in us and his love is perfected
in us" (I John iv. 12), and, probably representing the most
profound text in the whole of literature, "God is love and he
that dwelleth in love dwelleth in God and God dwelleth in
him" (I John iv. 8). The love here mentioned is not, of course,
of the vague, wordy and sentimental type but is deep, sincere,
self-giving goodwill. "Life is a chance to love", wrote Robert
Browning, and all communications that come to us from high
'levels' in the 'beyond' stress this same point.

As already said (Appendix III), many independent communicators have declared, and many physical researchers
have deduced, that the vast majority of communications from
surviving souls emanate from 'near-earth', i.e. 'Hades', or, at
best, lower 'Paradise', conditions.

People whose main concern is with the receipt of such
'messages' are mainly engaged in *verbal interchanges between
lesser (or intermediate, or psychic) selves*. Psychic communications
usually occur on the purely personal level: they are not necessarily more elevating than conversations between mortals.
St. Paul did not under-rate the service-value of psychic gifts,
but he (I Cor. xiii) indicated "a more excellent way"—a
spiritual way.

The main aim of true Christians is spiritual in nature:
psychical phenomena, if any, are incidental comforts and
means of service. Christians aim at achieving, and thereafter
acting upon (by way of service) the *experience* described by
St. Paul (Gal. ii. 20): "*I* [the lesser self] *live—yet not I, but
Christ* [the *Logos* or Christ-spirit, the Father-in-manifestation
who was uniquely incarnated in Jesus of Nazareth] *liveth in
me*" [in the Greater, Inner, Higher, Eternal Self, the Over-
soul, the Christ-in-You, which is a 'branch' of the *Logos*—
John xv, 5]. It is consciously to respond to the invitation of
the *Logos* (Rev. iii. 20): "*Behold I stand at the door* [of the Greater
Self] *and knock; if any man* [lesser self] *hear my voice and open the
door, I will come unto him and will sup with him and he with me*".

The Christian is not primarily concerned with the receipt of verbal communications from lesser or from psychic selves who have survived bodily death, but with experiencing (and thereafter so far as is possible, manifesting) the Presence, 'within' him, of the Living Christ.

Psychic truths (i.e. the existence of telepathy, etc.) are descriptive of 'Hades', and of 'Paradise' conditions. Scientific facts describe earth-conditions. Both differ from Spiritual truths. When Jesus (John viii. 32) promised, "Ye shall know *the Truth* and *the Truth* shall make you free", and when (John xiv. 6) He stated: "I am the Way, *the Truth* and the Life," He was referring to Spiritual Truths—those which describe the Nature of the 'Father', the nature of man and their relationship, through the 'Son'. Such Truths are not obtained by either long psychical 'development' or arduous experiment and observation: they are 'given' in the form of intuitions and inspirations from 'within'. They do not come through the psychic (=intermediate) self, nor through the intellectual studies of the lesser (=everyday) self, but are 'gifts' received through the 'Spirit' or Greater Self, and they are not fully grasped or understood until they are *lived* not merely passively accepted: the 'Kingdom of God' must be brought 'to earth'.

Spiritual Truths include the following: (1) "God is love" (I John iv. 8, 16); (2) "It is more blessed to give than to receive" (Acts xx. 35); (3) Peacemakers (etc.) are "blessed" (Matt. v. 1-48); (4) "We are members one of another" (Eph. iv. 25); (5) "Except a corn of wheat [=the lesser self, the 'Old Adam' of St. Paul] fall to the ground and die, it abideth alone; but if it die, it bringeth forth much fruit. He that loveth his life shall lose it; and he that hateth [=disregardeth] his life in this world shall keep it unto Life Eternal" (John xii. 24, 25); (6) "The Kingdom of God is within you (Luke xvii. 21); (7) "He [lesser self] that believeth in Me [the Cosmic Christ, the *Logos*], out of his innermost being [the Greater Self, Christ-in-you of St. Paul] shall flow torrents of Living Waters [=Spiritual Wisdom, Love and Power, which will animate first the intermediate, or psychic self and then the outer, lesser, everyday or physical self, bringing true health and victory over 'the things of this world']—John iv. 14, vii. 31—Syriac Version); (8) "I [=the *Logos*] am the True Vine and my Father is the husbandman. . . . As the branch cannot

bear fruit of itself, except it abide in the Vine, no more can ye
except ye abide in Me . . . for without Me ye can do nothing.
If ye abide in Me and My words abide in you, ye shall ask
what ye will, and it shall be done unto you. . . . Ye have not
chosen Me, but I have chosen you, and ordained you that ye
should go and bring forth fruit. . . . I will send unto you from
the Father the Spirit of Truth which proceedeth from the
Father: He shall testify of Me" (John xv); (9) "Judge not,
that ye be not judged" (Matt. vii. 1) recommends a tolerance
which few of us entirely possess. When we sit in judgment on
others, we may be right or wrong concerning them, but we
are inevitably judging ourselves. It is the lesser, outer, everyday self that judges—the self that also sins—the Greater, Inner,
Eternal Self understands and forgives. To judge others is to
live in the lesser self; (10) We need specifically and repeatedly
to *ask* for help in the 'daily round and common task': "Ask
and it shall be given you, seek and ye shall find, knock and it
shall be opened unto you" (Matt. vii. 7); (11) It is a Spiritual
Truth that, during physical embodiment, except on rare
occasions, we are temporarily exiles from our Father's House,
unaware that "the Lord is in this place", that we are all
'Prodigal Sons' (Luke xv. 11), apparently separated from our
Father. The meaning of the Parable of the Prodigal, according
to *The Oxford Cyclopedic Bible Concordance* (p. 219), is "Fatherly
love to the returning sinner". But its implication is universal.
Men are usually unaware of the Presence, within and around
them, of the loving Father, and they do not realise that 'behind'
and 'within' all their searches is a search for Him. As the
communicator of *The Coming Light* (Watkins, 1924, pp. 91-3)
said, human separation (and therefore loneliness)—produced
by physical embodiment—is necessary to enable each person
to develop an individual character. "But", he continued,
"until the reason for this is sufficiently grasped by the ego, he
seeks to escape from it by mingling with the crowd. . . . Yet only
by becoming still more lonely will he become less lonely. He
must go still farther into the centre of his being, until he feels
himself enwrapped by that consciousness of unity with his
Creator which for evermore will transform his loneliness, while
leaving him the abilities which the experience of loneliness has
developed. . . ." He insisted: "Escape from the aching void
is not effected by going into external activities, recreations,

etc., but by going into *what seems to be* still greater solitude *but is really* a consciousness of unity . . . not only with the Creator but with all one's fellows, both on earth and in higher spheres. . . . One becomes welded more closely with one's fellows. . . . But never does one attain this point by outward mingling with others, even with the choicest. One must reach back into the Divine innermost and *then* outward again."

This was said, centuries ago, by Plotinus: earthly loves change and pass: "They are not the things we truly seek—Yonder is the true object of our love." In 1937 Messrs. Mortiboys published a small book by 'A Physician' entitled *Crossed in Love*. The author pointed out that those who suffer loneliness through being 'crossed in love' should take heart, since it provides them with a great opportunity. He said: "The aching void caused by disappointment in the affections is largely due to the desire for the Infinite, which is, or perhaps should be, one's life-long search." On this view, he said, to lose a dear one, so far from being evil, affords an opportunity of obtaining "a glimpse into a higher form of existence, which might otherwise have remained a sealed book, helping the sufferer to realise the saying of St. Augustine, 'The heart of man was made for God and will not find happiness till it rests in Him'." J. I. Wedgwood (*Varieties of Psychism*, Theosophical Publishing House, 1914, p. 89) said: "So long as man is living in the separated consciousness of the personality, there is a sense of incompleteness—it bears witness to his pilgrimage in a land of exile."

Faith is not belief in facts taught by the Bible or the Church; it is the active realisation of Spiritual Truths such as those mentioned above: it is acting as if they are true, and therefore living in the 'Spirit' (Greater Self) in spite of suggestions to the contrary that may come from the 'world' and from the lesser self. This is the true faith: these are the "Words" which will "not pass away" (Matt. xxiv. 35). They lead to 'good works', but 'good works' will not 'save' in themselves: they must be products of the Spirit within.

It is possible to arrive at humanism—the self-sufficiency or worship of man—not only by way of over-emphasis on the physical sciences but also by way of over-emphasis of psychical phenomena. The idea that men can 'save' themselves does not accord with the Gospel or with the teachings received in communications. All experience is against it. Although we (lesser selves) must do our utmost, 'salvation' (true health of mind, body and estate) is "the *gift* of God" (received through the Greater Self in response to specific requests—Matt. vii. 7). It is not the claimable reward for 'works' done by the lesser self—"lest any man should boast" (Eph. ii. 9).

This essential matter is well expressed in the report, *Towards the Conversion of England* (p. 29): "As self-centredness is the essence of man's sin, it follows that every effort that he may make (even towards the good, and particularly every successful effort), only confirms him in his root sin more completely *because it is made from this centre*. Thus every new good which he achieves brings with it its own peculiar new evil. For example, even the attainment of humility, when regarded as his own achievement, produces in him the new sin of spiritual pride—pride in being humble."

The report continued: "Such is the tragic quality of man's fallen nature, which we term as Original Sin. Once the truth of Original Sin is recognised, it reveals the essential falsity of the humanist's basic article of faith."

'A.B.', communicating, made a typical statement concerning this conception of man's nature and his essential dependence on God: "However deeply plunged in the darkness of the material self, a soul may be raised to wonderful heights even in a few years by *relying entirely upon Divine strength for self-conquest and for the service of humanity*. Each must find his own gateway to the path. Behold the Christ! He is the Way!" (Mary Bruce Wallace, *The Coming Light*, Watkins, 1924, p. 65).

The importance of life in the physical body was stressed by this communicator (pp. 51-2): "Feel yourself so consciously one with the Divine that all outer tribulations will be to you as chaff, easily scattered. . . . The victory is to realise this joy and peace when apparently walking in outer cold and darkness. *You are on earth to achieve this conquest.* . . . Spiritual freedom means mastery of the physical senses, victory over the body and environment, after which you will tread easily the road with us . . . since the conquest, once won, is for evermore."

Similarly, the anonymous communicator of *Christ in You* (Watkins, 1910, p. 81) said: "Christ is God incarnate and dwells within your heart, so near that the feeblest whisper is heard, aye, before you speak. He hears and answers, for He is behind all thought and speech. . . . He only asks for your need of Him to fill you to overflowing with Himself. . . . Until the Christ fills the whole consciousness, man will ever be at war with himself, his brother and his God."

This communicator also stressed the importance of life in the Physical body (p. 36): "You should draw all from the spiritual first, thus feeding the Soul covering [Soul Body], and manifestation in the [physical] body must follow. Only *on earth* can man do this great and perfect work. Every spiritual truth is creative, and all your future is made by your conquests now."

Her communicator told Mary Bruce Wallace (*The Thinning of the Veil*, Watkins, 1919, p. 28): "At all times, and upon every question, heed the inner voice of the spirit. . . . Man *unaided* cannot hold the ball of Divine Wisdom, neither can he pass the treasure to others. He must rely on Divine Power. . . ." 'Private Dowding', communicating, said he had discovered "one great truth". It was this: "Empty yourself if you would be filled." He continued: "The Waters of Life can never flow through me until I have surrendered my whole self. . . . Somewhere within the soul there is silence. Attain unto it. It is a pearl of great price. . . . I begin to realise what is meant by the Still Small Voice of God!" (*Private Dowding*, Watkins, 1943, p. 35). 'Dowding' also stressed the importance of life in the physical body: "Many of the lessons in selflessness, self-control, the relation between reason and intuition, between intellect and emotion, are lessons which we should have learnt while still on earth" (*ibid.*, p. 73).

The basic conceptions which are transmitted from communicators (which some think are merely partial and subconscious minds of unlettered mediums) seem to the present writer to clarify certain conceptions held by some Doctors of Divinity (not only with exceptionally able, complete and conscious minds, but also with the advantage of comparing notes with each other).

Many people must have asked, how comes it that man, who was made 'perfect' ("in our image, after our likeness"—Gen. i. 26), was able to, and did, in fact, 'fall' and commit 'sin', for which he was excluded from the 'Garden of Eden' (='Paradise'), and on account of which he now needs to be 'reconciled' with his Maker? Again, how can a being who knows only 'good' (and who therefore has no chance of exercising his free-will in resisting the temptation to do 'evil') grow in strength, wisdom and understanding?

Communicators do not mention the 'fall' (of the Greater Self into partial physical embodiment) in orthodox terms at all. They say that, while the Greater Self is *a Cosmic and a Spiritual Being*, the physical body is essentially *an animal organism*, so that, after incarnation, our total nature necessarily includes animal tendencies and instincts. The body also acts like 'blinkers' and we seem to be separated from our 'Father' and from each other. Thus we are individualised and made self-conscious and thus conditions are provided in which development (and 'return') can eventually take place. On this view, 'the fall' was not itself a 'sin', i.e. a deliberate disobedience, but the necessary condition for advance and growth (which may terminate in co-operation with the divine plan).

Orthodox people, as Dr. W. R. Matthews has pointed out, often make the mistake of supposing that "they have all the truth and nothing more can be known". They can learn much, for instance, from psychical study. It will support their faith.

But people who are keenly interested in psychical matters also often make a serious mistake: they often suppose that knowledge of psychical phenomena and of the after-life is the central element in religion. This is not so. Although all knowledge is valuable, it is not the essential (I Cor. xiii. 2, 8). 'Knowledge' belongs to the lesser (and to the intermediate, or psychic) selves. Great knowledge may even be a handicap (Matt. xviii. 3).

One thing is certain: no movement, whether inside or outside the orthodox Church, that is mainly on the level of lesser selves (personalities) or of intermediate (psychic) selves, can possibly succeed and flourish. "Except *the Lord* build a house, they labour in vain that built it" (Ps. cxxvii. 1).

Students of psychical science are not necessarily among those who will not believe "except they see signs and wonders" (John iv. 48). As Sir William Barrett observed, "The psychic order, it is true, is not the Spiritual order. But I am convinced that, as our knowledge of the former increases, it will throw light on the conditions of access to the Spiritual order."

INDEX

INDEX